BURNING BANKS
AND ROASTING
MARSHMALLOWS

BURNING BANKS AND ROASTING MARSHMALLOWS

THE EDUCATION OF DANIEL MARLEAU

GREGORY DESILET

info@gregorydesilet.com

To order additional copies of this book, contact:
Xlibris Corporation
1-888-795-4274
www.Xlibris.com
Orders@Xlibris.com
63124

If a wizard were to offer you infinite extension of all your senses and you were to accept, you might lose the most precious sense of all.

—John Macksoud (1934-2005)

Above: Isla Vista Mural at 976 Embarcadero del Mar near Perfect Park circa early 1970s (artist unknown)

Acknowledgements

This project percolated for many years before I finally found time to write a draft during the late 1990s. Reading an early version of Malcolm Gault-Williams' *Don't Bank on America* (initially titled *Sunshine Revolutionaries*) inspired me to get down to writing. It prodded my memory and became an incomparable resource and time line to follow in reconstructing the pivotal events. Without Malcolm's work, my task would have been much more difficult. So my debt to Malcolm is deep and I thank him for producing an historical account of high quality and for help and motivation supplied through several email communications over the years I have worked on this project. Without excessive footnoting (which I have avoided in order to retain the style and flow of fiction) it would not be possible to note all the small factual details that have been recalled or confirmed through Malcolm's text. But I do want to note that the following major scenes are either cited directly from or supplemented (in addition to *El Gaucho* sources) by Malcolm's text: the Dean Evans bullhorn scene, the Bill Allen addresses to the crowd and radio interview, William Kunstler's speech, the exchange between the student and the police officer in the county jail, the Nancy Rubin and Stu Albert addresses to the crowd at the UCEN, parts of the dialogue at the Kevin Moran shooting, the Dean Reynolds scene, and the Kevin Moran memorial speech.

Acknowledgement must also be given to the UCSB student newspaper, the *El Gaucho* (which became the *Daily Nexus* not long after the 1970 events). Information acquired from the paper is noted in the context of the story with the exception of the first Tom Hayden speech—all portions of which were excerpted from the paper.

Special thanks are also due the UCSB Library Special Collections Department for extraordinarily helpful assistance provided during a research visit I made in 2000. Here I was able to acquire recordings of the Hayden and Kunstler speeches. All of the portions of the second Hayden speech (June of 1970) presented in the story were transcribed by me from the Special Collections recording. Information relating to administration officials, Isla Vista, and other documents relating to events of the period were also acquired from Special Collections.

The cooperation of Bill Macomber and the heir to John Macksoud's estate, Craig R. Smith, is also greatly appreciated. The words of Bill Macomber were composed from detailed class notes and the Macksoud classroom scene was transcribed and edited from a personal tape recording.

The critical commentary, cooperation, encouragement, and marketing assistance of close confidant and long-time friend John Riley have proven invaluable. Thank you, John! You are a gem and so is your wife Patty!

I would be remiss not to mention the encouragement and acerbic but often humorous commentary offered by my old (but not elderly) San Miguel dorm buddies over the years I have worked on this project—years during which they significantly contributed toward prodding me to complete it. Here particular mention should be made of Ed King, Bob Koch(endorfer), Mark Castleton, Vernon Alferd, John Karp, and, the recently re-discovered Michael Booth. Many thanks to Mike for his account of events and for information regarding the Kevin Moran shooting and inquest that is not widely known.

Also, the contributions of Omar Swartz and Scott Bonestell proved very helpful—Omar on matters pertaining to law and Scott on refinements of the cover photo. Phil Tompkins, Roger Seltzer, and Barbara Wilder were kind to read early script versions of this story and provide useful comments, and long-time friend Dave Pearlman was helpful with many suggestions, especially on structure and trimming of content on late drafts of the manuscript version.

Last, but never least, I thank my family, especially my wife Christine for her endless patience with my odd writing habits and occasional disappearance, for days on end, from the realm of the living. She was always there to throw out the life preserver and pull me back into the current of real life.

Photo credits: The image of Morro Rock was provided courtesy of Mike Baird, bairdphotos.com with additional thanks due Jayna at the Morro Bay Chamber of Commerce. The image of William Kunstler was provided courtesy of the *Daily Nexus*. The aerial photograph of Goleta Point was provided courtesy of John Rinaldi. All other photos are the author's.

Author Preface

The public events recounted in this tale are grounded in real events presented in substantially accurate chronological and historical detail. The characters of Daniel Marleau, Paul Canova, Melanie Lampert, Matt Baxter, Kyle Kincaid, Angie Wagner, Scott Lampert, Raymond Marleau, Officer Caldwell, Detective Newberry, Kevin Cink, William Andrew Arlington Jr., Ted, and Rob, while partly based on personalities of real persons should not be identified with real persons. The words and actions of these characters are entirely constructed and fictional. All other named characters are real persons whose names are preserved and whose words and actions are represented based on recorded transcripts, newspaper documents, and/or memory of witnessed events. In several instances these transcriptions include language that may be offensive to some readers. The words used are accurate to what was recorded and are retained in this account in order to preserve the violent emotional animosity of the confrontations.

On the evening of December 1, 1969 in a small auditorium in Washington D. C. Congressman Alexander Pirnie of New York stood before a large glass cylinder filled with 366 blue plastic balls. Each ball contained a slip of paper stamped with a date. Events of the previous score of months cast a gloomy backdrop for what was about to take place. In January of 1968 the North Vietnamese launched the militarily costly but psychologically lucrative Tet Offensive in response to which General Westmoreland requested 200,000 more troops. In the wake of failed war policies, President Lyndon Johnson decided not to seek reelection. Turmoil over civil rights and war policy escalated following the assassinations of Martin Luther King, Jr. and Robert F. Kennedy. In August, as the Democratic Party struggled to nominate a presidential candidate, ten thousand war protesters battled police in the streets of Chicago during their National Convention. Winning a narrow victory over Hubert Humphrey, Richard Nixon assumed the presidency and disclosed his "secret plan to end the war" as an escalation of bombings in North Vietnam. In response, anti-war protests soared and a radical anti-war group calling itself the Weather Underground launched a series of bombings of government buildings across the country. In March of 1969 the Chicago Grand Jury indicted Yippie, SDS, and Black Panther leaders for conspiracy to incite riots during the Democratic National Convention. In November, day-long gatherings called peace moratoriums drew a half million participants in Washington D.C. and over 100,000 in San Francisco.

This long whirl of events still churned in the national psyche when at precisely 8:00pm Congressman Pirnie selected the first ball from the glass cylinder. His action also met a strong headwind of cultural change. Over the past months, Neil Armstrong stepped onto the surface of the moon; Yale opened its doors to women undergraduates; Hair opened on Broadway; Tom Wolfe published a counter-culture manifesto in his account of the psychedelic road trip of Ken Kesey and the Merry Pranksters; waterbeds and mini-skirts flooded the marketplace; BankAmericards, automatic tellers, and pocket calculators attracted consumers; and Max Yasgur hosted a crowd of 400,000 at a three day music festival on his farm in Woodstock.

Pulling the plastic ball apart, the Congressman withdrew the paper and read the date: September 14. That meant I had won the lottery. But it wasn't the kind of lottery anyone wanted to win.

Men between the ages of 18 and 26 whose birth dates matched the dates on the first 100 balls drawn were certain to see military service, barring rare exemptions. Being number one in the draft lottery removed all hovering doubt about my induction. But since I was a sophomore at the University of California at Santa Barbara, I had the next best thing to an exemption—a student deferment.

12

Compared to immediate induction, deferment certainly qualified as a benefit. But it also held a notable downside. As merely a postponement, deferments gave those with low draft numbers a palpable sense of sitting on a steadily warming griddle. And as the number of deaths in the Vietnam War exceeded those of the Korean War and continued to climb, interest in ending the war increasingly trumped interest in classes. A month and a half after the lottery, events at UCSB stoked the griddle fire to a degree unsurpassed on any other campus in the nation. Like most in my position, I felt the heat. But I didn't immediately sense the rich possibilities for going from the pan into the fire.

*   *   *

Chapter 1

I made my way to Ocean Road, bordering campus. Eucalyptus trees trimming the west side extended straight down the road for over 200 yards before bending toward Isla Vista. The acid-sweet scent from the trees floated in the salty breeze off the ocean and hung in the air all along the road. The surf pounded faintly in the distance. I walked north, staying close to the tree line. Then, down at the far end, I saw it coming.

Even though I expected it, I was surprised, jolted by the strangeness of it. At the far end cruisers turned onto the avenue from the west, filing toward me at about ten miles an hour. On my left, I approached a side street, Seville Road, leading into Isla Vista. To my right, the entrance to the San Rafael Dorm parking lot opened off Ocean Road. I stopped and stood next to a large eucalyptus.

The lead police car slowly moved toward me, followed by ten or twelve more cruisers with still others coming. Then I saw a coach bus making the turn. And then another bus. Bus after bus wheeled around the corner.

To my left—at the entrance of Seville—several people gathered and stood watching the approaching cruisers and buses. A short, stocky guy wearing a faded tie-dyed T-shirt with a peace symbol on the back held something in his right hand—I couldn't see exactly what. The lead cruiser, now about a block away, continued slowly moving forward.

I removed my camera lens cap and read the light meter. Still enough light to shoot. Framing the lead car to include the caravan down the street, I set my hand on the focus—waiting for the cruiser to get a little closer. Then, a few feet before I thought the cruiser would turn into the parking lot, the guy in the tie-dyed T-shirt moved quickly into the frame. He reared back while stepping forward. When almost close enough to touch the cruiser, he used the full weight of his body to fling the object he held into the windshield. When he released it, his hand was no more than a few feet from the glass. A loud thud and crinkling sound followed as the windshield cracked out in every direction. The point of direct contact swayed inward.

The attack surprised me, but I pressed off the shot as the car swerved and slowed. An instant later another figure ran up to the cruiser, and, in the same way, hurled what looked to be a heavy iron pipe into the windshield. This time the glass exploded inward onto the cops in the front seat. The car pulled violently to the driver's left, swerving toward the opening that led into the parking lot, barely missing the fence bordering the lot. Several others joined the attack, throwing whatever they could lay their hands on at the approaching cars.

The row of vehicles accelerated to escape the ambush. But the added speed made it difficult to turn into the lot. Tires squealed and cars fishtailed and bounced into the air as they hit the driveway opening. The sound of broken glass and rocks ricocheting off metal resounded down the road. Finally, the line of cruisers broke off a hundred yards away where the police began using another entrance. The assault dissolved as quickly as it started.

Cops with helmets and riot shields emerged from buses parked in the lot. Now seemed like a good time to retreat. Keeping an eye on the forming groups, I backpedaled along the row of eucalyptus. Having withdrawn about half a block, I stood next to another large eucalyptus and waited. Two groups of cops in full riot gear hustled from the lot toward Isla Vista. While watching, I heard the rustle of dried leaves to my left. I leaned forward to look around the tree, expecting to see a few rioters sneaking along the tree line. Then a sickening wave welled in my stomach. Four uniformed bodies moved quickly toward me—only a few steps away! It made no sense!

They descended on me like open season on a sewer rat. The one closest to me raised his riot stick. I turned and ducked my head as he struck me hard across the back. I fell to my knees and raised my arms to protect my head while yelling out.

—Stop, I'm only taking pictures!

As soon as the words were out of my mouth I realized how ridiculous they sounded—as if the event were a photo opportunity for paparazzi. Three of them now vigorously cracked me with riot sticks across my back, legs, and arms. A blow glanced off my head, another off my hand on the back of my head. One of them taunted me.

—What's that puke? I can't hear you puke.

Another grabbed my camera, ripping the strap off my shoulder. Yet another knocked the glasses off my face and maced my eyes. I yelled again.

—Stop, I wasn't doing anything!

Even as I said these words, I knew it was more futility. They responded with another blow across the back and more verbal abuse.

—Shut up you stupid little fuck.

At this point I was completely blind, eyes stinging with mace. They stood me up, jerked my hands behind my back, and tied them with plastic handcuffs. The one who cuffed me ordered me forward.

—Move it puke. Your evening fun isn't over yet.

With that he pushed me forward. Stumbling along, I tried to blink the mace out of my eyes but could see very little. Finally, I could make out the ground and a few uniformed legs in front of me. More cops from behind joined the group that held me. One gave the order to spread out and prepare to sweep the street in front of them. Another pushed me again from behind.

—Keep moving. Now you pukes can make yourselves useful.

It didn't take long to figure out what he meant. Looking down through blurred vision I could see only the pavement in front of me but understood the situation when I heard rocks and stones bouncing off of it. Rioters in the street ahead threw at the cops whatever they could grab. Two other hapless captives joined me to serve as moving bales of hay between two angry mobs. A few moments ago I observed from a distance. Now I was literally the front line.

Edging down the street, prodded by riot sticks, I turned my left side toward the mob and tried to duck my head behind my shoulder. Rocks continued bouncing off the pavement around me. Several more stones careened off riot shields to my left, followed by a thud, a clunk, and the sound of metal rolling on asphalt. Someone had thrown a can full of soda. It hissed as the contents spewed out. Then I heard the whizzing sound of an object coming in my direction just in time to duck and turn my back. A stone the size of a walnut glanced off my shoulder and hit a shield behind me.

This was getting serious. The cops had helmets and shields, but I had nothing to protect my head or my face—and the cops could care less. As the struggle on the street mounted, rage and fear fought it out inside me. And rage was gaining the upper hand. These cops weren't law enforcement. They were nothing more than mercenaries hired to come in and kick ass. And any ass on the street was going to get kicked, never mind whose it was.

I wasn't feeling too kindly toward those throwing the rocks either. I had to get out of the middle of this, and I didn't much care how, since it was now clear there were no rules to any of this. One of the cops behind me shouted out.

—Keep moving puke. Anything hits me, I'm going to hit you just as hard.

I moved my hands. The plastic cuffs weren't cinched very tight. This might be one time my thin wrists would be an advantage. I worked my right hand through the loop to the point where I could pop it free with one quick tug. At my current level of adrenalin I was certain I could outrun even the fastest cop—especially since they were all weighed down with riot gear. One of them shouted a warning to the others.

—Watch out! There are two behind that dumpster at the corner!

17

Darkness had now descended over Isla Vista. Few street lamps, the loss of my glasses, and the mace still burning my eyes made it difficult to see. Running full speed in a getaway move would be little better than running blindfolded. I could hear rioters in front of me hustling in and out of spaces between the buildings. Every now and then they shouted: Off with the pigs.

Suddenly a bottle exploded against the street a few yards ahead, sending pieces of glass spraying across the pavement in front of me.

That was it! I'd had enough. Yanking my hands free of the cuffs, I bolted to the right. Immediately I was off the street and running between two apartment buildings. My thoughts raced with me:

—Two cops giving chase. One saying something to the others. Can't make it out. My place—only a couple of blocks away. Heading in the wrong direction. No good anyway. They'd follow me there. Street ahead, coming up fast. Got to choose—right or left? Right. Yes! Cops already swept past—up the street behind me. Dig in. Sprint toward campus. One still coming. Not too close. Don't look back.

I moved fast, considering that everything was a blur around me, but it got darker as the street neared campus. The street lamps on that end had been broken out. I knew I would lose that cop. There was no way he was going to catch me, even if I had to run all the way to Goleta. As I neared the row of eucalyptus separating campus and Isla Vista, I slowed because it became too hard to see.

—Another choice—right or left. Right again. Head for campus. Lose him south of the dorm. No cops over there. Oh shit!

Past the eucalyptus trees, I came out directly in front of a line of cops crossing Ocean Road. Putting on the brakes, I slipped on the leaves under the trees and fell to the ground. Then the cops were all over me—again.

This new patrol reintroduced me to their night sticks, handcuffed me again, and dragged me off to their staging area in the San Rafael Dorm parking lot. With all the excitement on top of having not eaten much that evening, I was beginning to weary. But my night on the town had just begun.

* * *

Chapter 2

At the parking lot I was searched for weapons and then made to stand against the side of a school bus along with three other handcuffed bodies—one of whom had blood splattered across his forehead. Even though we were more than two blocks from the scene of action, shouts and the sounds of broken glass laced the air along with occasional whiffs of tear gas. The cops in the parking lot were not well organized for handling the large number of those arrested. First they stood us against the school bus, then loaded us into the bus, then pushed us out of the bus, then marched us to another bus where we stood for what seemed like over an hour. All the while, more handcuffed and disheveled captives swelled the group.

Finally they loaded us into the bus only to discover they had too many for one bus. But they crammed everyone into one bus anyway, pushing people together until the isle filled and some were sitting on top of others. I was one of the lucky ones who had a seat with no one on top of me. Packed well beyond capacity, the bus moved out of the lot and onto Ocean Road. It continued off campus and onto El Colegio Road. As we passed by the intersection of Embarcadero del Mar, I could see heavy smoke rising from a fire in the middle of the street several blocks south toward the ocean. Isla Vista looked and felt like a war zone, lacking only a few tanks in the streets. I wondered if it would come to that as the overloaded bus shuddered down the road.

After turning north on Storke Road, the bus continued for about another mile until it reached Fire Station #11 where it pulled into the lot next to the building. I thought they would be taking us to jail somewhere in Santa Barbara. The Fire Station made no sense.

The cops unloaded everyone from the bus and marched us into the bay where normally the fire trucks would be parked. The bay was lit up as bright as daylight. My eyes had to adjust to the light. When I could see more clearly, the sight was stupefying. I had never seen more cameras and reporters in one place. Every newspaper, radio, television, magazine and pamphleteer operation within a hundred miles must have been represented. Television cameras, news cameras, and microphones were everywhere—flashbulbs popping right and left. The cops were parading their spoils of war—no doubt anxious to bolster their sagging image following the previous night's events. With a feeling of dread, my overactive imagination pictured footage of myself front and center on television news the next day—along with commentary about the rounding up of radical criminals in the community.

Several guys who weren't cooperating well enough with our herders—along with another who was complaining about the tightness of his handcuffs—were slammed up against the brick wall and treated to a spew of threats and invectives. I sensed this was more for the benefit of the news media than a concern for keeping order. The cops were obviously all too willing to show they weren't taking any shit from "street pukes." To reinforce that point, one of the cops went around tightening everyone's handcuffs. My cuffs had been cinched tighter than the first pair, but were not painful. Now they were painful. At this point it was obvious that it would do no good to complain about the cuffs. It occurred to me it would be wise not to attract any attention at all. I could feel myself stuffing the anger, storing away lumps of resentment that wouldn't be dissipating anytime soon.

All the prisoners from the bus, including myself, were lined up against the east side of the bay facing the brick wall. We were told to touch the wall with our noses and not to move a muscle. A few who were apparently not following these orders precisely enough were made examples of by being shoved to the floor and pressed flat on their stomachs. The picture-taking continued along with what sounded like interviews with some of the cops.

As I stood against the wall, the sense of outrage continued building in me. It was fueled further when I thought about the camera. They had no right to take it. I tried to visualize how it had happened, tried to remember any little detail that would help lead to who might have it.

The command to move again forced me out of my thoughts. They were finally herding us back onto the bus. Off to some other media event in Santa Barbara perhaps. Perhaps to be displayed on the stage of some theater. I imagined being paraded around all night so the residents of Santa Barbara's white stucco haciendas and palm tree gardens could view for themselves—close up and personal—live specimens of the rank elements causing all the trouble in the squalid flea market of Isla Vista. As the bus pulled out of the fire station, I sank deeper into depression.

However, instead of turning onto the freeway toward Santa Barbara, we continued past it and onto a frontage road. We followed the frontage road for four or five miles then turned north up an incline. The bus pulled to a stop alongside what appeared to be a large new building. We exited the bus and were led single file up a short flight of steps, across a loading dock area, and through a small door at the side of the building. Once inside, I could see we had entered a new facility—a jail that had not yet opened for business. I found out later it was the new county jail and that we were its first occupants.

They put us all in a large holding cell. The cell doors operated electronically but apparently were not yet wired. The cops had to open and close the doors manually using a large, clumsy-looking metal key. None of them were too happy about that. Due to the lack of familiarity with the new jail and the manual locking and unlocking of doors—or perhaps due simply to petty mean-spiritedness—the cops did not take anyone out of their handcuffs. Each one of us waited our turn in the holding cell—hands feeling worse by the minute with over-tightened cuffs—as the cops searched, booked, and fingerprinted us one by one. Consistent with a general attitude that none of us deserved civil treatment, the cops refused phone calls or toilet privileges. They definitely wanted everyone well invested in the thought that jail was an experience we would take pains to avoid in the future.

Somewhere between two and three in the morning I was finally booked and led to a cell. Two officers took a group of ten of us down a corridor, through three doors—each one of which had to be manually keyed and pushed open with considerable effort. Once inside these doors, we were led through a door opposite a long row of eight foot high windows. This door opened into a rectangular barred room, perhaps forty feet by twenty feet, with two long tables and benches—all bolted to the floor. Beyond this room were two smaller cells, probably twenty by twenty. We were deposited in the one on the left. It contained four beds, bunk style, on the far wall and six on the right wall. An institutional lidless toilet protruded from the middle of the wall on the left. Journey's end for the evening. Most made use of the toilet, then, without much negotiating, everyone took a bunk and fell asleep.

Morning began with the sound of urine splashing into the toilet bowl. It was followed by the industrial strength power flush unique to institutional plumbing. One decided to be the first to take a dump in the thing—an indignity and breach of basic privacy no one was in a hurry to experience. Use of the toilet continued every so often for the next couple of hours.

The cell next to ours had been filled with ten more captives. I recalled having vaguely heard them escorted in sometime before dawn. The cops brought food in and set it on each of the two tables and then unlocked our cell door and retreated, locking the door to the outer room.

No one talked about the circumstances of their arrest. No one talked about much of anything relating to what had happened in the streets. Talk, what little there was of it, centered mostly on complaints—complaints about the food, the

21

beds (no blankets, no pillows), the handcuffs, the treatment during the booking, the denial of phone calls.

Through most of the morning a steady flow of new inductees marched down the corridor toward other cells. I estimated the cops must have jailed over three hundred people by now—from all I had seen last night and this morning.

After a lunch of Wonder bread and baloney, followed by the trotting out of more complaints, things quieted down for a while. Most of us sat or lay on our bunks. A month ago I couldn't have imagined I'd find myself here.

*   *   *

Chapter 3

Saturday morning, in mid January, I sat across from my roommate Matt at the small kitchen table in our spartan one bedroom apartment on El Nido Lane in Isla Vista. He ate from a bowl of cornflakes as he eyed eight by ten photographs. I had left them on the table late last night after returning from the Devereaux photo lab. Several of these photos were taken at a meeting of the Radical Union an old friend cajoled me into attending two weeks ago. Matt glanced at me as he pointed to the photos.

—How'd he talk you into that boot camp for wannabe revolutionaries?

—I was curious—as much about him as the meeting. I've hardly seen him the past couple of years.

—You don't exactly move in the same circles.

—That's been part of it.

—What's the other part?

—I think Canova wants a break from the past. I remind him of who he was.

—He could pick better company than those RU types.

—Afraid they'll live up to their name?

—You've heard those cranks. They carry so much venom you're likely to get snake bit hanging out with them.

Matt pointed to the *El Gaucho*, the campus paper, on the table.

—Fanatical diatribes—that's all the left is since Bobby Kennedy got ripped off.

Matt and I got along well but weren't matched as roommates if you counted political persuasion. We met the previous year in San Miguel dorm as fourth floor residents. His short stature combined with fastidious attention to appearance and an appetite for military board games earned him the moniker "the fourth floor Napoleon." But we had at least three things in common: a similar standard for tidiness, a love of Dostoyevsky, and a desire to get into the more independent Isla Vista apartment life. Raised in Orange County, he hewed conservative with a libertarian tack that included opposition to marijuana laws and one or two other liberal positions. But his views were not hard to predict. I picked up on his comment about "diatribes" and tried to needle him.

23

—What do you know about the left?

Matt smirked scornfully.

—Take the "Chicago Eight," for example. Ought to be the "Chicago Hate." Just watch those RU groupies surfing Tom Hayden's wave of screed for all it's worth. You going?

—Of course. Photo opportunity.

—Bull. You're into it. Why not admit it?

—I go with an open mind. What are you going to do? Join ROTC?

—Close. I'm hitting the beach.

I shook my head, grabbed my camera, and opened the door as Matt called out.

—Oh, I almost forgot. A chick came here last night while you were at the lab. Said to tell you the drama queen stopped by to say hello.

—Nice of you to remember.

—I wasn't sure how to break it to you. We had a cozy chat.

—Right. Like I'd be worried. Her from Chatsworth and you from Orange County. Opposites like that don't attract, they explode.

—You're jealous already. Why does she call herself the drama queen?

—Because she's a drama major who thinks highly of herself.

—How'd you meet her, anyway? She's doesn't seem your type either.

—She isn't. She's business. If you can make her, be my guest.

I closed the door and walked down El Nido Lane onto campus. Arriving early at Campbell Hall, the university's largest auditorium, I took a seat near the front and loaded film. The hall soon filled to standing room only.

Tom Hayden, one of the "Chicago Eight," had come to campus to speak. He and seven others were indicted following the 1968 Democratic National Convention in Chicago. They allegedly violated a statute signed into law by President Johnson in April of 1968. The statute imposed a five year penalty on anyone conspiring to use interstate commerce for purposes of fostering, encouraging, or promoting civil disorder—otherwise known as a riot. Crossing state lines legally constituted "interstate commerce." All the members of the Chicago Eight crossed state lines when coming to the convention and were now held responsible for violent confrontations between police and protestors.

Presided over by Judge Julius J. Hoffman, the trial attracted constant national media attention. Altercations between the staid 74 year old Hoffman and the eight defendants transformed the courtroom into a farce that at times rivaled the bizarre antics of a Marx Brothers movie. Nowhere in the country were the lines between the radical left and the Establishment status quo so sharply drawn as in Hoffman's Chicago courtroom. Political divisions over the war in Vietnam, civil rights, and basic liberties played out daily in exaggerated extremes and passionate intensities that, if taken as an index of the national mood, suggested nothing less than the dawn of civil war. In fact, most commentators on the trial were quick to point out that members of the Chicago Eight who spoke outside Illinois exposed themselves to the same indictment they were being tried for—crossing state lines to incite a riot. But with the growing national news media coverage they received, nothing seemed to daunt the Chicago Eight. They continued to speak out at every opportunity. Most of these opportunities came at liberal university campuses.

Stepping to the podium after his introduction, it didn't take Hayden long to stride into the explanation for what had led to the Chicago Eight Trial.

> As for the Democratic convention, Richard Daley thought it was necessary to show that he hated hippies and protesters as much as George Wallace—that's one theory. This is a conspiracy that saw Hubert Humphrey and Lyndon Johnson as pawns rather than in command. But I think two conspiracies were actually going on. First, an election year plan to be the party of law and order and, secondly, an attempt by the ultra-right to overthrow the government and establish in the justice department, the White House, and the Pentagon people who had ideas that were immediately consistent with the FBI and the CIA. And they have accomplished that. I mean, look at a man like Klinedinst who announces—and Will Wilson—both of whom have announced that radicals should be rounded up and put in detention camps—and who have said that the left in this country is a group of ideological criminals. These are people I would consider to be ultra-rightists.

As he spoke, Hayden leaned to his left at the podium. My angle from the front left wasn't good so I moved to the center aisle to kneel and take a few close-ups. Listening as I moved, I imagined how the conspiracy he pictured might play as a Hollywood melodrama. So his next trope didn't come as a complete surprise.

> And if you have seen the movie "Z"—how many people have seen the movie "Z"? Just won the New York Critics Award as the best movie of the year. And it was played, by the way, for the first time in the United States at the Panthers United Front against Fascism Conference—which a lot of people didn't take very seriously last July.

The movie is about Greece, which is not so far from America—and I'm not making a reference to the Vice-President. It's about Greece and it sketches out the way that a police state operates—the way it first overthrows the government but leaves it formally intact and then eventually finds it necessary to overthrow it altogether. I think that "Z" is a movie about what happened in Chicago and what's happening elsewhere and that everybody should see it.

As I moved to the side aisle for a different angle, framing more of the first few rows of the audience, I noticed the red hair and beard of anthropology assistant professor Bill Allen seated in the second row. He had recently become a campus celebrity in the wake of the controversy over his failure to gain tenure. Popular with students, his cause had been adopted by the Radical Union and a petition circulated around campus for an "open hearing" regarding the tenure decision. Hayden's next theme no doubt caught Allen's attention, since his classes were notorious for critical discussion of the Vietnam War.

In times of crisis it is always the objective of the government to create the specter of an internal enemy, a devil inside the country preventing progress. In 1968 there was a tremendous desire in the middle class for some kind of change. And on all the campuses there were people who wanted university reform. The government said it was in favor of more student power—even Richard Nixon said that. But they also said first we have to get rid of the troublemakers who raise the question. The chief obstacles of implementation were the people who raised the question in the first place. The same with Vietnam. It's the Vietcong who are the obstacle to self-determination in Vietnam. If only we could remove the Vietcong, we would withdraw our forces and let the people have their freedom. This is the kind of double-talk we get. I don't even know how to describe the seriousness of it.

Hayden threw his arms up to punctuate his exasperation.

People who come to our trial can't believe what they see. And our trial is nothing compared to what's happening to the Illinois chapter of the Black Panthers. Chairman of the Panthers was shot in bed. He was assassinated by an invading force of State's Attorney's police. This is during our trial. I don't think people even begin to comprehend what happened. That's why you have to see the movie "Z." You have to see it dramatically rather than hear about it in speeches. The way in which Fred Hampton was assassinated—during a 4:30am raid after having been secretly drugged with secanol—is enough evidence to indicate to people that somewhere near the center of our government is a group of fascists—who are employing time-honored techniques that nobody seems to believe could come to America. They are applying these time-honored techniques all around us.

Hayden then turned to anecdotes from the trial, including John Voight's visit to the courtroom, an account of the testimonies of Alan Ginsberg and Arlo Guthrie, and a thorough berating of the childish antics of the judge. He continued for several more minutes until a commotion to his right off-stage caused him to pause. Apparently it was time for him to conclude. He summarized his remarks about the fascist conspiracy and the need for bold action and ended on an ominous note.

I think we have to develop the attitude that some of us are going to have to spend the revolution in jail. And some of us will be out in the streets. But being in jail is better than being murdered in bed. And sometimes I think that being murdered in bed is better than living a normal life in American society.

The person who introduced him then returned to the podium and stood beside him.

Tom needs to leave in order to speak to another gathering at UCLA. On our way out of the building we can thank him by giving a donation to the Chicago Eight Trial Defense Fund. Also at the doors please take the time to sign the petition for an open hearing for Professor Bill Allen of the Anthropology Department. Assassination is only one of the more extreme ways that powers that be get rid of so-called troublemakers. Professor Allen has been singled out and his contract unfairly terminated because of his political views. He needs your support, so everyone who has not signed the petition please do so now. Thank you.

I followed the exiting crowd into the lobby and found Canova manning a table for the Bill Allen petition. His northern Italian charm, crowned by kinky blond hair, had attracted two co-eds. They smiled in conversation with him as they signed the petition. I stood a few paces from the table watching when I heard a voice from behind.

—I recognize that camera!

I turned to see the drama queen approaching.

—Hi Melanie.

—I never forget a good camera.

Her smile flashed rows of perfect teeth set against high cheekbones, fair skin, blue eyes, and long straight blond hair. She was average height but not average looks. Her awareness of that fact wasn't endearing. She carried on as I lagged behind, searching for a retort.

—We have a lab date yet?

—I guess you'd like to see some glossies?

—Yeah, I haven't heard from you. What's happening?

—Well, I need to read up on processing a little more . . . you know, to improve the odds of making you come out good.

She pushed me with her right hand.

—You're awful! I can't believe you said that!

I smiled, pleased to have taken a shot at her fortress of self-confidence. But despite her bravado, it took work to overlook her assets. With stoic resolve, I clung to the inner voice of wisdom that assured me she was more interested in getting her prints than in me. So I turned to business.

—The lab is really busy right now and I need a stretch of time to do everything. I'll stay in touch on how soon I can work something out. You still sure you want to be there?

—No offense, but I want to be there.

—I understand. When I get the day set, I'll stop by. If you're not there I'll leave a note on your door. I'll try for a late afternoon or early evening slot. Hopefully we won't have a conflict. Meanwhile, don't lose that film.

—Like that's going to happen!!

Melanie rolled her eyes. Everything about her tone and mannerisms, from her matter-of-fact delivery to her slight tilt forward at the waist, spoke of The Valley. She exuded girlishness and carnal maturity in an amusing and disarming blend.

As I said goodbye to Melanie, I looked toward Canova and saw the two women signing the petition leaving. Canova nodded to me and held out a pen.

—Hi Marleau, your name on here yet?

I shook my head and walked up to the table.

—No, I haven't signed it.

—Now's your chance. Over half the student body has—not that it matters much to the Anthro Department and the administration.

—Does that surprise you?

—It could bring things to a head.

—You mean ultimatums?

—Something like that.

—The Radical Union figures this list of names gives them a mandate for that?

—That would be getting ahead of things. There'll be a scheduled rally for support. Hopefully the majority of signers on this petition will show. If the administration continues to stonewall, then it'll be up to the crowd to decide what to do.

—Good. Nothing like a mob for clear-headed action.

Canova let out a sigh, then, with a knowing smile, leveled a stare at me and held out the pen again. I shrugged, took the pen, and signed the petition while changing the subject.

—How's the store coming?

—It's nearly done. You should take a look. I'll be there the rest of the day.

Canova prepared to open a used book store on Pardall Road in the community next to campus. I told him I'd stop by in the afternoon.

* * *

Chapter 4

The place Canova and I now called home—Isla Vista—counted as unusual by any standard. The University and Isla Vista sit alone together ten miles north of Santa Barbara on a rise of sandstone called Goleta Point that juts into the Pacific like the corner of a football field. The lay of the land along this entire section of coastline is counter intuitive. The ocean lies directly south rather than west because of the way the land mass bulges near Santa Barbara. Bordered by the ocean to the south, the Devereaux Slough to the west, the Goleta Slough to the north, and the University to the east, Isla Vista filled a confined corner. By the late 60s that corner was home for over 11,000 residents—mostly students.

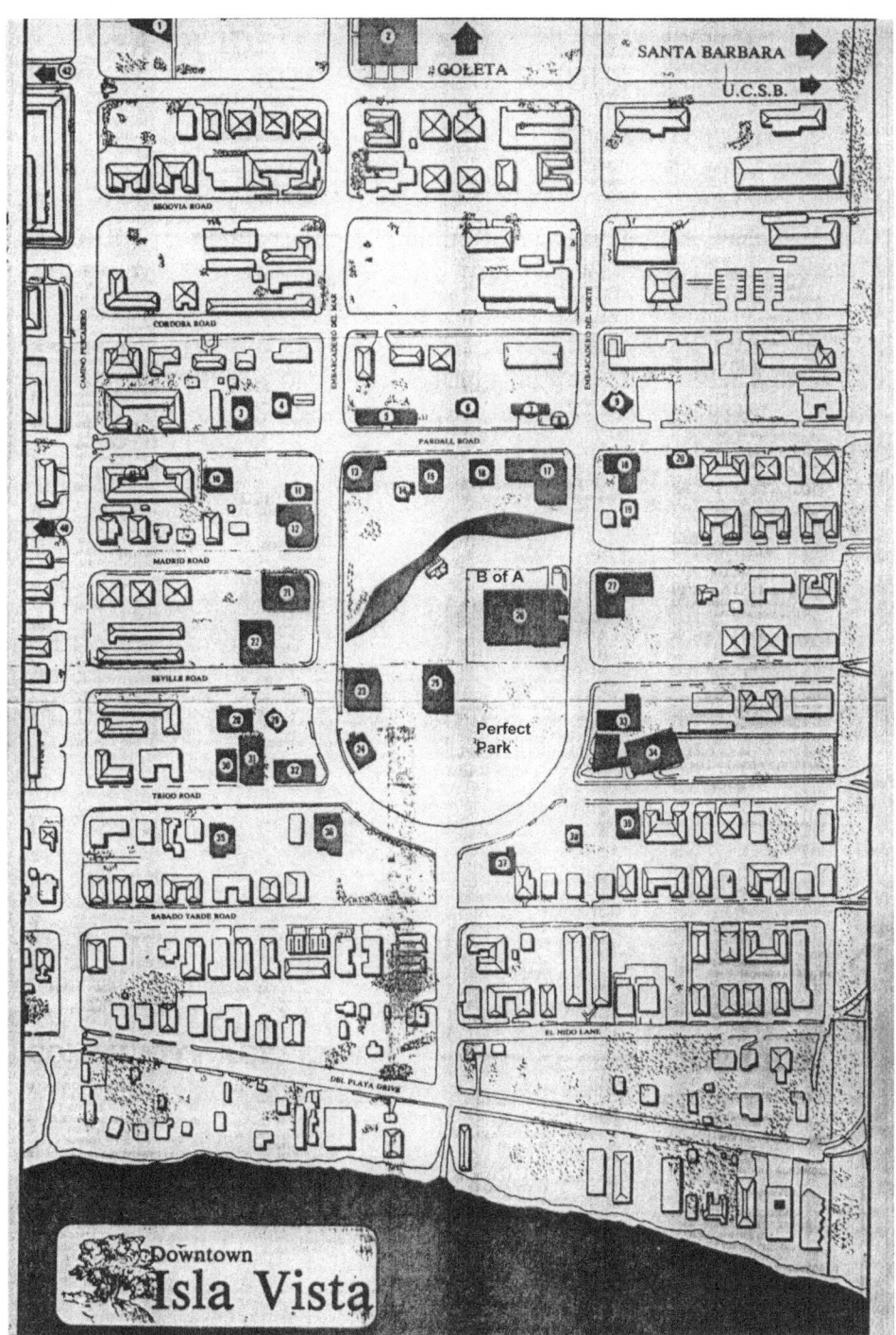

GOLETA

SANTA BARBARA

U.C.S.B.

B of A

Perfect Park

Downtown Isla Vista

Two arteries connect Isla Vista to the rest of the world. Storke and Los Carneros Roads branch south from highway 101, the old El Camino Real, for about a mile until they intersect El Colegio Road, which runs east into campus. Five streets extend like fingers south from El Colegio toward the ocean. The two streets closest to campus—Embarcadero del Mar and Embarcadero del Norte—form what residents call "the loop" because of the way they meet at the south end in a half circle only a block from the ocean. A block further east and parallel to the Embarcaderos, Ocean Road and a long row of eucalyptus trees divide Isla Vista from campus.

Most of the commercial development in Isla Vista lay along the loop south of Pardall Road within half a mile of the ocean. Although filled with record stores, realty offices, coffee houses, fast food dives, book stores, a pool hall, and two small markets, several lots in the loop area remained vacant. By '69 a large lot at the southern end had been commandeered by locals and named "Perfect Park." Perfect Park was anything but perfect—little more than a dirt field inhabited by a few hardy weeds.

The "park" presented a stark contrast to a large white building sitting by itself on the northern edge—the Bank of America. As the only bank in Isla Vista and with primly columned architecture, it stood out like an embassy in a third world country.

From the University at Goleta Point the coastline extends briefly north, forming the eastern edge of campus, then sweeps east into Goleta County Beach and Park.

East of the park, intermittent beach fronting estates, avocado orchards, and swatches of inland suburban residences fill the corridor to Santa Barbara where the scenery then changes to a Mediterranean landscape dominated by palm trees, manicured gardens, white stucco buildings, and red tiled roofs—all ascending gradually up the hills overlooking a small harbor.

During the 60s, the UCSB campus became the buffer between the increasingly estranged worlds of Santa Barbara and Isla Vista. Visually the campus reflected these extremes of lifestyle. Narrow, two-story, wood-planked barracks handed down from the war era when Goleta Point was a military base mixed oddly with newer university constructions—multi-story, quasi-resort style towers displaying faux balcony grids and designer cinderblock facades.

Even from Goleta Point, gazing out on the cobalt sea rimmed by the Channel Islands, the sense of extremes persisted. The campus had all the natural charms of a first class seaside resort except for one thing—the oil. Several miles out in the channel, three oil platforms sat like anchored galleons taking on black gold. With all the subtlety of reality breaking in on a dream, the oil managed to permeate everything—from clumps of sticky black tar washed up on the white sand beaches to the faint but discernible odor of petroleum mingled with the scent of eucalyptus from the stands bordering Ocean Road. In the sea, the sand, and the air, the oil was inescapable.

People new to the area would first think to blame the off-shore drilling for the tar on the beaches. And Union Oil did contribute a major oil slick to the channel in '69 from a pipeline blowout. But the tar was part of the local ecology before the off-shore drilling began. So much oil lay under the seafloor it oozed up naturally and washed ashore even before Spanish ships sailed through the channel. Chumash Indians used it to seal the bottoms of their sea-faring canoes. The tar was especially prevalent on the beaches at either side of Goleta point and the beach fronting Isla Vista.

Locals were not happy about the small black patches that collected on their feet when walking barefoot along the beaches. Cans of solvent kept by front doors spoke to the remedy for that problem. But against the beauty and pleasures of living by the sea, however, the tar weighed as a small complaint.

But owing to its size, dense population, substandard housing, and proximity to affluent Santa Barbara, Isla Vista garnered the tag line: "one square mile of reality surrounded by paradise." Growth came rapidly along with the University expansion in the late 50s. As the University dorm housing project failed to keep up with the increasing enrollment, developers descended on Isla Vista like homesteaders in a land rush. Since the area was unincorporated, it fell outside city building codes. Consequently shoddy, slapdash construction proliferated. Within only a few years of use—combined with minimal maintenance—much of the housing acquired an unkempt and shabby appearance sufficient to prompt some to tag the area as a "white ghetto."

Isolated at Goleta Point, Isla Vista emerged as a demographically unique community with few adults over the age of twenty-five. The students who resided there—most of whom were living away from home for the first time—experienced a sudden and unparalleled degree of freedom. Inclinations prohibited at home were freely indulged. By the late 60s, Isla Vista emerged as drug central between L.A. and San Francisco, and county authorities found themselves filling the parental vacuum—much to the annoyance of newly liberated students. Local underground newspapers alerted residents to the drug scene with front page headlines like "The Narcs: How They Work and How to Stop Them." As an unincorporated area, policing came under the jurisdiction of the County Sheriff's Office, headed by Sheriff James Webster. Webster had hired a captain with credentials from the FBI in narcotics enforcement and, with deployment of several zealous narcotics agents in Isla Vista, appeared to many residents to be taking his job too seriously.

Lines were drawn and sides chosen. Attitude toward drugs, particularly marijuana, became a litmus test for whether a person was in or out, hip or straight. The stakes involved made it understandable why the mood in student

communities had become paranoid and polarized. Possession of even a small amount of marijuana was a felony punishable by up to five years in state prison. Dealing or even encouraging a minor to smoke marijuana could earn an offender up to life in prison. Anyone caught merely using marijuana would serve from 90 days to a year in county jail, and, if a student, would be subject to suspension or expulsion from the University.

As divisions polarized between the marijuana tolerant and intolerant, separate political cultures evolved. The drug culture gave new impetus to the old politics of the franchised versus the disenfranchised. From the point of view of students, the issue was simple. Students had no power. On campus they had little or no voice in administration policies or decision-making. In Isla Vista they had no voice in community issues, because, being unincorporated, Isla Vista fell under county commissioner decision-making. Male students under 21 years of age were subject to a military draft even though not yet old enough to vote. Similarly, students under 21 who smoked marijuana violated laws over which they had no control. Not being of voting age, they had no political muscle. Last but not least, while attending the University most students were dependent on someone else—parents or banks—for financial support.

Despite being "liberated" from the family in the sense of having their own place for the first time, students were disenfranchised in every way that mattered politically. They were expected to embrace the rules without having a voice in making the rules. Consequently, while tasting freedom, they continued to feel the pinch of Mother Hubbard's outgrown shoe. Constrained by a system that continued to view them as dependent children or worse, students easily identified with every sign of repression on the local and national scene. And representatives of repression were not wanting.

Union Oil had recently catapulted to the top of the list of local "oppressors." In January of '69 one of Union Oil's two drilling platforms in the Santa Barbara Channel experienced a drilling accident and subsequent blowout sufficient to produce an 800 mile long oil slick along the channel. A significant quantity of this oil ended up on local beaches, including the beaches around UCSB and Isla Vista.

35

As part of a one year commemorative protest of the previous year's oil spill, a group of environmentalists and students organized a march and sit-in on Stearn's Wharf—the Santa Barbara pier. Stearn's Wharf continued to be an important staging area for Union Oil and the march sought to advance the cause of discontinuing oil drilling in the channel. Drilling was regarded by many as not worth the risk of future oil spills.

Secretary of Interior Walter Hickel suspended drilling for a brief period after the Union Oil accident, then allowed it to continue against the protests of many Santa Barbara residents. Soon after this reversal it became obvious to many why Hickel changed his mind. He had been Chairman of the Board and principle owner of the Anchorage Natural Gas Company. When becoming Secretary of Interior, he resigned as chairman and sold his shares but retained substantial stock in a conglomerate that owned the gas company—Alaska Interstate. And this company purchased all of its natural gas from—you guessed it—Union Oil. It occurred to many in California, including a majority in the State Assembly, that Hickel had a direct conflict of interest. In the revolutionary spirit of 1776, many on campus viewed the march on the pier as a kind of Boston Tea Party where, instead of spilling tea, the point was to stop spilling oil. The Stearn's Wharf protest achieved sufficient notoriety to earn national television coverage. But although the Stearn's Wharf sit-in had been billed as the major local event of the season, the growing controversy over the "firing" of Bill Allen threatened to upstage it.

*　　*　　*

Chapter 5

Nearing the row of shops housing his fledgling business, I spotted Canova at the edge of the vacant lot behind his store. He crouched in front of a circular slab of wood. Turning the slab over, he began spraying something across the surface. Moving closer, I saw it was a section cut from a huge eucalyptus tree over which he held a can of Raid. Hundreds of gyrating ants covered the slab. Seeing him wince against the toxic cloud, I offered advice.

—You should try talking to them.

He stopped spraying and turned around.

—What?

—Talk to the ants.

Flashing a knowing smirk, he played along while examining the cluster of ants.

—Tried that.

—What'd they say?

—Said go to hell. They were winning, so I had to call up chemical reserves.

He held out the can, gave it several shakes, and fogged the ants again.

—What do you want with that mangy slab of wood?

—Can't you see it? A table top for the store. I'll put a smaller stump under it for support and that'll finish it off.

—It'll smell really nice once you get that Raid soaked into it.

He aimed the nozzle of the can at the wood again, releasing several more blasts.

—My capitalist partner has me on a tight budget.

—Who might that be?

—The University. Don't tell anyone, but my scholarship money is launching this hope and prayer of a business.

Most of the ants on the slab of wood now curled up and dropped off. Canova swept away the remaining few with a piece of cardboard.

—That'll spread you thin.

—I'm moving into the back of the store, so that saves rent. Got a sizable stock of books now—all paid for. Sales should start generating income soon.

—Have any help watching the store?

—I'll be here most of the time. But I've got a guy who'll help out a few hours here and there so I can get out when I need to. Mostly I'll just borrow notes and skip classes. I'll do the reading and take the tests, but I'm not sweating the details.

—Adventure in commerce, 1A.

—Main thing is to get the store hyped and keep it going—whatever it takes.

He motioned toward the slab and I helped him lean it against the stucco wall of the building. He stood back and studied it as if it were a work of art. After a few seconds he broke his focus and turned to me.

—What are you doing right now?

—Standing here.

—Got plans for the weekend?

—Nothing big.

—Come with me. I'm leaving for Morro Bay.

I knew he didn't have a car or money so his basic plan quickly took shape in my mind.

—Riding the thumb?

—The only way to fly.

—What's in Morro Bay?

—Enlightenment.

—I've only got a couple of bucks.

—That'll do.

—How do we eat?

—Spare-change-it along the way.

—Where do we crash?

—On the beach. In the woods. Get creative, go native.

—I don't know. Seems so planned out, having a destination and all.

—Right. We'll dispense with that. We wind up where we end up.

I lobbed him a you're-too-accommodating look and asked to see the store before we left. We entered through the back door into a small room he had sectioned off from the main part of the store. To the right was a toilet room with sink and next to it a small coat closet. On the left wall two by fours famed a platform holding a small twin mattress and a counter covered with dishes, hot plate, and an assortment of other kitchen items.

Sweeping aside a tie-dyed sheet pinned over the doorway, Canova led me into the store. Not much wider than a railway car, the walls on both sides were lined to the front with ceiling-high selves. The smell of fresh cut pine from the newly installed shelves filled the air along with a hint of incense. An old oak school desk sat in the far right corner by the front windows along with a potted plant on each side. All the shelving space held books and many more sat piled in rows in the middle of the room. Canova explained these would be given away or tossed—the unusable remains of boxes of books purchased at garage sales and flea markets in the Los Angeles area over the past several weeks. Two threadbare stuffed chairs in the back corners of the room and a large batik linen pinned to the middle of the ceiling completed the furnishings.

Passing on the opportunity to chide him about the rustic décor, I congratulated him on the impressive selection of books—a selection dominated by art, history, literature, philosophy, and criticism. I shared his interest in the liberal arts and could have spent several hours examining the books. But he was in a hurry to get on the road. After he grabbed a jacket from the closet, we left by the back door and walked toward El Colegio. As we ambled along, he pointed to my camera.

—You go anywhere without that thing?

—I need the practice for my journalism class.

—I'll try to be newsworthy.

Before I could reply, a rust-mottled Buick pulled over in response to his soliciting thumb. The driver regaled us with details from his afternoon on the rare high surf at Goleta Point before dropping us at Storke Road and highway 101.

Within ten minutes of our arrival at the on-ramp, a 50s era Mercedes convertible roadster pulled toward us. I immediately recognized the car but was surprised by the driver—Kyle Kincaid, a philosophy TA. Several years older than Canova and I, in his late twenties maybe, Kincaid's tan-weathered face and short-trimmed beard conveyed a well-traveled look. He rolled the Mercedes alongside us. I told him we were heading to Morro Bay and he said he could take us as far as Avalon. I motioned for Canova to take the passenger seat. I squeezed into the small space behind the two front seats while doing the introductions.

—Paul's an old friend. We go back as far as junior high in Santa Rosa.

Kyle nodded toward Canova as I continued.

—Kyle's a TA for Macomber. I had his section in philosophy last quarter. He had us playing pool for our final grade.

Canova threw up his hands and turned toward me.

—Why don't I get classes like that?

I continued explaining as Kyle put the Mercedes up to speed northward on highway 101.

—Actually, like real life, it was harder than it sounds, right Kyle?

—Something like that.

—Kyle's the only guy I know who can give as good as he gets with Macomber. What are you doing with Bill's car?

—Won it from him in a poker game.

—Jeez, that's high stakes poker for campus life.

—Bill likes living on the edge. One night he pushed his luck and I got luckier. We worked out a deal, though. He keeps the car so long as I can borrow it whenever I want.

—What's in Avalon?

—Visiting Terry. We were in Nam together. I'm sure he wouldn't mind if you crashed for the night. You could go on in the morning.

Things were falling together. Although I wasn't a fan of hitching, Canova's planless plan was working. Just raise a sail and trust a favorable wind to come along.

Around twilight we approached the ocean-side community of Avalon near San Luis Obispo. Kyle guided the Mercedes through streets veiled in thickening fog and finally pulled into a covered driveway alongside a small, ranch-style, wood-frame house. We entered through the kitchen where Kyle introduced us to Angie—an attractive, dark-haired woman sitting at the table smoking a cigarette and sipping a beer. I didn't know whether she was there for Kyle or Terry. She glanced at us and said hello. Kyle repeated the introductions when Terry entered from the living room. Beardless, with a mop of blond hair, Terry seemed slightly younger than Kyle but probably wasn't. Immediately friendly, he invited us to join them for spaghetti. When Kyle explained our situation, Terry said he would find us a corner to bed down in his living room. We had barely opened our mouths in thanks before he handed us beers from the refrigerator. Terry's agreeable manner contrasted with Angie who eyed us silently from her seat at the table, coolly blowing smoke from her cigarette.

While we ate, talk turned to Bill Allen. Terry had heard about the controversy and wanted to know more. Canova knew Allen, so he offered to explain.

—I had Allen for a class last quarter. He teaches ethnography but grounds it in current events. He focused a lot on the economics of farming, United Farm Workers, politics of the war, and related stuff. He's competent enough, but it's obvious why they're axing him.

—Why's that?

—He doesn't wear a tie to class.

Terry grinned and played along.

—Well yeah, I mean how can they let that sort of thing go on?

—Right. He's as good as gone because he looks like a hippie—long hair, beard, sandals, work shirt. And get this. You know one of the reasons they gave for dropping him? He doesn't keep the proper "social distance" between himself and students. Can you imagine that?

Canova winced to punctuate his disbelief. Terry showed little surprise but prodded him for more.

—They also said his teaching is below standard—even though he gets high evaluations from his students. They fault his teaching because he refuses to give multiple choice tests and doesn't give enough Cs. It's all pretty sick.

—Let me guess. His publications and research are lacking, too.

—You got it. Hell, he's published as much as the average assistant prof and yet they say he hasn't published enough. He even has a book under evaluation. Plus he's gotten a grant from the National Science Foundation and done research on a tribe somewhere in tropical Peru. What do they want from the guy? It's clearly a political thing. They don't like his radical attitude and his student sympathies. It threatens their control on the direction of the department.

—Well, you know he's getting off easy. At least they haven't accused him of being a communist.

—Not yet anyway. Angela Davis has a case. She can fight because she's uncovered a contradiction in university regulations. But Allen has no leverage. Rules were followed, but not fairly. Yet he can't challenge that because of confidentiality. Everything is done behind closed doors. All they have to do is list reasons without justifying them. They can be completely autocratic. Allen is screwed. He really has no recourse—other than kicking the walls.

Terry leaned back with a sigh.

—The great University! Alma Mater! You know, the space for abuse has always been there in the system, the rules. Only now it becomes more visible as lines get drawn between right and left, straight and kinked, low and high . . .

As he spoke he pulled a small, white, rolled paper from his shirt pocket.

—Speaking of high . . . ARPR anyone?

Canova smiled, but with a curious look.

—What?

—Already rolled pocket rocket. How about an after dinner smoke? Too much talk of politics gives you a sour stomach.

Having never smoked—unless I counted the second hand smoke inhaled at rock concerts in Robertson Gym—I declined. Terry, Kyle, and Canova went around the corner into a section of the living room divided by French doors. That left me sitting in the kitchen with Angie and the dishes. She broke the silence.

—You don't smoke?

—No.

—You don't smoke. You don't cuss either, do you?

She leaned forward, smiling slightly, and looked me in the eyes.

—Bet you're still a virgin, too.

She said it in an odd way that didn't sound entirely insulting. As she stared at me she put her right hand in the side pocket of her jean jacket, pulled out a cigarette, and lit it. Annoyed and challenged, I searched for a comeback. Out of the corner of my eye I noticed a Tarot deck lying on the counter and gestured toward the cards.

—You know, reading people isn't as easy as reading those.

—Depends on the person . . .

I thought she had finished as she paused and took a drag on the cigarette. But then she completed the sentence on the exhale.

— . . . doing the reading.

—You read well, do you?

—Maybe we'll do a reading sometime.

—Why bother? You're talking like I'm already read.

My face reddened as the double entendre hit me. She came close to laughing and got up from the table.

—Do you do dishes?

—I'm paralyzed in both arms.

She reached in a drawer, pulled out a dish towel, and threw it toward my face. I reacted instinctively and caught it with both hands.

—Your arms look okay to me.

Outmaneuvered, I stood up and helped her. As we washed and stacked the dishes, she informed me about the Major and Minor Arcana. She had shifted to a less aggressive tone but one that still retained a measure of condescension. There was something about her I liked, but she wasn't making it easy to like her—a deliberate act I sensed. I couldn't decide whether it was me in particular who put her off or whether the pose of being put off was part of her style. When we were almost finished, the telephone rang from another room and she went off to answer it.

I washed and dried the last few dishes. After moving into the living area, I sat down on a chair on the other side of the closed French doors and picked up a magazine. Feeling alienated, I drifted asleep in the chair until sometime later when Canova woke me. He wanted me in the other room so I could better hear what was on the stereo. While listening, he showed me the album cover as the Paul Butterfield Blues Band played East/West. We talked some about music, then Canova changed the subject.

—So Kyle, you were in Nam?

Kyle nodded, then just stared at Canova. I had seen his uncanny stare before. Head steady, eyes wide open and unblinking, his gaze pierced through you, yet in a way strikingly calm and lacking in hostility. After the silence grew awkwardly long, Canova gathered himself and pressed on.

—So what was it like?

The music, although not very loud, took over the room. I wondered if Canova had blundered into asking the wrong question at the wrong time. Finally, Kyle spoke up.

—What do you want to know?

—I don't know. Anything you feel like talking about.

Kyle let out a slight snort of a laugh.

—Who *feels* like talking about Nam?

—Yeah, I guess that was a stupid way of putting it.

Never shifting his gaze from Canova, Kyle then spoke evenly, sometimes with short pauses between sentences.

—Being there isn't like anything you can imagine. The way you live now—you wake up and think to yourself—what class do I need to get to today? In Nam you wake up thinking I could lose my arm or leg today—or maybe even get my head blown off. Things can happen anywhere to anybody, accidents happen, but out there death is *the* happening thing.

Without changing expression, he then leaned slightly forward.

—There are guys out there who're doing nothing but trying to kill you.

Leaning back again, he continued at the same calm pace.

—I can sit here and tell you this but there's no way you can understand it, no way you can feel it, until you get thrown into it. When that happens, it'll rearrange everything. You'll never be the same.

Kyle pulled a roach out of the ceramic bowl he used as an ashtray. Pinching it carefully between his thumb and forefinger, he struck a match with his right hand, and moved the flame up to light the roach. He took a drag, held his breath for a few seconds, and then blew the smoke toward the ceiling.

—Nobody can live like that. Nobody can do it.

He shifted the roach to his right hand.

—Do you know how you get through it?

Kyle paused for so long I began to think he wanted one of us to answer. But we said nothing. Apparently having worked something out in his head, he continued.

—You get through it because you stop living. One day you discover you're dead already on the inside. You're a walking corpse. Sure, you tell yourself stories about how you'll get through it. But deep inside you know it's already over. You begin to sense your life doesn't matter. How can it matter in a place where every day you wake up knowing you can take a hit and be gone just like that? And for what? In some corner of yourself you let go. When you do that, you die—die on the inside. But that dying doesn't kill the ugliness of what you see around you.

The stereo had stopped playing. Silence filled the room.

—It only kills the fear. When you go dead on the inside, your fear dies too. That's what needs to die—because you get sick to death of feeling it. But when the fear goes, everything that matters goes with it.

Seeing the roach was fried, Kyle squeezed it between his thumb and forefinger and moved them back and forth. What remained of the roach shredded into the ashtray he held below it.

—Believe it or not there are guys who come over to Nam eager for the fight. They come over with this thing about how facing down death is like the way to cross over, the way to cross into *real* life—like somehow they're just shadows until they pass that test. They get over that quick. Living with death every day is how to become a shadow. It sucks the value out of everything. And when that happens—which it does—that's when the real fight begins.

Kyle stopped again and stared directly at me. He said nothing but continued to stare until it seemed like he stared through me—maybe even somewhere past me into who I might become. Unable to take the stare any longer, I broke the silence.

—What's it like for you now?

—When you get back—if you get back—the fight isn't over. You think it's over, but it's not over. When you get back, that's when you find out what you're really made of—when you have to figure out how to put value back into what you took it out of. You have to find a way to reverse that. But it doesn't work so easy in reverse. When I got back from Nam, I found myself acting—playing a role like some character on a stage—pretending it all mattered, taking it seriously. I had the idea that if I played the role long enough I'd forget I was acting. On a good day I do forget.

Seeing I wasn't pursuing it, Canova took over.

—And on a bad day?

—On a bad day? I remember everything. Some things stay as clear as yesterday. Have you ever touched a corpse?

Canova and I shook our heads and waited for Kyle to continue. But Kyle looked toward a voice coming from the far side of the room.

—You telling lies again? He's so full of shit.

The voice was Angie's. She leaned against the door jam where one of the French doors stood open. Canova and I looked up in surprise. I didn't know if she had been there for a while or had just arrived. The look on her face didn't show whether she was kidding. Angie was hard to read. Kyle gazed at her and just smiled.

*   *   *

Chapter 6

The next morning Canova and I awoke at daylight. The blankets Terry had given us didn't make the floor much of a bed, so we were more than ready to be on our way. The others were still sleeping, so we left a thank you note on the table and let ourselves out through the kitchen door. At the freeway we caught a ride in the back of a pickup truck. The wind noise in the truck bed made it difficult to hear, so we didn't talk much on the ride to Morro Bay.

Though we had been friends since junior high, Canova and I had not seen much of each other since his year in Italy on a study abroad program for high school seniors. And before he left I spent most of the summer at the UCSB high school juniors "get acquainted with university life" program. Before I returned to Santa Rosa in mid August, he had left for New York on the first leg of his trip to Italy. He spent the next year in Bologna at the equivalent of an American high school—but with emphasis on Greek and Latin and classical history and philosophy. This curriculum better suited Canova's ambition for something more challenging and exotic. The "plodding monotony"—as he called it—of instruction at Santa Rosa High was second only to his genealogy among reasons why he was eager to spend a year in Italy.

The first time I saw him when he returned to Santa Rosa in late July of '68 confirmed changes. He was visibly different. His sand-colored hair, usually cropped short, was now nearly shoulder-length and he wore loose-fitting clothes purchased second-hand in Italy. Though he had picked up some flavor from Italy, I gathered his experience there had not turned out to be everything he had hoped. He seemed genuinely glad to be back in California and didn't volunteer much in the way of details about his time in Italy. Instead we talked about the future.

We had both tested for the California Regents' Scholarship—a four year award, including room and board with tuition, based on academic merit and a qualification interview. We jokingly swore that if the other won, it would be the end of the line for our friendship. With unbelievable luck, we both won four year scholarships. And we picked the same campus—UCSB—because it was far enough from home and not too close to Los Angeles—a freeway clogged smog zone that held little attraction for us. Though we drifted apart again in our freshman year, we reconnected in the fall of '69 while taking a Hugh Kenner class on Yeats and Eliot. Then in early January he persuaded me to join him at the weekend strategy meeting for the Radical Union. But the trip up the coast would be the first we had spent any length of time together since high school days. With the opening of his used book store he had changed his relationship to books. Rather than read them, he would now buy and sell them. I was curious about what else had changed.

After a half hour ride, Morro Bay came into view from the highway. I passed through this area once a few years back on a family vacation. Aside from its small fishing fleet and oyster farms, I couldn't recall much about the place. But there was one thing no one could forget—the rock—dominating the setting just as I had remembered. Framed by the white sandy curve of the shore and the deep blue of the bay, it stood conspicuously solitary only a few hundred feet from the waterline. Rising as a huge, conical, foliage-covered monolith some 500 feet above the water, the eye couldn't reconcile it with the surroundings. It looked surreally odd—more like something dropped from outer space than anything nature had wrought in the course of time. I viewed it through the camera lens and pressed off a shot.

Our ride took us into town and we spent most of the day wandering through the streets and exploring places around the bay. We didn't walk out on the pier until late afternoon. Canova found some kids fishing and bought a flatfish from one of them. At a market a couple of blocks from the pier we talked another hitcher into buying us a bottle of wine. Then we made our way to the dunes on the North side of the bay.

We had the place to ourselves, along with our choice of two elevated iron fire pits. I wandered off in search of driftwood while Canova cleaned the fish. After canvassing the dunes, I found only two large pieces of driftwood. I managed to break them down, but we still needed kindling. With Canova's knife I shaved off strips of wood and added wadded sheets from a newspaper I had picked up earlier in the day. Neither of us knew much about campfire cooking but it didn't take long to figure out the logs we were using wouldn't burn to grilling coals anytime soon. We threw the fish on anyway—opting for flame broiled—and opened the bottle of wine.

The fish had been searing only a few minutes when the wind started to gust. Before long, it blew apart the newspaper and kindling, fanning a ribbon of smoke and ash across the dunes. Canova tried to reassemble the fire while I whittled more strips off the remaining driftwood. The wind continued gusting and the pit billowed smoke. Canova gamely mumbled something about how the smoke would make the fish taste better. We stood together on one side of the pit, blocking the wind and swigging wine. The wind shifted direction. We shifted with it. Canova grabbed more paper. The wind gusted again, blowing ash onto the fish. We obstinately persisted, feeding the fire with more wads of paper and bits of whittled wood. It became a grudge match between us and the wind.

Finally, our aggravation with the wind peaked, breaking the threshold of mere frustration into the farcical. We started to laugh. Then we couldn't stop laughing. Soon we could barely function. But just as we were becoming completely useless, the wind let up and we were able to get a hot fire going. For a while the fish progressed nicely. Then the wind suddenly returned and blew out the fire. At that point we said to hell with it.

Gingerly flipping the fish onto a picnic table, Canova poked at it with the tip of the knife blade. Parts of the meat seemed cooked, so he sliced off a piece and chewed on it. He raised his eyebrows in surprise at how good it tasted. But when I sampled it, I found he was joking. It was barely edible. As darkness crept across the bay, we pushed the table on its side to block the wind and took cover on the sand behind it. We ate pieces of half-cooked fish with bare hands, drank wine, and made jokes about our mockery of a meal. When the jokes dwindled away, Canova changed the subject.

—Who was the babe I saw you with at Campbell Hall?

—That was Melanie. A friend in the Drama Department introduced me to her. She said she wanted some photos for an ad agency. You won't believe how that went!

—You mean the photo shoot?

—Yeah, dig this. We meet at this small studio on campus that has screens and lighting. She's looking nice, wearing a short skirt and a long sleeve white blouse with a collar. So I do some close-ups. Then she motions me back for some full body shots. I take three or four, and then she stops me and unbuttons her blouse.

—More cleavage?

—No. She unbuttons all the way and takes it off! And there's nothing underneath! She's naked from the waste up!

Canova let out a long whistle.

So I lower my camera and say to her—Like, what are you doing? And without the slightest self-consciousness she says—Never mind. Just keep shooting.

—So what did you do?

—I froze. Finally, I said—Never mind?? Easy enough for you to say! But she's unflappable. She tosses me a smile, then says—C'mon, don't make a big deal of it. Just keep shooting. So I gather myself and she poses and I shoot. Then, just as I'm starting to breathe again, she reaches behind her skirt. In a flash she unzips, steps out, and places it on a chair.

Another whistle from Canova.

—And she has *nothing* under the skirt! Now she's standing in front of me buck naked!!

—Jesus! To hell with bookselling. I want to be a photographer!

—She sees me staring at her, struck dumb, laughs and says—C'mon, snap out of it. Just keep shooting and watch the lighting.

—So what's this babe up to?

—I'm not sure. She must be angling for a spread in some men's magazine. Anyway, we finish the roll and she goes behind a screen and puts her clothes on. But she's not done with surprises. When she comes out, she asks me for the film. I tell her I thought she wanted prints. She says she does, but she wants to hold the film. And when I develop the roll and make the prints she wants to be in the room with me.

—Can't blame her there. A shady guy like you might peddle them on the street. She paying you anything other than the cheap thrill?

—I'm not cheap. We agreed on seventy-five dollars plus materials.

—She pay you?

—Due on satisfactory completion of prints.

—You'll never see her again.

—I already did, stupid—at Campbell Hall where you saw her. Anyway, I thought about that, so I slipped her an unexposed roll.

49

—Very slick.

I told Canova the friend who introduced me to Melanie said she grew up in the Chatsworth area of L.A.—famous for being a part of the film community. Chatsworth might offer opportunities for actresses of all stripes. This fueled more speculation about her designs.

Gradually the subject changed. Knowing that camping on the beach would be hard and cold, we weren't in a hurry for sleep and talked on into the night. But eventually we got too tired to make any sense. I slept fitfully for a couple of hours before the cold finally forced me wide awake. Jacket and newspaper weren't enough insulation from the sand. A damp chill had sneaked in all the way to the bones and the wind was rising again. I sat up and leaned against the table top. A few minutes later Canova woke up and joined me. We knew it was too cold to sleep, so we headed into town looking for someplace warmer.

After wandering down several streets, we retreated from the wind in an alcove at the entrance of a small hardware store. We sat against the doors and Canova pulled a joint from his shirt pocket.

—Want some?

—Where'd you get that stuff?

—Terry gave me two for the road.

Canova lit the jay, took a drag, and held it out to me.

—What the hell. Maybe it'll dull the chills.

I held it as if I were squeezing an insect, slowly drew air through it, and choked out the smoke along with a question I'd been meaning to ask.

—What do you make of Angie calling Kyle a liar?

—Doesn't matter. He made sense to me.

—What were you thinking when he was talking about Nam?

—I was thinking I'm glad I got number 267 in the lottery. I'd cut off toes before I'd go into that meat grinder.

—I'm basically screwed. I got number one.

—Jesus! I didn't know that.

—I'm deferred for now. I don't believe we're getting out of there any time soon.

—Would you actually go to Nam?

—I think about ways to stay out.

—Like what?

—I don't know.

—Leave the country?

—I'd never do that. Warts and all, the U. S. is still the best.

—Go to jail?

—Doubt it.

—You can't go to Nam, man. It's a crazy, immoral war.

—And student deferments? Where's the morality in that?

Canova threw what was left of the roach toward the street.

—A government with its act together wouldn't put us in a war with no clear purpose.

—So how do we end it?

—That takes radical action.

—Radical Union action?

—Why not? It's a step in the right direction.

—Everything's so black and white with them.

—Sometimes, like you just said, you take things, warts and all—especially if you want to make a difference.

—Everyone wants to make a difference. But that's a lot easier than making progress.

—You're skeptical. That's good, I guess. But things are heating up. A guy with your draft number has too much at stake to watch it all from behind a camera. You'll get into it before summer's here. You won't be able to stop yourself.

—Wanna bet?

It was a manner of speaking, but Canova took me seriously.

—I'll bet you that camera of yours. You won't need it anyway when you stop watching and start doing.

—Yeah? And what do I get if you lose this bet?

—How about the satisfaction of standing up for something? But since I'm asking you to put up something material, I'll give you half my store—so long as you agree to work it with me and split the hours.

—You serious?

—Of course.

My thoughts ran as I tried to catch up with whatever motives might be lurking behind this bet. He knew my wheels were spinning.

—C'mon. What do you say?

I could think of reasons not to bite, but the folly of any attempt to predict my behavior was too tempting. I wasn't interested in partnering his store so much as challenging his challenge.

—Fine. You're on. But are you sure you know who you're dealing with?

—Marleau, my man, I've known you since junior high. Who do I know better?

Chapter 7

Around sunrise the wind let up, so we roamed the streets and found an open cafe. Between us we had enough change for coffee and donuts. By noon we had seen enough of Morro Bay and returned to the highway to thumb our way back to Santa Barbara. Before long we got a ride, but it took us only as far as Santa Maria—a small, quiet town off highway 101, not ideal for hitchhiking.

Two hours later we still waited for a ride. Four others—parked on backpacks and rolled sleeping bags—had joined us on the gravel shoulder of the on-ramp. It seemed someone had to take the blame for this downturn in our plan, so I turned to Canova.

—Next time you have a bright idea, share it with your tooth fairy, okay?

—C'mon. You've had such a good time you'll be writing home about it.

—What I'll be writing is new lyrics to "Born under a Bad Sign."

—Thank me when you're rich off that.

As we sat minimizing our prospects, a candy-apple-red muscle car rolled up the ramp past four eager faces and stopped directly opposite us. An all-American-looking beefcake stuck his head out the window.

—Want a ride?

We were immediately on our feet. Beefcake opened the door, and pulled the seat forward. Canova squeezed into the back as I threw a shrug and a "we-were-here-first" look toward the other hitchers.

We settled into the seat, the door closed, and the coupe growled through gears toward the freeway. Beefcake turned to face us and pointed to the driver.

—This here's K. C., not to be confused with "Casey" like "Casey at the bat." Stands for Kevin Cink, Cink with a "C." So you see how he got the nickname "Kitchen." But I save that for when he's really cookin'. I'm William Andrew Arlington Jr. but you can call me "Junior."

I took care of the pleasantries.

—I'm Dan, he's Paul.

Canova raised his hand in a slight how-do-you-do gesture but said nothing Thinking this greeting a bit cool, I attempted to make polite conversation with Junior.

—What make is the car?

—'68 Charger R/T, 440, four speed, four barrel. It's mine but I let K. C. drive 'cause that's what he does. Besides, I'm nippin' a bit.

Junior pulled his hand from between his legs and raised a bottle of Cuervo.

—You want a shot?

I shook my head. Junior looked toward Canova and Canova waived off the bottle. The thought crossed my mind it was good Junior wasn't driving just as he handed the bottle to K.C. who took two large swallows before passing it back to Junior. That wound me up a few turns. Reading the double-take I gave K.C., Junior smiled.

—Needn't worry. K.C.'s a professional. Drives stock cars for a living.

I failed to see his point and felt more uneasy. Then Junior turned to K.C. and asked him to show us what he could do. K.C. didn't need persuading and immediately gunned the accelerator. In an instant the speedometer reached 90 mph. The afternoon traffic provided some obstacles. But K. C. nonchalantly weaved the Charger, pulling within inches of a car then whipping past it. After doing this several times, he approached two cars cruising nearly parallel. The blocked path slowed him down, but not for long. He accelerated and slid between them, with only a few inches to spare on either side. The blood drained from my face. Junior let out a yell.

—Wohaahh, K.C.! Outa sight. That's balls for glory. The Kitchen is cookin'.

He swigged another shot of Cuervo and, sporting a horsy-tooth grin, turned to Canova and me.

—How'd you all like that? Ain't he the starch?

Realizing I had forgotten to breathe, I sucked in air and felt my chest expand against a cold sweat clinging to my shirt. Canova wasn't saying anything either so Junior kept probing.

—Hey, I think you overdid it K.C. These guys don't look so good. But I think they're impressed.

Noticing Canova eyeing him, Junior returned the gaze until Canova finally gave him the response he wanted.

—That was crazy.

Feigning surprise, Junior turned to K.C.

—Hey, K.C., he thinks you're crazy.

K.C. said nothing but grabbed the bottle from Junior and took a chug. He handed it back to Junior who turned to us again and went on a roll.

—He's not crazy. He's just good. What'd you mean, crazy! Sure you guys don't want a shot of this? Looks like you could use it. You know, K.C., I think these guys are the crazy ones. Shit, we're offerin' 'em free booze here. What's the deal?

He tipped the bottle again.

—You two oughta loosen up, have a drink, come on down to L.A. with us. We're partyin' and we'll acquaint you to several stone foxes tonight.

The party I wanted to join was back at the Santa Maria on-ramp. They were luckier than they knew. I glanced at Canova. He stared out the side window. Junior turned back to K.C.

—I can't believe it! It's one thing to turn down Cuervo, but it's a whole n'ther thing to turn down babes. They ain't sayin' nothin' K.C.

Junior made another pass at the bottle and shifted his head back and forth, facing K.C. or us depending on whose attention he wanted.

—Shit, I think I'm onto 'em K.C. I think I'm onto 'em. A little shy, that's all. But hell, that's okay. We can deal with that. Everybody's gotta have a first time—'cept for K.C. here. Christ, he can't even remember a time when he wasn't screwin' somethin'. But whaddaya think, K.C.? The foxes can handle the situation, can't they? The babes can handle the babes. It'll be a night to remember. 'Course, that's a manner of speakin'. In the mornin' you're lucky to remember your name. Hey, what're you doin' K.C.?

Junior had good reason to ask. K.C. had driven entirely off the freeway and onto the median attempting to pass two cars on the right. The Charger rattled and shook, bounding over small rocks and twigs among the dirt and weeds. Seeing the uneven median slowing progress, K. C. floored the accelerator. The car lurched forward then fishtailed. Struggling to maintain control, K.C. refused to let up and Junior shouted.

—Hey, what the hell, K.C.?

About 300 yards ahead the median abruptly changed to heavy shrubs. Certain there was no way to avoid a crash, I braced myself for the worst. But just before we were about to slam into the bushes, K.C. yanked the wheel, throwing us back onto the freeway while almost side-swiping a car to the right. Back on the paved surface, the Charger fishtailed again but K.C. brought it back under control. Behind us the sound of repeated horn honking faded in the distance as Junior continued shouting.

—Jesus Christ! Nice goin', K.C.! Nice goin'. I think you've showed off enough for now. Can't you see I'm tryin' to talk here? Now keep it on the road for Jesus' sake.

K. C. grinned and spoke for the first time.

—Relax. Gimme the bottle.

But Junior kept the bottle and, flaunting another fatuous grin, turned to us.

—He's just tryin' to show off. Hope he didn't scare you any.

Canova and I said nothing while eyeing him with a cold stare. He turned back to K.C.

—You know K.C., I'm goin' to cut you off. You might've chipped my paint back there. I'm goin' to cut you off. No more for you, partner.

K. C. peeked toward Junior and complained.

—Shit, I haven't had any yet. Give me the bottle, damn it.

Junior handed him the bottle and continued facing the front. He seemed temporarily content to let us stew in our predicament. I glanced at Canova who now glared at the back of K.C.'s head. We needed to do something. Junior grew more menacing with every swig. I thought about ordering them to pull over and let us out, but something told me that was exactly what they wanted—so they could refuse and continue toying with us. Inner currents collided. Fear vied with anger mixed with obstinate machismo. The latter seemed to be winning. I refused to play into their hands and ask to be let out of their little game of "chicken," so I settled into the seat and watched the landscape fly by.

Junior couldn't shut up for long. He blathered on about the party in L. A. and repeated his invitation several times. Finally Canova surprised me by casually answering Junior while continuing to stare out the window.

—Nice of you to invite us, Junior, but we've got business in Santa Barbara.

Surprised by this move, I searched for an assist. But what I came up with sounded stupid even to me.

—Yeah, pressing business.

Junior pounced all over it.

—Ohhhhh, *prrressing* business. K.C., they've got *prrressing* business in Santa Barbara. But what could be more pressing than partyin' down with the babes? I think the business they've got in L.A. is much more *prrressing*, for sure.

Junior spewed more nonsense about how he wanted to introduce us to Hugh Hefner. I was convinced they weren't going to let us out at Santa Barbara. After that I wasn't sure what they would do—they probably didn't know themselves. They were making this up as they went. As drunk as they were, and more in the bottle, I pictured us upside down in a ditch in south L. A.

K.C. continued driving erratically—slowing to 85 mph, then gunning to 95 or 100 mph, weaving in and out of cars. Canova and I lurched forward and backward as he hit the brakes and then the accelerator. There was only one good thing about his driving. At the speed K. C. averaged, we were rapidly approaching Santa Barbara. After enduring another twenty minutes of insolent tripe from Junior, our destination finally appeared on the horizon. I told them to let us out at the next exit. Junior made a point of acknowledging the instruction in an exceptionally loud voice.

—Did you get that, K.C.? We need to let them out up here at the Storke Road exit.

The exit came and went with K.C. never even entering the right lane. Junior pretended to be annoyed.

—Jesus, K.C., you missed their exit.

Then he pretended to explain.

—You know, when he gets in a groove drivin' you just can't get him to stop. You've got to have good kidneys in the car with K.C.

At this point, I thought Canova had lost his mind. He extended his hand to Junior.

—Maybe I will have a shot of that.

Junior raised his eyebrows, paused, then finally reacted.

—I'll be damned. Well that's more like it.

I watched, astonished, as Junior handed the bottle to him. But as Canova took the bottle, he let it slip through his fingers to the floor of the car. Then I understood. The contents began gushing out. Junior made a quick lunge for it, but Canova grabbed it first and fumbled it again. Now only a few drops remained in the bottle. Turning the tables on Junior, Canova offered a mock apology.

—Damn. Sorry about that Junior. Clumsy of me.

Junior glared menacingly at him.

—Son of a bitch!

To my further amazement, Canova had more cards to play.

—There's a liquor store at the next exit. I'll buy you another bottle.

At a loss for words for the first time, Junior kept repeating "son of a bitch" to himself as he turned back to the front. Ready for anything, I waited to see what he would do next. Finally he growled to K.C.

—Pull in. This asshole owes us a bottle.

I didn't like the tone of his voice. It was missing even the jeering pretense of affability that had been in it before. K.C. took the Hollister exit and Canova pointed out the direction of the liquor store. Then, as we entered the parking lot, Junior suddenly reached back and grabbed my camera. I had placed it on the seat between Canova and me. Taken by surprise, I yelled at him.

—Hey, what do you think you're doing?

—I'll just keep this 'til you get back with the bottle.

Seeing my camera in his hands, a switch tripped inside me. Junior got out and flipped the bucket seat forward.

—Let's go jerkoff.

He stood at the end of the open car door. As I stepped out, pent up rage burst out. I threw myself at him with a tackling move. We hit the ground hard with me on top. The fall stunned him, but he out-weighed me by several pounds and was able to roll on top of me. Canova, who had followed me out of the car, grabbed him from behind by both arms and pulled him away. Pumped with adrenalin and fuming with rage, I landed a blow to Junior's midsection. He wheezed and doubled over.

By this time K.C., roused from his liquored haze, rolled himself out of the car and rounded the front of the Charger. I delivered another blow to Junior. Too juiced and outraged to know better, K.C. kept coming. Canova let go of Junior and, as K.C. rushed him, deftly stepped aside and shoved him to the ground. He then grabbed the back of my shirt and pulled me away from Junior. With an angry lurch, I spun free of his grip. He got in front of me and backed me up.

—Cool it. That's enough. Let's get out of here before the cops show up.

Cussing and spewing, K.C. stood up and moved toward us again. Together we pushed him into Junior who was on one knee to the side of the Charger. K.C. fell over him and onto the pavement again. I noticed my camera next to the car and grabbed it. As we backed away, K.C. shouted after us.

—You faggot welching assholes! You're gonna pay for this!

We raced down Hollister for a long block, then turned the corner, and went down a side street. I pulled up behind a fence and squatted down to catch a breath. Canova caught up with me.

—They won't follow us.

—Maybe not, but they're thinking about it.

I sucked in a few more breaths.

—You did good dropping that bottle.

—Yeah? That pummeling you gave Junior shut him up for awhile. I've never seen you that mad.

—Nobody touches my camera.

—I'll remember that.

—Now you know why I don't like hitching.

—It's just shit luck.

—You never know when you'll run into cretins like that.

—You can't breathe without taking risks.

—Risk is one thing. Worthless risk is another. If we wound up in a flaming wreck with those shit-for-brains, we'd be thinking what a lousy way to go.

—C'mon, shake it off. Let's hitch a ride to I. V. You need to learn some trust, man.

I knew what he was doing but I wasn't ready to cool off.

*   *   *

Chapter 8

The week passed quickly since Canova and I spent Monday on the return from Morro Bay. True to Canova's expectations, the administration made no concessions on an open hearing for Bill Allen. So the Radical Union set a deadline of noon Thursday for a response and called for a rally of support in front of the Administration Building at 11:00am. Near the start of the rally I stopped at the philosophy lounge on the sixth floor of Ellison Hall to pick up a recording a teaching assistant had made of the philosophy class I'd missed on Monday. After getting the tape, I exited at the west end. Ellison Hall stood on the southeast corner of the quadrangle in front of the Ad Building and each floor had a small balcony overlooking the quad. At the edge of the wall, I peered over the balcony.

Well over two thousand students filled the quad sixty feet below. The rally marked the culmination of six months of progressing conflict between Radical Union led students and the administration regarding the Bill Allen firing. Words from a loudspeaker already filled the air. I was surprised to recognize the voice. Canova had public speaking experience and the Radical Union evidently decided to test it. Standing near the front of the Ad Building, he raised his voice and pointed to the entrance behind him.

—Arrogance. We're here today because of arrogance. The issue is simple: the administration has violated a constitutionally protected right. Professor William Allen's fundamental right to due process has been trampled—first by the Anthropology Department, then by the administration. We're here today because we refuse to tolerate abuse of power.

Lifting the camera, I framed him standing near the entrance to the building and drew the image closer with a zoom telephoto lens. He spoke into a microphone extending from a long chord plugged into a box balanced on someone's shoulder. The crowd whistled and applauded his words as I pressed off the shot and advanced the film. Wanting to get closer, I left the balcony. Canova's voice penetrated the walls as I descended the stairwell

—We're here today because we expect the University to be an example instead of a disgrace when it comes to practicing responsible government.

A roar of approval resounded in the stairwell.

—We're here today to demand a repair and a remedy. An open hearing for Bill Allen to repair the injustice. Student participation on tenure review committees to remedy abuse of power in the future.

Another roar from the crowd.

—In June of last year the Anthropology Department notified Professor Allen that, with the end of his classes this year, his contract would not be renewed. And what were the reasons given? He was told: insufficient research, insufficient publications, and insufficient teaching standards.

Exiting the stairwell, I knifed through the crowd as a chorus of boos filled the air.

—When Professor Allen rightly complained about the unfairness of these so-called insufficiencies—none of which was true—he was then given another reason. He was then told that the real reason was his "attitude." Now this reason began to get a little closer to the truth. They said his "attitude" was—get this—inconsistent with the "master plan." That's right. The "master plan"—something devised by the tenured faculty of the department.

Another chorus of boos. Reaching the middle of the crowd, I raised the camera, framed Canova's head in the viewfinder, sharpened the focus, and released the shutter. He then lowered his voice and projected a sarcastic tone as he continued describing the key events.

—And when Professor Allen complained about the vagueness of that reason, he was then told something else. First they cried "insufficient," then "inconsistent," and now they shifted to, of all things, "indiscreet." Yes, it's true. He was told that he was fired because of his failure to keep the proper "social distance" between himself and his students. In other words, he was too friendly and helpful to students. Incredible!

More boos and exclamations went up from the crowd along with derisive laughter from several in front.

—And when he complained about the arbitrary and subjective nature of that reason—guess what? That's right. He was given yet another reason. He was then told the department was "redefining" his teaching slot in order to fill the need for a full-time archaeologist. This reason came straight in the face of the fact that Bill Allen is, among other things, a trained archaeologist!

To the left of me someone called out.

—Way to go, Bill!

A scattering of cheers rose around the quad.

—The litany of groundless and shifting alibis only serves to prove what the real reason is for Bill Allen's dismissal: the tenured professors in the Anthropology Department just don't like his *politics*. They were right in saying

59

the problem was his attitude—only what they meant was his *political* attitude. He's too radical and anti-authoritarian for their taste and therefore they want to get rid of him. Well we're here today to inform the Anthropology Department what Angela Davis had to inform the Philosophy Department at UCLA—that in this country tenure decisions are made on merit and not on political views and affiliations.

A roar welled up throughout the quad, trailing off with dispersed whistles and the sound of clapping hands on the west side near North Hall—home of the Anthropology Department.

—So, in response to this injustice, we—the students of this University—put together our petition with 7,776 signatures—over half the student body. We presented that to the Anthropology Department and the administration calling for an open hearing on Bill's case. All we wanted was a fair and open review of his case in order to bring some objectivity to it. And what did we get in response? We got a big, fat autocratic "NO." Are you all happy with that response?

As one voice the crowd shouted a deafening "NO." Sensing a swell of emotion, Canova pushed the crowd further.

—When is the administration going to wake up and get it? Tenure decisions are made on merit, not politics!!

The crowd cheered again.

—When are the Regents of the University of California going to wake up and get it? Tenure decisions are made on merit, not politics!!

Another surge of cheers swept across the quad.

—Well, I'll tell you when they're going to get it. They're going to get it today. The administration has our ultimatum: either they accept our demand or we shut this building down and keep it down until they give us an open hearing!!

Everyone erupted into wild applause and hollering. As the ovation of support continued, Greg Knell approached Canova.

Knell was Associated Students Vice-President and also a spokesman for the Radical Union. Knell and Geoff Wallace were key organizers for the Radical Union along with Bill Allen. As one of few faculty members of the Radical Union, Allen's participation largely accounted for why the RU had become instrumental in mobilizing support for his cause.

In the spring of 1969 the local chapter of the Students for a Democratic Society (SDS) had teamed with the Black Student Union (BSU) and the United Mexican-American Students (UMAS) to create a radical coalition. They sponsored candidates for all the Associated Students elective offices. This coalition won two of the Vice-Presidential positions and enough seats to control the Student Legislative Council. Having sponsored candidates for elective positions on the student newspaper, the *El Gaucho*, they also gained control of the paper. By the fall of '69, several members of the local SDS broke from that group, which they regarded as too disorganized, and formed the Radical Union. By controlling the Student Legislative Council and the student paper, the RU positioned itself to set the agenda for student politics.

The signature total on the Bill Allen petition had reached the memorable number of 7,776. Many were already making analogies between the current "revolutionary spirit" marking the fight for student rights and the revolutionary spirit of 1776. The revolutionary agenda included not only the fight for student rights on campus but the larger fight in support of oppressed groups of every sort, including the Chicago Eight, the Black Panthers, the United Farm Workers, those subject to the draft, members of branches of the Communist Party such as Angela Davis, marijuana users, and anyone else who could show abuse by an agency of established powers.

Knell and Canova exchanged a few words. Then Canova faced the crowd again.

—Greg has just told me that Vice Chancellor Buchanan has a statement to make in response to our demands.

Canova turned toward the front of the building where three men emerged and moved into the group of campus police gathered at the entrance. The tallest of the three, a balding man in necktie and blue suit, continued past the police line and through a section of the crowd to where Canova and Knell stood. They talked for a few seconds, then Canova turned to the crowd.

—Vice-Chancellor Buchanan would like to say a few words.

Buchanan took the microphone.

—I'm speaking to you on behalf of Chancellor Cheadle who is currently abroad on University business. I want to begin by reading to you the statement I received on Tuesday from the students responsible for circulating the petition for Bill Allen. Listen to this:

> On behalf of the 7,776 people who called for an open hearing for Dr. William Allen, we express our indignation at the administration's response to the petitions. The administration's statement can only be viewed as a total disregard of the wishes of the majority of students. For this reason, we must reject that statement and insist that the administration accept, by Friday noon, the students' call for an open hearing.

On hearing the Radical Union statement read to them, the crowd erupted into cheers and applause. Buchanan continued.

—It's my understanding that many of you here may not have been aware of the fact that the administration had been handed an ultimatum. That piece of information did not appear in any of the campus publications over the last two days. Ultimatums are not a productive way to move us all toward a resolution, and I think the few responsible for handing over the ultimatum would have been wise to have made their intentions public before doing so. I doubt there would have been broad support for it.

Someone shouted above an uproar of heckling.

—That's not true. We *all* gave you the ultimatum.

Buchanan ignored the comment.

—As it stands, I want to repeat emphatically what I said earlier this week about Professor Allen's case. The decision to let his contract lapse is *not* a politically motivated decision.

Another voice from the crowd shouted at him.

—Then give us an open hearing.

Others whistled and applauded. Buchanan labored on.

—It has been the policy of this administration to encourage student participation at all levels of campus activities—with the exception of academic personnel matters.

A scattering of boos resounded across the quad.

—Those matters must remain in the hands of professional peers and the administration. Peer evaluation and confidentiality are essential to maintaining academic standards and fairness. For those reasons and as a matter of principle we cannot have an open hearing in Professor Allen's case or in any other case.

This brought a roar of disapproval from the crowd.

—Please! Hear me out! In consideration of the degree of dissatisfaction and suspicion relating to the decision concerning Professor Allen, I have ordered an emergency session of the Academic Senate Committee on Privilege and Tenure to meet at one o'clock. They will discuss the Allen decision to see whether, in their view, the matter warrants further review by the Committee. I have asked them to try to have a decision for me by four o'clock this afternoon. In the meantime, I must ask you all to disperse and allow normal traffic in and out of the administration hall.

With that news, Buchanan retreated quickly into the building. Many in the crowd continued to boo the Vice Chancellor but the response was more subdued than before. With Buchanan's message about the emergency session of the Academic Senate Committee, the ball was now clearly in the Allen strategists' court. So after several minutes of discussion around the microphone, the man of the hour, Bill Allen himself stepped forward to speak.

—I want to say something about what we just heard. But first I want to say thanks for the support from friends like you all and the members of the Radical Union—who put together the petition drive. I thank everybody here, man, and everybody who signed the petition for an open hearing. Seven thousand, seven hundred, seventy-six—that has a nice patriotic ring to it.

Whistles of approval filled the air.

—That's overwhelming support and it ought to overwhelm any resistance on the part of *these people*.

His last two words echoed scornfully around the quad as Allen pointed to the Ad Building.

—The principle of an open hearing goes beyond my own case. We can't allow unfair decisions to hide behind a wall of confidentiality and closed doors. The decision-makers need to be accountable. All we're asking for is an open hearing. They won't give us one and that's insane. Who do they think they are?

The crowd broke into a chant.

—OPEN HEARING! OPEN HEARING!

Allen grinned, waited for a few seconds, then interrupted the chant.

—Now let me talk about what we're doing here. Some have suggested that we break in and take over the Administration Building. I don't think we ought to do it. We're just going to get our heads busted because they've got pigs all over this campus. I don't think we ought to let them get us into this thing where they can point at us and say "you've been violent." You see, no matter how they want to skew the use of that word, we don't have to be violent to show them where we're at. Like, we're all here and they're scared shitless, right now—you know what I'm saying?

The crowd roared in approval.

—The other thing is that we have a decision to hear and I hope that decision is ready by four o'clock. I hope that on the basis of that meeting we'll be able to make a decision about what we should do from there on out. Right now, what I think we should do is harass them by being here and by being like the people we're supposed to be, like "Woodstock Nation" people. And you ought to have a good time while you're waiting around and do whatever you have to do. Somebody might be able to make some runs for some stuff.

The ambiguity of the word "stuff" brought laugher from several in front.

—And then, what I think we should do is wait here until four o'clock and if they say "No," then we ought to make a decision, then, about what kind of shit we're going to take from these people. So, right now, lean against the windows, but don't break them, because they construe that as being violent. And, you know, there's a misconception of what kinds of things people are violent towards.

They talk about violence in relation to things, not in relation to people, in this society, and we think that violence towards people is a lot worse. So as many as can stay, let's stay put until four o'clock.

Temporarily placated, the crowd dwindled as many went off to afternoon classes. A significant number, four to five hundred, remained to continue the sit-in around the Ad Building and, in effect, keep it closed to normal business. As the remaining protesters settled in for the wait, the loudspeaker was made available to anyone who wanted to speak. Several others among the Radical Union used the opportunity to say a few words.

I followed in the direction Allen had taken toward the south end of the Ad Building. Around the corner, the campus radio station, KSCB, had set up a table from which they now conducted an interview with Allen. In the first question I heard, Allen was asked how he would react if the statement from the Committee was negative and what he would recommend the crowd do at that point.

—Well, I'll have to talk to them. I mean, it's the crowd that makes the decision. I don't make the decision. Decisions are made by the crowd, not by me. It's as simple as that. I don't think that this building should be taken in light of all the force they've amassed to protect it.

Allen paused. The anger and frustration in his facial expression mounted as the conviction that the Committee's response would be "negative" grew clearer and more ominous in his mind. Finally he continued, with an audible mixture of that anger and frustration in every word.

—There seems to be something basically wrong when we can't even talk over the issues. We can't even have an open hearing. Fuck! What kind of a situation is that!?

While listening to Allen vent, I switched to a 50mm lens and loaded another roll of film. In the process, activity near the entrance to the Ad Building caught my attention. Those gathered near the front windows had taken rolls of newsprint and taped these to the glass. Moving closer, I heard someone saying the paper had been put up to keep photographers inside from taking pictures of the crowd. That news made me suddenly aware of the possibility that some in the crowd might not want me taking their picture.

No one had hassled me yet, but a few unfriendly glances I had noticed earlier began to make sense. Some were definitely sensitive about who was aiming cameras at them.

After the glass along the front of the building had been covered, someone fastened a bicycle lock across the outside door handles to secure the doors and keep unwanted photographers inside. With these precautions taken, the crowd settled down and three musicians with flute, guitar, and bongos began entertaining while everyone waited. Making my way through the remaining crowd, I found Canova on the north side of the quad.

—Why didn't you tell me you had a starring role today?

—Didn't know myself until last night. Everyone was beat from the overnight occupation of Stearn's Wharf. I didn't stay overnight, so they asked me to step up today.

—You got the crowd going. Maybe you've found a new calling.

Canova waived off the suggestion.

—I don't like the spotlight that much. Plus I've got the store to run. But I can handle it when needed.

He gestured toward the camera on my shoulder.

—Why don't you get on the ramparts instead of the sidelines. Photography's a nice hobby, but it gets in the way of really being here.

—Nice try. Keep in mind some people aren't here at all.

—Are you sticking around for the afternoon?

—I planned on it.

—Good. The more bodies in this crowd the better. I need to get back to the store. I don't think we'll have any word from them this afternoon. They're not going to cave in. Not today anyway. Things won't get crazy until tomorrow.

—What's on for tomorrow?

—We'll meet about that tonight. Why don't you come? You could help shape what happens.

—In my view they've gone too far already—shutting down the building. I'd be shouted down like Buchanan.

—And maybe you'd hear things that would change your mind. But suit yourself.

He turned and headed off through the crowd. I felt an edge in his tone and in the way he cut through the conversation. He was pushing hard—not only on the crowd and me but on himself.

After a half hour or so the crowd wearied of the flute and guitar so the bongo player took up a driving beat and rallied everyone into chanting "Seven, seven, seven, six—no more bureaucratic tricks." But the monotony of the chanting wearied me so, despite what I had promised Canova, I decided to leave. Then, just as I was walking off, a man with a black patch over his left eye exited from the side of the Ad Building. Carrying a bullhorn, he moved to a position near the main entrance and faced the seated demonstrators.

Everyone knew the eye-patch man—Robert Evans, Dean of Men. The patch gave him a militaristic appearance—an association with Israel's General Moshe Dayan—who had been a media icon since the Seven Days War. And then there was the showing of *Casablanca* two weeks ago in Campbell Hall as part of the Council on Arts and Letters Bogart Film Festival. The Nazi Commandant also wore a black patch over his left eye. The common knowledge that Evans was a World War II veteran only contributed to the aura of martial authority. Consistent with this image, Evans wasn't wearing the look of a man who was about to appease the crowd.

Squeezing my way through the crush of demonstrators sitting along the front of the building, I positioned myself a few yards to the left of Evans and readied the camera. Following his radio interview with KCSB, Bill Allen had rejoined the crowd and now sat only a short distance to the left of where Evans stood. After surveying the crowd like a field marshal gauging the strength of the enemy, Evans raised the bullhorn and began to speak.

—Will you listen to me! This is now declared a violation of University regulations.

Allen began to heckle him.

—Oh no!

Without changing expression, Evans repeated himself.

—You are in violation of University regulations.

Allen taunted him again.

—Oh no!

The crowd joined in with a volley of hoots and howls. Before Evans could begin again, Allen continued.

—Who's the U-ni-ver-si-ty?

He drew out each syllable so derisively Evans stopped and turned toward him. They shot menacing looks at each other. Then, in disgust, Evans turned away and increased the resolve in his voice.

—You are disrupting this facility.

This acknowledgement met with a predictable chorus of cheers. Evans plowed on, raising his voice to counter the din.

—If you do not move, action will be taken.

Joined by several others, Allen repeated what had become a sarcastic mantra.

—Oh no!

Someone else called out.

—Are you threatening us?

Another voice from further back in the crowd shouted at Evans in a tone demanding response.

—When are we going to have an open hearing?

Evans pretended not to hear and instead replied to the previous question.

—That is not a threat. That is a statement of fact.

Sitting cross-legged directly in front of Evans, a guy wearing a headband over shoulder-length long hair shouted at him.

—Pig!

Evans looked down at him and scowled. His voice then turned unmistakably threatening.

—What's your name?

The protester stood up directly in front of him, leaned forward, and snarled back.

—What's your name?

When he stood up, I recognized him as Joe Melchione—a photographer for the *El Gaucho*. With a reflex move, Evans lowered the bullhorn between them.

67

As Melchione leaned further toward him, Evans defensively raised his arm. As he did so, he struck Melchione in the face with the bullhorn, knocking off his glasses. Startled and falling backwards, Melchione flailed momentarily with his arms to find support. He succeeded in righting himself and lunged toward Evans. Then pandemonium broke out.

Some in the crowd stood up and tried to move between Melchione and Evans while others became involved in a pushing and shoving match. Suddenly the sound of broken glass rang out at the entrance of the building. Everyone sitting near that area, including myself, jumped up and scrambled backwards. The police inside had broken the glass doors—because they were locked from the outside with the bicycle lock—and were moving to defend Evans. They swung nightsticks right and left and clubbed several people in front of me. Retaliating while in retreat, some demonstrators threw rocks at the police—most of which missed and hit the windows of the Ad Building, breaking out more sections of glass. Released from the crowd, Evans maneuvered his way through the police and back into the building. A few demonstrators recovered and moved toward the entrance while shouting at the police.

—Pigs. Fucking pigs.

This provoked the police and they charged again. They were able to grab one of those who had shouted at them, dragged him away from the others, and, despite his furious kicking and swearing, succeeded in wrestling him through the entrance and into the building. Then, in a line of retreat, the rest of the police disappeared into the building. Seeing the end of the assault, the crowd slowly reclaimed the area it had occupied before the charge. Greg Knell took the microphone and attempted to regroup everyone.

—This building's going to stay shut down until the administration changes their minds. Now listen up! One of our sisters was trampled by your chicken-shit retreat, man, so don't run that fast. Watch where you're going. If anyone falls, pick them up.

Someone from the crowd interrupted.

—We all saw what happened here. Evans hit one of us. I propose we get together and sue that man for assault!

Knell ignored the suggestion.

—Let me explain what happened. People were painting the windows, including newspaper on the windows, so they couldn't take pictures of us. Dean Evans came out and declared it an unlawful assembly. Joe Melchione bent over to listen closer to the bullhorn and Dean Evans shoved him. He shoved him three times and then he hit the dude. Then the pigs charged through the door and started busting people. A few people got carried away.

Knell's explanation that Melchione "bent over to listen closer to the bullhorn," sounded silly enough to induce a few laughs from the crowd. There followed some discussion of who got busted by the police and what to do about it. Then, suddenly, the entire crowd grew silent.

Stepping through the broken glass at the entrance, Evans returned and walked toward Knell. This stunned everyone, as no one could imagine what he was doing. When he stood next to Knell, he asked to use the microphone. Grumblings could be heard from a few in the crowd. Taken by surprise, Knell hesitated but finally agreed.

—All right. Let's let Dean Evans speak.

Evans took the microphone. As he spoke, I maneuvered for a better camera angle.

—I came out of the building in order to tell the group in front of the doors, that were pounding on the building, that were blocking the doors, that they were in violation of University regulations. One young man pushed up to me and I pushed him back.

The mood of the crowd remained more angry than curious. Someone shouted at Evans.

—That's assault and battery, motherfucker!

Another joined in.

—You should have turned the other cheek, then.

Allen piled it on.

—Listen to him! He's telling you he's a fool!

Evans persevered.

—Another man kicked me from the rear.

Evans could have helped himself, I thought, by leaving out that detail. Predictably laughter and cheers went up all around. Evans ignored them.

—I tried to get the identification of the man in front of me. He did not give it. People were starting to swing at me and that's when the police came out.

Someone shouted out.

—Liar!

Again Evans ignored the taunt.

—The police came out. They thought I was in trouble.

Another shouted at him.

—You start the trouble and we'll finish it!

Undeterred, Evans slogged on.

—I'm asking you people to disperse. We were, quite frankly, afraid you would do just what you have done: break windows.

A disapproving howl went up from the crowd. A voice from behind yelled above the noise.

—What did you do, you motherfucking pig?

Steeling himself, Evans pressed on.

—We did not want to make a big deal out of this. My objective is to prevent disruption of the administration building and to prevent disruption on this campus.

Another angry voice called out.

—Why'd you fire Bill Allen?

Again Evans passed over the bait.

—What is taking place here is a disruption. It is a violation of University regulations. I am asking you to stop blocking the building and disperse now.

Evans handed the microphone to Knell and walked back toward the building amidst a chorus of boos and howls. As everyone stared at Evans retreating into the building, Knell—clearly anxious to rebut—raised the microphone and launched into a sarcastic reply.

—Not to correct Dean Evans, but I'd like to tell what really happened. Now the windows—no windows were broken. That is a lie. The police did not charge because the windows were broken, that is a lie. The first window was broken when the police charged through the doors. They broke the doors coming through. The doors were locked and they just came through them. And there was no disruption. They sent all the employees home and they locked it up. They shut the building down, we didn't. We would like to have done it. They did it for us. So that's two lies from Dean Evans.

Sensing his slide toward petty vindictiveness, Knell checked himself and switched direction.

—Now you people have to realize, you know, it's not Dean Evans who's reacting. It's not the campus cops—who had their first exercise in a long time—that are reacting. This is the reaction of the University of California that refuses to liberalize the way this University is run. Now, with the administrators, I'm sure they didn't want this to happen, man. If they thought they could let us sit here, let us shut this building down without Ronnie Reagan and the Regents shitting on their head, they would have let us do it. They were forced into this. You know, we don't want to direct anything at Dean Evans, man. It's the Regents. It's the people they represent in society.

Questions from the crowd about what should happen next followed, along with a short discussion of raising bond for the guy who was dragged into the building. Then the talk turned to a recounting of the day's successes and the need to continue the protest on Monday.

If the Committee on Privilege and Tenure had met that afternoon, no evidence of it was made public by the administration. The promised four o'clock deadline had now passed. The front of the building had been secured with plywood. Most of the staff inside were now gone.

Among the protesters, many broke off into conversations and general merriment. Allen continued talking to a group on the north side of the building. The musicians started up again. A guerrilla theater group began performing what appeared to be a symbolic reenactment of the day's events. Having seen enough, I shouldered the camera and walked off, with mixed feelings, toward Isla Vista.

As I left the quad, a group of thirty or more broke into an odd dance, locking hands into a circle—moving together to meet in the center and then moving backward to reform the circle. An outer circle then moved clockwise while an inner circle moved counterclockwise—a carousel of gleeful celebration.

*   *   *

Chapter 9

After Bill Allen's derisive taunting of Dean Evans, I saw no way the administration could be maneuvered into cutting him any slack. Allen not only wanted concessions, he wanted to wrest them from the administration with all the finesse of a good bitch slapping. No administration in the land of Reagan could succumb to that kind of pressure and live to tell about it. Either Allen overestimated the power of the mass of signatures on his petition or he didn't care about retaining his job—because he had definitely burned bridges. But those signatures did count for something. Despite the fact that many may not have known what they were signing, the signatures represented a substantial number of students and Thursday's rally brought many of them to the administration's door. A possible way out, it seemed, would be a compromise that would deny Allen an open hearing but grant the students some voting power on the Academic Senate.

The previous year students had already been invited to participate on Academic Senate committees. But this gesture had been labeled "ceremonial" by the Radical Union because the participation included no voting privileges and thereby no real power. The administration fought the voting privilege issue because it appeared to give away too much. From the point of view of most faculty, granting student voting power amounted to throwing a monkey wrench into the decision-making machinery. Most students attended universities for four or five years, then they were off to pursue careers elsewhere. They weren't around long enough to witness the effects of their decisions. The student influence, as primarily a nomadic influence, potentially threatened the long term quality of the university. Tenured faculty believed they had a higher stake in the future of the university. But in the last couple of years many younger faculty had come over to the student side, acknowledging that student participation could be healthy rather than detrimental. This faculty support added new credibility to the student position.

The Allen confrontation presented the administration an opportunity to come out looking good by moving more in the direction toward which momentum had already been building for some time. Giving students some representation in the tenure voting process would be in effect only token power and could work beneficially—keeping faculty more attentive to evaluation of teaching skills. Student power might make it more difficult to deny tenure to professors who happened to excel at teaching but not at publishing. Allen may have dug too deep a hole for himself but others could still benefit from the momentum generated by his case. In the face of overwhelming student support for an open hearing, it seemed possible the administration would concede something.

On Friday morning the number of students in front of the Ad Building steadily grew until by ten o'clock the crowd in the quad area exceeded three thousand. Chief Lowe of the campus police twice announced that demonstrators would be subject to arrest if they didn't leave. Despite this threat, the crowd continued to grow and the building remained closed. As I made my way through the tensing crowd, I found Canova near the entrance. He told me what he knew about the progress of negotiations.

—Early this morning Geoff and some students from Legislative Council put together a proposal asking for a commission to be formed today. It would be half student and half faculty/administration. They'd review the Allen case and make a recommendation by Monday. Then, over a two week period, they'd study the long range possibilities for reforms that would include a student voice in hiring and firing.

—So what happened?

—Buchanan didn't give Geoff's proposal more than a glance. Within fifteen minutes he sent back some bullshit reply. Something about how he would "encourage" all department chairmen to organize meetings with students to discuss the question of student input.

—Yeah, that's bullshit.

—The closing of the building is forcing his hand and he's taking a hard line. He said he won't discuss the situation any further until we lift what he calls our "siege" on the building. But that's not the worst of it.

—What do you mean?

Canova leaned closer.

—I don't want everyone hearing this yet. Someone on the negotiating team says Buchanan already contacted Webster. That can mean only one thing. He doesn't intend to negotiate.

—What kind of manpower can Webster raise?

—He'll get outside help.

—But it could take days to put together the army they'd need to control this crowd.

—What do you think Webster was doing all night? Buchanan probably made his decision late yesterday after the thing with Dean Evans.

It didn't take long for the rumor of Buchanan's request for outside police to begin circulating among the crowd. No further communications issued from the administration. Anticipating the worst, two RU members specializing in tactics took turns addressing the protesters—preparing them for an encounter with police. They instructed how to respond in case of a tear gas assault, passed out white arm bands to volunteers manning first aid stations, and gathered a list of phone numbers to be given to those who might be arrested.

Despite the threat of tear gas, injury, and arrest, the crowd continued to grow. But the possibility Buchanan might be bluffing vanished at precisely two o'clock as a caravan of coach buses appeared along Mesa Road behind the Ad Building. They slowly rolled into the parking area near Robertson Gym and came to a stop. For the first time in the history of the campus outside police had been called in to maintain order.

As the cops unloaded from the buses, I moved to the west side of the Ad Building for a better view. After forming columns in the parking lot, they marched single file along the access road and lined up on the north side of the building. I couldn't believe the numbers. It was a small army. By the time they were all together on the west side of the building, I estimated the manpower between

250 and 300. I learned later that deputies had been gathered not only from Santa Barbara County but from departments all the way to Ventura County to the south and San Louis Obispo County to the north. The group also included officers from Santa Barbara City Police and the California Highway Patrol. All were equipped with visored helmets, night sticks, tear gas masks, mace cans, and Plexiglas riot shields.

After grouping on the north side of the field west of the Ad Building, the police took final instructions. Then about two thirds of the group moved single file across the lawn toward North Hall.

From there they continued into the corridor between North Hall and the Ad building. I stood to one side—framing, focusing, shooting—thinking I might capture something of how unreal it all seemed.

As the majority of police filed along the walkway in front of North Hall, it became clear that the first area of major confrontation with the crowd would take place on the south side of the quad. As the line of police marched forward, the few who were standing directly in their path moved aside. Nearing Ellison Hall at the southeast corner of the quad, the line stopped, facing North Hall. Then every other cop in the line did an about-face and moved forward about ten yards toward the crowd in the quad. This created an empty space between what were now two rows of uniforms, one facing south and one facing north.

I took a position midway in the quad only a few feet away from the line facing north. The entire area had grown eerily quiet—with only the sound of a few shifting bodies or a word or two spoken in a low voice. Gazing upward to my left, I noticed the stairwell balconies of Ellison Hall overlooking the quad were lined with bodies—all staring motionless at the scene below.

Across to the south, a wall of bodies strained against each other to look over the parapet along the large second floor patio area of North Hall. And over to the northwest, a few others from the administration side leaned over the parapet of a similar patio extending out from the second floor of the Ad building. Everyone watched and waited.

The police stood motionless for what seemed a long time. No one knew the degree of violence they were prepared to use, but I noticed they were not carrying their riot shields. Finally, one of them gave a command I couldn't hear. In response they all pulled out riot clubs and held them forward with arms slightly extended in front of their bodies, grasping the handle in their right hand while resting the tip in their left. On television news I had seen this tactic used to move protesters in Berkeley. The police would slowly advance forward. Those who didn't move would be clubbed as hard as it would take to get them to move. The Berkeley police encountered few who would stand ground and take the beating.

But that was Berkeley—a place of urban warrior cops and seasoned protest groups. This was Santa Barbara—a place of palm trees, sea breezes, and upper middle class ambiance. Most of these cops were used to dealing with cooperative crowds and the students were accustomed to sitting in classrooms.

As these thoughts crossed my mind, the line of police slowly began moving forward. In response, those nearest the line edged slowly backward, staring eye to eye with the police. Here and there someone would test their resolve by lagging too close to the line. In every case the cops answered with a forceful shove of the club. I was now in the front row of the retreating crowd—aiming my camera up the line toward the Ad Building, framing and shooting. After pausing too long for a shot, I received the same shove I had just seen given to others and stumbled into two people behind me. As the line of police moved mechanically across the quad, more police spaced further apart took up positions on the south side to keep protesters clear of the area that had just been swept. Half the quad had now been cleared.

With continued retreat, it seemed any leverage the protesters had would soon be lost. On Thursday the organizers set the goal of keeping the building closed until the demand for an open hearing was met. If they allowed police to clear the area with a simple sweep and secure the entrance to the building, business as usual could resume. The administration would gain the upper hand and no longer need to negotiate anything.

The crowd could up the ante, refuse to yield, and force the police to start beating and arresting them. In Berkeley that might have been the chosen course. Earlier this seemed to be what the leaders were preparing the crowd to undertake. But that would have been overkill.

Television news cameras had arrived in advance of the police. This was now a bigger local news event than the Stearn's Wharf sit-in. Bill Allen had already been interviewed by local television. The mere deployment of outside police on campus was all that was needed. Tomorrow pictures of the "invasion" would be all over the campus newspaper and in all the local news media. That would fuel the radical agenda more than any speech or petition. Looking at the disbelief on student faces all around the quad, I sensed it may have been a big mistake to call in the cops, and Buchanan had blundered into it.

I continued retreating north along with the crowd and the advancing line of uniforms. Within a few more minutes they succeeded in clearing the entire quad. Segments of the crowd now gathered at the south and north ends, and, for the moment, there seemed to be no plan among the demonstration leaders for what to do next.

Then shouts came suddenly from the east side of the quad. In the area between Campbell Hall and Ellison Hall a scuffle broke out. Several demonstrators hit the ground as they were beat with clubs. Cops nearby struck at other demonstrators and for a few seconds the situation looked like it would explode into greater violence. But this action created an opening. A huge section of the crowd that had previously retreated from the quad had circled around Campbell Hall and now broke through the weak link in the police perimeter. Within minutes the quad area filled with students again. Jubilant cheers rose from the newly formed group in the quad and from others observing from beyond. Now it appeared that the police had accomplished nothing.

The campus radio station had set up in front of one of the old military barracks on the north side of the quad. I was now close enough to overhear a student reporter.

—There's just plain too many people for this amount of police to handle. The only way this crowd can be contained is by circling them. A sweep just won't work. In Berkeley it works because the sweep area is pretty well sealed. Around here, it's not sealed. They can just go around a building and come back again.

But the KCSB reporter turned out to be wrong. After several regroupings, several more sweeps, and finally the addition of a few more men, the police succeeded in clearing the quad area and securing the front of the building. But it took well over two hours. Many students had already left, realizing the goal of keeping the Ad Building closed for the day had been won.

The administration could claim victory for freeing the Ad Building. But the use of outside police, combined with the clubbing of several students, left them looking like the Gestapo.

Bill Allen was clearly pleased with the day's events. A group had gathered around him on the lawn west of the Ad Building. I didn't see Canova, so I assumed he had already returned to his store. Allen praised those remaining for having befuddled the police all afternoon. He then urged everyone to return tomorrow and continue the demonstration.

—I don't want to stay here all night. They don't run any business at night and normally very little during the day. Tomorrow we'll make sure they do even less.

Several whistled and applauded.

—I think that, hey, you people really voted today. It was far out! Just remember that you didn't just vote to have an open hearing, but you voted to have a vote in what the hell goes on at this University.

As everyone cheered, I headed back to Isla Vista. Allen clearly didn't get it. Student voting power was as far away as ever. But the blame wasn't all his. The administration had also blown it. Today they made themselves ugly—just as the protesters had on Thursday. It had turned into a contest for who could get uglier—the radicals or the administration.

*   *   *

Chapter 10

On Monday Buchanan initiated phase two of his counter offensive against the radicals. He called a press conference at ten o'clock in the Ad Building. He was joined by Sheriff Webster and James Walters, chairman of the Academic Senate. Buchanan announced he had called for an emergency meeting of the Academic Senate to be held Tuesday at one o'clock. At the meeting, resolutions concerning an open hearing for Bill Allen and the issue of student participation in personnel decisions were to be presented and voted upon.

But as questions were answered during the press conference Buchanan's strategy became apparent. Gathering the contested issues into resolutions and putting them to a vote gave the appearance of granting the Allen case and the student power issues further formal and fair consideration. But the possibility that the Academic Senate would seriously entertain the question of an open hearing was predictably dampened by Walters in response to a question from a *Santa Barbara News Press* reporter. Walters restated the view, dominant among the faculty, that open hearings conflicted with the principle of confidentiality in personnel appraisals. For that reason they would not likely get Academic Senate support.

Since confidentiality and the exclusion of students and non-tenured faculty from the tenure decision-making process were policies of the University of California and not just the Santa Barbara campus, the question was asked whether Buchanan or the local administration even had the authority to grant an open hearing or student participation on tenure issues. Seizing the opportunity to take pressure off the administration, Walters fueled the notion of the Senate's limitations. He noted the question had never arisen before but that he doubted the Senate had such authority.

It also came out in the conference that, in response to a letter of grievance sent to the Committee on Privilege and Tenure by Bill Allen on December 5th of last year, the Committee chairman, Professor Harry Girvetz, had begun a review of Allen's case on January 27th. Apparently this Committee included the question of the need for an open hearing as part of its review process. When asked whether the Committee's recommendation on this matter could affect the administration's decision, Buchanan answered that it depended on what the recommendation was. If they decided against an open hearing, then that's all there was to it. But if they made a different recommendation, then the administration would consider it.

This response seemed to leave the door open on the question of an open hearing. But this waffling was consistent with Buchanan's strategy. The conference was a thinly veiled session of buck-passing—but only simulated buck passing since the buck wasn't really being passed. The relevant decisions were already made. No one believed the Academic Senate and the Committee on Privilege and Tenure were likely to propose anything that would contradict the administration. Passing these issues over to these governing bodies for review, while giving the appearance of greater deliberation and fairness, actually served to buy the administration more time. Buchanan's next announcement took everyone by surprise and revealed why buying more time would be useful.

—Indictments have been issued this morning by Sheriff Webster for the arrest of 19 participants in Thursday's and Friday's unlawful assemblies. All those indicted are charged with four misdemeanor counts of trespassing, failure to disperse from the scene of an unlawful assembly, remaining present for purposes of disturbing the peace, and participating in an unlawful assembly.

He went on to read a list of those indicted, all of which, it turned out, were members of the Radical Union. With this move the administration adopted a well-proven Machiavellian tactic: to quiet a barking dog, don't step on the tail, cut off the head. Surprisingly, however, the list did not include Bill Allen. Probably the administration calculated his arrest would prove needlessly inflammatory.

Those indicted were forced to turn themselves in later that day in order to avoid the possibility of increased bail, which was set at a thousand dollars each. As further inducement toward compliance, Dean Evans also put those indicted under suspension. If they did not submit to the indictments, they could face expulsion from the University. Suspension also meant that even if the accused got out on bail, they would now be ineffective in continued protests because the suspension barred them from campus. Ignoring the suspension and returning to campus would then give the administration the excuse for expulsion. The administration had clearly decided to play hardball.

That afternoon the 19 who were indicted turned themselves in at the County Sheriff's office in Santa Barbara. Bill Allen, more animated than ever, continued to lead students in protest marches near the Ad Building—now under the continued protection of a police perimeter. I followed the protesters, recording the events with more photographs.

At one point Allen led the crowd into North Hall with everyone clapping and chanting "Open hearing now." That created enough of a disturbance to disrupt several classes. The crowd then occupied the section of the building containing the Anthropology Departmental office, effectively closing it to normal business. After shutting down the department, the crowd then left North Hall and conducted a

serpentine march through the first floor of the campus library.

The 19 arrests were a constant topic of conversation among the demonstrators. Questions were circulating about how the administration came to arrest just these people among all of those who had played an active role in two days of demonstrations. How and why had these particular members of the Radical Union been selected? Questions also circulated about how Canova had escaped being among them.

I hadn't seen Canova all morning, but I found him watching the protestors marching out of the library. When I asked him where he had been, he answered in an irritated tone.

—Making phone calls at the ASIA office—raising bail money—until word came around that the cops had inside help.

—What do you mean?

—An informant, of sorts. Apparently they had a photo or photos—from the retreat we went to. They matched faces with surveillance photos taken at the demonstrations. Just like that they finger the key people.

—But if that's true, how'd they miss you? Aren't you "key people"?

—I've been asking myself that. So has everyone else.

As Canova stared coolly, I suddenly sensed what was coming next.

—They're all thinking it was *you*.

—Me!?

I recalled the dozen or so photos I had taken at the ranch where the Radical Union met. There were others with cameras. But I was new and hadn't been overly talkative. I would definitely count as an "outsider."

—Yeah, they really think it was you. They know it had to be somebody fairly new. That list includes you and me and four or five others—but especially you.

—So what did you say to them?

—I told them I'd ask you.

—Christ, you know I wouldn't do that!

—I still need to ask.

He was plainly angry with me but now I was equally hot.

—No! Is that clear enough for you?

Even though innocent, it unnerved me how guilty I suddenly felt and how much I sensed that was visible to Canova.

—They think it was you and because I brought you in they put us together on this. We're both under suspicion.

—I didn't do it, okay!?

Canova looked unpersuaded but eased off.

—I'm trying to make sense of it. Help me out here. How do you explain this?

I shook my head. Uneasy in the guilt role, I deflected attention back to him.

—So they're giving you a hard time?

—Let's just say, thanks to you, I'm sidelined for a while until this gets sorted out.

—What do you think we should do?

—It wouldn't hurt for you to cool it with the camera. I thought that thing would get in the way but I didn't think it would come to this.

—I should talk to them.

—They won't believe you. They won't believe either one of us right now. And who can blame them?

—God! They must be pissed off, getting burned like that.

—Sure. But they'll turn it to some advantage—not that that'll make heroes of us. Getting busted has its uses. The more the administration looks like Nazis the more vehement protest gets.

—You mean violent?

—The violence is coming from the administration. But if they keep cracking down and giving nothing up, pressure builds.

—Then what?

—Something snaps. That's when *change* becomes possible.

Canova walked away in the direction opposite the marching protesters.

*   *   *

Chapter 11

The next day's *El Gaucho* confirmed Canova's account. The Santa Barbara 19, as they were now called, had been arrested with the help of photos and testimony obtained from an unnamed source that had infiltrated a strategy meeting of the Radical Union. The police matched these photos with photos taken from the demonstrations. And while the District Attorney's Office did not press for conspiracy charges, the information strengthened the charge of collective intent to disturb the peace. The use of an informant infuriated Allen sympathizers and provoked them to add espionage to their growing list of "Gestapo tactics" used by the police and condoned by the administration. No name had yet been made public, but I anticipated word would soon get around the rumor mill that I was the informer. Wanting to duck that kind of attention and potentially adding further fuel to it, I chose to leave the camera behind when I went onto campus Wednesday.

The demonstrations continued with another noon rally held north of the library—this time without the core leadership of the Radical Union. Bill Allen spoke briefly about the arrests and the need to continue pressure, but made no direct proposals for action. He left with word that he would be meeting in a strategy session with those indicted. After the rally, what remained of the RU leadership—in angry reaction to the arrests and rumored approval from Allen—marched the crowd to the Faculty Club, located near the lagoon west of the University Center (UCEN). They broke into the building and chased out the few faculty who were there.

The break-in went unopposed by the police, all of whom remained near the Administration Building. Once inside, protesters removed much of the furniture and used it to barricade the access road to the Club. Then merriment and mayhem reigned as the crowd consumed the Club's alcohol and food, sang protest songs, and skinny-dipped in the swimming pool.

I viewed the antics from an overlooking vantage point in the San Rafael dorm parking lot. Watching the increasingly scandalous spectacle, I regretted not having the camera and thought about getting it. As I watched, I noticed Melanie approached along the path from the Speech and Drama Building. Her slightly nasal voice increased her disdainful tone.

—The natives are restless today.

—You mean savages, don't you?

She pointed toward the swimming pool.

—Gawd! Those people are naked!

—Allen's supporters are letting it all hang out today. They should hoist the Jolly Roger with a sign that says, "Screw you." The Senate's in session right now voting on some resolutions. Clearly no one puts much stock in those activities.

—It's stupid. How do they think that's going to help? It only proves what the administration already thinks—students aren't responsible enough to have a say in how things are run.

—The whole thing has degenerated. Nothing good's coming out of it. It's depressing. An opportunity was there, but they really blew it. We all blew it.

—Looking at this I don't think we deserve change.

Melanie turned to leave. She was heading into Isla Vista, so I walked with her. I shifted the focus away from campus politics.

—I couldn't schedule the lab yet. Some class is making use of it this week and part of next. I should at least be able to schedule something next week.

—The sooner the better.

Suddenly words jumped out of my mouth as if someone else were speaking.

—Before then, would you like to do something?

—What do you mean, "do something?"

—Right. I mean something like a date. You know . . . we could go see The Band. They're at Robertson Gym Sunday night. Why don't I get some tickets?

—I like The Band.

I took that to be something like "yes."

—Since you don't have a phone, assume I get the tickets. Let's meet at my place. We can head over from there.

—What time?

—Make it seven.

I walked her to the corner of Pardall and Embarcadero del Norte and then we parted paths. I couldn't believe I asked her out. It must have been because seeing her at that moment was unplanned. That didn't leave time to weigh every crazy idea that popped into my head. Despite her looks I wasn't even sure I liked her. I was surprised she accepted, but in her case I couldn't be sure of the motives. Maybe she wanted more photos. Maybe she didn't even know what she wanted. Then I recalled her conduct in the studio. She didn't act like a woman who didn't know what she wanted.

I returned to the apartment late in the afternoon. Matt sat on the three cushioned Danish couch in front of the cinderblock bookcase dividing the living room from the desk squeezed in the space behind it. He browsed the campus paper as we listened to KCSB. The Academic Senate upheld the resolution stating they wouldn't support open hearings. They also voted down the resolution to set up a special commission—half students, half faculty—to review the Allen case. Only one resolution passed that catered to students—something that suggested departments examine ways to include student and non-tenured faculty input for evaluations and hiring decisions.

Matt reached back and lowered the volume on the radio behind him. I took a beer from the fridge, sat down on a chair in the kitchen, and shared my disgust with the news.

—Whole thing's a bust. The administration stinks. The RU stinks. Students get the shaft. Something good could have been worked out. Allen and company seem more interested in burning bridges than in building them. Now, instead of progress, we have regress. They've brought a police state to campus. It all really stinks.

—Hate to say I told you so about that pack of fanatics.

I took a sip from the beer and didn't answer.

—Allen's starting to lose some of his halo, especially when you find stuff like this even in here.

Matt held up a copy of the day's *El Gaucho* and began reading.

> What had originally been cited as official course evaluations sponsored by the Anthropology Department and favorable to Bill Allen were in fact only an experimental instrument wholly designed by Acting Assistant Professor Manuel Carlos. The official departmental evaluations were not nearly as favorable toward Allen.

He tossed the paper aside as he continued.

—Allen's supporters twist things in his favor. Most students didn't even have the facts when they signed his petition. The Anthropology Department put out a statement today that refuted most of the paper's claims about Allen's publishing and experience. You can't trust either side, but I trust the faculty more than the radicals.

—I heard someone talking about Girvetz's speech at the Senate meeting—about how the faculty fought with the Regents to get peer review on tenure decisions. He said if the Senate were to give away power to students it would mess up what they had fought to gain. You'd think, knowing how it feels, he'd be more sympathetic. Instead he treats students like the Regents treated the faculty. Who'd trust this guy?

—I think he's right myself. We're not the faculty's peers. They're entitled to evaluation by their peers.

—Sure, but students could have a voice. The way it is now just puts more division between faculty and students. Besides students need to stretch themselves—take more responsibility.

—They're stretching themselves alright. Picture them swilling gin and swimming nude in the Faculty Club pool.

—That doesn't help anything, I'll grant you that. But the Faculty Club is just another symptom of the problem. The tenured faculty get treated like aristocracy. There should be a Faculty-Student Club where students can go and have more social interaction with faculty.

—That's crazy, then the faculty would have no place to get away from us!

—Look at the way you think. Why get away from students?

—Because they get tired of dealing with problems all day. And that's what students mostly are—walking problems. Not to mention the walking accidents going somewhere to happen. That's why they screw up things like demonstrations and sabotage their own credibility.

—You're unbelievable. There must be a prune-faced old professor under that skin of yours.

*   *   *

Chapter 12

Sunday night the music from Big Pink came to Robertson Gym. The timing for a concert couldn't have been worse from the administration point of view. Rumors circulated on Thursday that Buchanan would cancel the concert in order to eliminate the excuse for a crowd to form. If he had considered such a move, by Friday it was clear he had decided against it—probably for fear that canceling the concert might trigger a larger disturbance than any that might result from having it. But he delayed the time of the concert to seven thirty so additional security personnel could be brought in.

Rob Gym, as everyone called it, was little more than a covered cinderblock rectangle with bleachers on two sides. Its location 200 yards west of the recently besieged Ad Building accounted for administration concern about the concert. Although I expected even more, police were everywhere around the gym. By the time Melanie and I entered, three thousand or more people filled the hall. A three foot high platform had been set up at the south end, just inside the wall separating the entrance lobby from the main auditorium. Melanie and I maneuvered to a place on the floor near the platform, already set with drums, keyboards, and sound equipment. No members of *The Band* had appeared yet but the lights were dimmed and the smell of marijuana heavy in the air.

Not long after we arrived, someone I didn't recognize, wearing an army surplus jacket, approached a microphone on stage. He spoke about the

Santa Barbara 19, alerting everyone to the collection baskets circulating for contributions to their defense.

When *The Band* finally emerged, the lights dimmed further as two spots lit the stage. They got everyone feeling good by starting with "Up on Cripple Creek."

Toward the middle of the show they played "The Day They Tore Ol' Dixie Down." It didn't take coaching from Robbie Robertson for most in the audience to hear the lyrics as "The Day They Tore the Ol' Radical Union Down."

Following this song, I left Melanie, moved closer to the stage, and took several photos. Feeling a dry throat from inhaling second-hand reefer smoke, I entered the corridor behind the bleachers to find a drinking fountain. Over the fountain, I was surprised to hear my name.

—You Marleau?

I looked up from the fountain to see the guy in the army surplus jacket standing next to me. Before I could speak, Canova entered the corridor from the restroom next to the fountain. He introduced the guy in the jacket as Nolan, a member of the Radical Union. Anticipating an interrogation about the photos, I cut Nolan off before he could speak.

—Okay, listen. If you think I gave any photos to the cops, you're wrong. I haven't given them anything and I haven't talked to them. It wasn't me.

Canova interrupted.

—It's not about that.

Nolan glanced at Canova and turned back to me.

—Relax. It's like this. The cops are looking for photos. They want to harass the Radical Union—the leaders—on every possible violation they can work up. We know you've taken photos of the demonstrations. They'll get around to you soon.

Not expecting this change of direction, I had to shift gears.

—Well . . . I don't intend to help them out.

—That's good. But they have things called subpoenas. It would help us out if you would turn over to us, for safekeeping, any photos you have.

—Turn over to you?

—From the last few days. It's hard to say what might become . . . relevant, you know?

—You want all my photos from the last few days?

—No need to worry. They'd be kept in a safe place—with our attorney—until the possibility of more indictments blows over. Our attorney can fight the subpoena.

I glanced back and forth between the two of them, my brain racing. I wondered whether Nolan was serious or whether he was cooking this up as some kind of ruse to smoke out any involvement I might have with the cops—like maybe I had already given my photos to them. But I wasn't going to play along just to prove my innocence. I didn't like the idea of handing my photos over to anyone—especially the Radical Union.

—I need my photos.

Nolan continued pressing.

—The cops are going to get rude on this. I don't think you understand what they're capable of. If you don't work with us, they eventually get to you and force you to cooperate with them. Is that what you want?

—I don't think the cops even know I exist. And even if they did, they probably have more photos than they know what to do with. A lot of people were taking pictures.

—Not as many as you might think. And I wouldn't bet they don't know you exist.

—I'll take my chances. I think you're being paranoid.

I walked back to where I had entered the corridor and opened the door. The volume of the music increased. Nolan got in the last word as Canova stood leaning against the corridor wall.

—You're wrong. Think it over. But don't take too long. Things are happening fast.

At the end of the concert the lights came up revealing the cloud of smoke floating above the crowd. But the pacifying effects of music and marijuana turned out to be insufficient to keep the peace. As people poured from the hall, police constrained the avenues of exit so much that pushing and shoving commenced. By the time Melanie and I were outside, we could hear shouting in the direction of the Ad Building. Unsure what was happening, more people began pushing and shoving. Now we could hear a few rocks and a bottle hitting the pavement on Mesa Road. A skirmish had broken out between a few concert-goers and the police. We were squeezed into a row of cops with their batons out. I grabbed Melanie and tried to pull her in my direction but she resisted and stared at one of the cops. He spoke to her by name and with an annoyed tone.

—There are better places to be tonight, 'Lanie.

—Dan, meet dad.

Speechless, I glanced at Melanie. Her father swept us inside the police line and away from the crowd. He turned to me.

—Coming here wasn't smart. Events like this right now are just an excuse for a riot. Rocks and bottles are already flying around. You need to get her out of here on the far side of the gym. And keep your eyes open.

Melanie exhaled an audible sigh.

—Dad, it's okay.

—No, it's not okay. This is already a mess.

More shouts and commotion could be heard further up the police line.

—Dan, say goodbye to dad.

Melanie pulled me with her in the direction her father indicated.

—Nice to meet you, Mr . . . .

Suddenly I realized I didn't even know Melanie's last name. We moved quickly around the gym, across Ocean Road, and into Isla Vista. On the way to her place I asked her to tell me more about her dad. But she wasn't in a mood to talk about him, so I made small talk about the concert. At the door to her apartment she fumbled with the key and swore at the lock. Once inside she switched on the lights and lit up a cigarette before sitting cross-legged on the raised mattress she used as a couch.

—You smoke often?

—Not often. Just when I want to calm down. It slows my brain.

She gave me a cold look. Apparently the question annoyed her. I shifted to the real issue.

—So what's going on between you and daddy?

—He's a cop—ten years Santa Barbara Police. He's putting me through college, but I wish I could do it alone.

—Where's your mom?

—She lives in Chatsworth, but she can't help much financially. I take his money, but I wish I didn't have to. I feel strings attached, like tonight. He has all these ideas about how I should manage my life. He needs to back off. But he won't as long as he's paying the bills. Do you know what I'm talking about?

—Guess I'm lucky. I have a scholarship.

—Jerk! Just kidding. Make the best of it. You *are* lucky.

I sat down beside her but quickly sensed she was irretrievably distant. So I said good night and told her I would catch up with her in a day or two about times for the lab work on her photos. As I was closing the door, she surprised me by calling me back.

—I'm sorry I'm such a bitch tonight. Let's get together again. I promise I'll be in a better mood.

We decided on a beach rendezvous later in the week.

*   *   *

Chapter 13

After the previous weeks' Faculty Club incident and the Academic Senate meeting, the predominate mood on campus shifted. The unity of the "spirit of 7776" broke apart—partly because of the controversy surrounding the unofficial student evaluations of Bill Allen but primarily because most students did not support the Faculty Club takeover. Although the key leaders of the Radical Union were not present because of the indictments, the majority of students held the Radical Union responsible. Nevertheless, a substantial number of students defended the Club takeover and continued to accuse the administration of flagrant disregard for student concerns.

On Monday the Radical Union called for a campus-wide strike where students would suspend class attendance until the administration granted an open hearing. But coming in the face of declining support for Allen, the escalation from demonstrations to a strike proved to be poorly timed. The strike failed to gain sufficient support and, within a few days, momentum for the student power initiatives completely withered.

In the days following the Faculty Club takeover the *El Gaucho* bulged with angry letters to the editor and opinion columns from all sides of the issues surrounding the Allen demonstrations. While some accused students of violent tactics because of the Faculty Club incident, others accused the administration of violent tactics with the use of off-campus police.

A letter to the editor submitted by a cop who had been among those brought in from outside drew wide attention on campus and showed the division of opinion even among the cops. I thought of Melanie's father and how different the opinion seemed from what I had gathered of his views.

> I had the misfortune of being on duty Monday last as a member of one of the supporting police agencies called in to quell the "insurrection" involving the dismissal of Professor Allen and the subsequent blockading of the Administration Building. Our initial response involved the "moving" of a large segment of students across the plaza to the north of the Administration Building, an exercise which proved extremely distasteful to me what with some of the

"stick work" that I witnessed on the part of my fellow officers and of which I too was guilty.

After much of the active portion of the demonstration was over, I had the enlightening experience of talking with many of the students who happened by my assigned position. I was honestly amazed by the friendliness, open-minded curiosity and intent of purpose expressed by these young people. One of the lads offered to purchase for me a subscription to your paper.

Naturally their questions to me dealt with my purpose in being there at all, at least under these circumstances, and beyond a point, I was at a loss to explain away my presence. (The Nuremberg syndrome, just following orders). My discomfort was increased with the realization that some minutes before I was wading through these same students, bridging the generation gap to the "tune of my hickory stick." This latter realization sickened me and I vowed (to myself) never to return to this campus under these circumstances—short of moving to Canada anyway. No punks, they.

Past conversations with some of my peers and a few guarded remarks on the transportation buses leaving your campus have indicated that I am not alone in some of my "liberalized" thinking. So I would ask that your readers reflect before disdaining all policemen as fascist tools, pigs, etc.

So hopefully some day soon there will be no need for such conflicts when people can sit down and discuss their differences without being held accountable for the rash and ill-advised actions of the violent few among them—the few that too often mold the general image.

Peace be with you,
A cop

For others "peace" was a kind of seduction that crippled the cause. On the editorial page under the title "Friends of the Revolution" Morris Friedell wrote a short parody using Samuel Adams (the instigator of the famous Boston Tea Party), a group of negotiators, and King George:

A: Look, Sam, this idea of dressing up as Indians and dumping the tea into the harbor sounds groovy, but it will only hurt our cause.

B: That's right. It will harden the King's position, and now that he's set up an ad hoc committee there is new hope for negotiation.

Sam: We know about the last four ad hoc committees.

B: This one is different. It has been instructed to make a preliminary report within a month. So he's now taking us seriously, and it's no time to be provocative.

C: The important thing is not to antagonize the British citizenry. We need their support in our struggle. You know how John Bull worships commerce. If we disrupt it we will immediately lose his sympathies.

D: And how will our own silent majority react? When the average Bostonian misses his morning tea he will blame us rather than the King.

E: We must first educate our fellow Americans, increase their level of political awareness. We must vastly broaden our program of Lockean discussion groups. Then in five years we will have a solid base of informed support.

F: Gentlemen, our goal is revolution, and revolution is not a tea party. Our strategy must be organized clandestine cells and cadres, while lulling the enemy into a false sense of security. Then when we strike we will be invincible.

C: Why doesn't the British citizenry support us? Because they believe that we are crude, uneducated, irresponsible frontiersmen. This "Indian" thing will only confirm their stereotypes. Instead, join my group and help us finish our 500 page "Dissertation on Governance," which will appeal to their sense of justice.

G: Sam, you know we like you and appreciate the energy you've devoted to the cause. You've been getting a lot of negative feedback here, and maybe you ought to get in touch with your feelings and examine your motives. Does your penchant for the dramatic stem from a personal bitterness at having failed to make it within the system?

E: Rather than, say, from a developed political consciousness? If Bostonians were educated to fully support the boycott, no tea would be taxed because no tea would be bought.

H: Gentlemen, we have business to attend to. With your permission I would like to present to you the tentative program for tomorrow's rally.

All (except Sam): Hear, hear!

Division of opinion spread on campus and fell predominantly but not neatly between students and faculty. But as the Allen protest dissipated into newspaper exchanges, a spate of relative calm swept across campus and Isla Vista—even though clouds of greater confrontation lay on the horizon. But for the moment, the weather belied storm clouds as sunny, calm days continued rolling in off the Pacific.

Blue skies suited the date I had with Melanie on Thursday afternoon at the Isla Vista Beach. She waited at the end of the ramp where El Embarcadero runs down to the beach. We strolled west along the sandstone cliffs. As I pointed out which of the Channel Islands was Santa Rosa and which was Santa Cruz, she told me about the band she played in when she was in high school.

—Our music was a mix of jazz—with a Latin feel—and some rock and our own version of swing. On the rock side we were influenced by some all female groups like *The Clingers* and *Fanny*. On the swing side I always liked Duke Ellington's stuff. So I suppose there was something of him that came through in a few of our songs. You ever hear of Dan Hicks?

—Yeah. Sid Page, the guy who plays fiddle, went to my high school.

—Our sound was a little like theirs—but without the fiddle.

—So what happened to the band?

—The lead guitarist and I were involved—then we had a falling out.

We reached a quiet place up the beach. I pointed to a rise of sand near the cliff and we went over to it and sat down. Melanie pulled two apples from her backpack and handed me one.

—So why'd you break up?

—He got to be so suffocating. We had to do everything together. That turned me off. I needed more space. He couldn't deal with that. It got ugly.

—Did he get violent?

—No. Just *very* temperamental.

—What did you do about it?

—I wrote him a farewell song.

—Yeah? How does it go?

—It's not that good.

—C'mon, I want to hear it.

—All right. But don't laugh.

She cleared her throat, looked toward the ocean, and recited the words in a half-singing voice.

> I know I call you a good friend,
> But don't see me as your day's end.
> Even if I always begin,

Clear and fresh as a newborn sin,
Don't turn and start in on me
When I'm just tryin' to be free.
Don't turn and tell me where to go
When the path is not one you know.
I'm not sellin' myself to you,
I'm findin' myself for me.
So don't tell me the sky is blue,
Just let me go and let me see.
Just let me go and let me be.

When she finished, she wouldn't look at me. I sensed this wasn't a concern about what I thought of her so much as what I thought of her song. Melanie wasn't shy, but, like most artists, she did fear the critic. The song was not exceptional, and, since she already acknowledged that, I went easy on her.

—Nice lyrics. Take the last two lines. Seeing deepens being. That's what I like about photography. Framing through a lens helps you do more than look. It helps you really see.

—You think so? So what did you "really see" when you photographed me?

That question caught me by surprise. Stalling for time, I clumsily shifted focus.

—Speaking of which, why do you want those photos?

Staring out to sea, she hesitated a while before answering.

—I want to be independent. That requires money.

—You're going to sell them?

—I know a guy in Chatsworth, met him through a friend. Says he can sell me in the "men's magazine" trade. I can get decent money for it. So I promised him a portfolio.

—You must want independence a lot. Why not get some kind of loan?

—I don't want to borrow money. That's no way to independence.

We both stared at the surf. Finally she pushed me over.

—Hey! You didn't answer. If you can "really see" with that camera of yours, tell me what you saw.

I pulled myself around and looked her in the face.

—Aside from a great body, what I saw was a woman who really doesn't trust men.

She took a bite out of her apple without taking her eyes off me. Then she turned toward the surf and spoke with a tone of dissatisfaction.

—You stole that from my song. Very clever—like a fortuneteller. But never mind. So what about you? What kind of music do you like?

I thought about telling her how changing the subject only confirmed what I was saying, but decided not to push it for now.

—Music?

—Aside from The *Beatles.*

—I like *The Beatles.* But . . .

—But what?

—They don't quite do it for me. They rock and roll and get you feeling good, which is okay. But a group like *The Doors*—they rattle the cage. They take you to the edge and shade off into the dark.

—You mean like evil?

—No, just darkness. Something you can't see to the bottom of, something with no name. Listening to *The Doors* doesn't just move you along—it puts you in the current. *The Beatles* brush up against it—like with that extended chord at the end of "A Day in the Life." That chord takes you into the dark. But *The Beatles* back away from that. I can't think where they evoke that again after *Sergeant Pepper*—except maybe in "I am the Walrus." *The Doors* are more edgy, more electric.

—Electric?

—Plugged into high voltage. They want to get burned and they want to burn you.

Melanie stared at me with a blank expression, but then slowly started to crack a smile. Finally she broke into a laugh.

—What? What is it?

—You get such a serious look on your face.

I smiled and pointed to the surf.

—You up for getting wet?

—No, it's too cold.

We went to the edge of the surf and Melanie walked along the sand as I waded barefoot through the water. As I turned to pick up a piece of driftwood, I noticed a guy approaching from the east end of the beach. He looked familiar. After a few more paces I saw it was Kyle. When he came up to us, I introduced him to Melanie.

—Hi Kyle. I've seen you before, walking on the beach.

—I get out here a lot. You too?

—Once in a while. It's good for the head.

They looked at each other for a few seconds without saying anything, so I turned to Kyle.

—You seen Bill recently?

—No, I've been at Berkeley for a few days.

—How are things up there?

—Not as crazy as here.

—Yeah?

—More weather blowing in, too.

—What do you mean?

—Kunstler's coming on Wednesday.

—I heard he's bringing Jerry Rubin with him.

—That's changed. Nancy Rubin's coming instead.

—How do you feel about Kunstler?

—Things get interesting when people from Chicago come to campus. I've got to keep moving to get back for a class. Nice meeting you, Melanie.

He walked off toward the Devereaux end of the beach. As Melanie and I continued toward Isla Vista, she asked how I knew Kyle.

—I had him as a TA in Existential Philosophy last fall. At the end of the quarter he asked the class to meet him at the UCEN. There were only six of us. The Prof—Macomber—left the grades for the TAs. We'd all heard stories about Kincaid—how he played poker, how he picked up a clarinet and made music without even a lesson, how he hung out backstage with the Grateful Dead. I guess he even spent time in Nam. Plus we'd all seen how he held his own with Macomber. All in all, he's a living legend around campus.

—It's weird how he looks at you without blinking.

—I've never seen anything like it. He fixes his eyes on yours and doesn't let go, but for some reason you don't feel like he's trying to stare you down. Anyway, getting back to the story. So when everybody arrives at the UCEN, Kyle motions for us to gather around. He says we're going downstairs to the pool tables and our final exam will be Eight Ball. Grades will be determined based on who wins and who loses.

—He wanted you to play pool for your grade?

—Exactly. We each had to pair up with someone else and play one game. Then everybody had to play another game with a different opponent. He said those who lose both games get a "C." Those who win one and lose one get a "B." And those who win both get an "A."

—For a philosophy grade? Did anyone complain?

—Well, at first we're all smiling and thinking this is just a joke—Kyle's weird sense of humor. But Kyle's got his poker face on. When we see he isn't laughing, we all start complaining. What about the papers we wrote? What about some being better than others at pool? We air all these complaints—and more—but Kyle waives them all off. He says philosophy is about life and life is about what we do in situations we haven't chosen. This game isn't going to be fair. You haven't made the rules. There are elements of luck as well as skill. And you're going to be judged for what you do. The pressure is on. Welcome to real life. So for a few seconds we're all speechless. Then Kyle starts passing out pool cues. At that point everybody got sweaty palms.

—So how did you score?

—Well I'm decent with a stick, but it's amazing what a little pressure can do to your game. I got a "B" because I won one and lost one.

—So is that the grade that got recorded?

—Sure thing. It was no joke. So you noticed him on the beach before?

—Yeah. He may be weird but he's cute.

—Cute? Bull!

Melanie grinned, happy to mess with my head. We stopped at the top of the ramp into Isla Vista. She had to go to practice for a one act play. I thought I'd steal a kiss from her, but as I leaned over to brush her lips she pulled me toward her and swirled her tongue in my mouth. I quickly forgot the remark about Kyle.

*   *   *

Chapter 14

In the days following the Allen demonstrations much of the talk around campus and in the *El Gaucho* revolved around the administration and its reaction to the crisis. Due to mistakes by the Radical Union and revelations contradicting claims about Allen's publishing and teaching record, the campus now stood divided in its support of Allen. But many students still viewed the administration's repressive use of outside police as an abuse of power in lock-step with the actions of established power brokers in other political arenas: for example, the Nixon/Agnew crackdown on activists in the anti-war movement, the Union Oil resumption of drilling in the wake of the Santa Barbara Channel oil spill of 1969, and the Bank of America support of the growers in opposition to the United Farm Workers Union. The more thoroughly abuse of power registered locally and personally the more students identified with perceived abuses at the national and global level. For many at UCSB and on campuses around the country a "big picture" emerged from the darkroom of apathy and misinformation. The familiar parts of the "big picture" took shape in radical papers in a litany that laid out like a sideways corporate tower:

Money rules.
Corporations control money.
Money buys elections and politicians to represent corporate interests.
Government of the people becomes government of the corporations.
Through control of government, corporations control state owned universities.
Universities function as research centers and training grounds for corporate interests.
Corporations engineer contracts and co-opt agendas supporting their interests
Corporations marginalize those who criticize and undermine their interests.
Corporations authorize police crackdown on forms of dissent.
Corporations control money.
Money rules.

The cold truth was simple: the system was a lie. The system was a Cosanostra. It had the appearance of legitimacy and used the force of law whenever it could be used to its advantage. But underneath the veneer of legitimacy the system exuded corruption through a small minority of executives willing to use Machiavellian means to achieve self-serving ends. The system was not America. It was Amerika—a subtle version of a fascist state, all the more sinister because it was so well hidden behind democratic mirrors.

Over and against these monolithic concentrations of self-aggrandizing power stood a thin line of loosely organized, poorly financed, but firmly committed resistance activists and demonstrators. In between the relatively small minorities of those who wielded power and those who opposed them lay Middle America—a mass of people all more or less duped by those in power but who nevertheless were capable of having their consciousness raised by the resistance. With the help of Middle America the tide could be turned and a better society, a better future, could be built.

For many on university campuses, this was how the big picture had looked for several years. Now, at UCSB, in the wake of the failed Bill Allen demonstrations and the military approach used to quell them, it was a picture shared by a larger number of students and faculty than before.

The big picture got even bigger for students and residents of Isla Vista on Tuesday, February 24th. Late that afternoon, on leaving the Isla Vista Market, I saw a huge column of smoke rising above a large crowd at the intersection of Embarcadero del Mar and Seville. As I walked closer, I saw the smoke came from a County Sheriff's cruiser that had been tipped over and set afire.

Seeing Canova standing at the edge of the crowd, I asked him what had happened.

—The pigs busted Lefty Bryant over by Johnnie's Cue. Then a fight broke out between the pigs and some of his friends. The ones in this cruiser ran across the park to help them. That's when someone slashed the tires. The pigs finally split with Lefty in another cruiser and left this one. So some guys rolled it, drained the gas, and torched it.

—How many were there?

—Pigs? I don't know. Four, I think. At first there were only two busting Lefty. Look at this thing!

—What was the bust for?

—Some real bullshit. The said they had an L. A. warrant on him for armed robbery. They all know he wasn't involved in any robbery. Arresting him is just part of Webster's strategy. They want to clear the streets of as many radicals as possible before Kunstler gets here. I heard three others from the Radical Union got busted this afternoon, too.

—Seems pretty stupid to me, busting someone on the street in the loop. Webster can't figure out what kind of mood that's going to create?

—Webster thinks busting some people off the streets will intimidate these hippies. It's the macho thing you'd figure from a John Wayne wannabe like him.

—So what are you going to do?

—I'm going back to the store and keep an eye on things. Webster won't take this lying down. The pigs will be back. Best not to be caught flat-footed when they come.

In response to the torched cruiser Webster ordered more police into Isla Vista. The situation escalated. The next day I learned that the ill advised arrest turned into late night street rioting with bonfires and burning dumpsters throughout the loop. Lacking sufficient numbers and riot gear, the cops made no move on the crowd, and for several hours maneuvers between rioters and cops amounted to a standoff. Finally, in the early morning the crowd dispersed.

Keyed up by an evening of street rioting, the entire community looked toward Kunstler's arrival with high anticipation—some with foreboding, others with great excitement. As one of two attorneys representing the Chicago Eight from the trial's beginning in April of '69, Kunstler had become an icon of the protest movement. With the completion of the trial on February 18th, his fame continued to spread in the wake of a split decision. The jury had acquitted all the defendants on conspiracy charges but had convicted five defendants (Hayden, Hoffman, Rubin, Dellinger, and Davis) on the lesser charge of crossing state lines with the intent to incite a riot. Two days later they were each sentenced to five years in federal prison and fined $5000. The five were currently in Cook County Jail while Kunstler worked on an appeal and bail arrangements.

The Radical Union hoped Kunstler could, as Hayden had done, ignite a resurgence of momentum toward change on and off campus. But the timing of the Kunstler visit, in relation to the newly aggravated tensions and the rioting that had occurred the previous evening, was more accidental than orchestrated. The Kunstler speaking date had been booked weeks ago. Geoff Wallace—member of the Radical Union and research editor for the *El Gaucho*—had seen Kunstler speaking about the Chicago Eight trial on the late news in early January. Based on what he heard that night, he was certain Kunstler would have much to say concerning autocratic abuses of power and tactics of repression of dissent—all of which he regarded as highly relevant to the Allen situation. He picked up the phone and a few days later Phyllis Bennis, the Associated Students Lectures Chairwoman, had secured a February speaking date. Also, Nancy Rubin—Jerry Rubin's wife—volunteered to join Kunstler.

In addition to the previous night's rioting, tensions were heightened because of the controversy that had arisen from the University's approval of the Kunstler speaking engagement—an approval many local and non-local observers did not realize had been given several weeks prior to the current disturbances. The most vocal opponent of the Kunstler appearance had been State Senator Robert Lagomarsino. He was quoted in Tuesday's *El Gaucho* as saying there was still too much turmoil on campus concerning the dismissal of Bill Allen. This was not the time to bring in a visitor whose only purpose would be to "stir up trouble."

Lagomarsino's remarks were especially relevant in the combined context of the Allen demonstrations and the Chicago Eight trial. Since the Chicago Eight had been indicted and five convicted of violating the 1968 Johnson statute regarding "interstate commerce" and promotion of civil disorder, crossing state lines and giving speeches that could be construed as inflammatory had become a more sensitive and potentially dangerous act. Now Kunstler and Nancy Rubin would cross state lines in coming from Chicago to California. If any riots were to break out following their visit, they would be subject to the same indictment handed the Eight. Some claimed Lagomarsino's remarks were strategic, designed to set the stage for holding Kunstler and Rubin accountable for any disturbances that might arise following their speeches.

Even before he left Chicago for Santa Barbara, Kunstler was accused of being the trigger for rioting that had occurred the previous night in Isla Vista. So the events of Tuesday afternoon and evening, as well as the Lagomarsino complaints, were very much on everyone's minds when Kunstler and Rubin arrived. Given these circumstances, the turnout at the stadium was not surprising. The situation had the makings of a showdown—a major test of wills between law enforcement and what many were now calling the local faction of "the Movement."

*   *   *

Chapter 15

William Kunstler and Nancy Rubin arrived at the Santa Barbara Airport a little after one o'clock on Wednesday, February 25th and were on time for their scheduled talk at the University stadium at three o'clock.

Having detoured to the I. V. drugstore to buy film, I didn't get to the stadium until after Nancy Rubin had begun speaking. The crowd was enormous—between six and seven thousand. It nearly filled the oddly "L" shaped stadium and far exceeded the attendance for football games. But the animated and exuberant mood of the crowd was not far removed from what would be expected at a football game. A sizeable platform had been set up on the field facing the stands near where the stadium formed a right angle. People swarmed around the base of the platform as Nancy Rubin spoke into a microphone extending from a sole lectern resting on top of it. Her concluding remark stuck in my head: "When there is no justice in the courtrooms we may have to take to the streets." On that portentous note Nancy then introduced William Kunstler.

Although he didn't look it, Kunstler was three years older than my father. As he stood at the lectern with weathered, suntanned face and sunglasses perched on top of a full head of long dark but graying hair, he looked seriously wise. That someone of his generation had risen to become the legal point man for the protest movement and now stood in this stadium to inspire a group of people half his age imposed a good measure of what I had learned in a psychology class to call "cognitive dissonance."

But Kunstler had good liberal credentials. I had read about him in *Time Magazine* last fall. Born in New York City, educated at Yale and, like my father, a veteran of World War II, he earned his law degree at Columbia and began his practice in the early 50s. In the 60s he sided with disenfranchised minorities and provided legal service for groups like the Congress of Racial Equality and Martin Luther King's Southern Christian Leadership Conference, and, later, the Student Non-Violence Coordinating Committee. But it was Kunstler's acquaintance with Charles Garry—the attorney who had represented Huey Newton and the Black Panthers in Oakland—that brought him to the Chicago Eight Trial. Garry, who was initially in Chicago to represent Panther Bobby

110

Seale, planned to head the legal team for the entire Chicago Eight until he fell ill and needed gall bladder surgery. When Judge Hoffman refused to postpone the trial for Garry's surgery and recovery, Kunstler was brought in as his replacement.

Standing before the crowd at UCSB stadium, it was obvious Kunstler did not draw a sharp line between representing his clients and representing their causes. His practice of blurring that line had earned him the respect of people in "the Movement"—as well as a lot of suspicion from those in his own generation. He immediately addressed the subject of the anti-riot statute and the street violence of the previous night.

> When I came to O'Hair Airport, this morning, to get the plane to Los Angeles, I picked up a copy of *Chicago Today*, which, by the way, is the stepchild of the *Chicago Tribune*. The *Chicago Tribune*, an arch-conservative newspaper, had editorialized heavily against the Chicago Eight and the street violence that had occurred during the Democratic Convention.
>
> It says: "KUNSTLER VISIT SPARKS RIOT"—and it's in no small headlines. It's these three lines on the top. And I thought, as I was flying out, how this deadly law of interstate riot could so easily be applied. They were a little early, because I hadn't come yet. When I read in the papers, this morning, about what happened in Santa Barbara [Isla Vista] yesterday, I thought I would make some comment about it, because I think I should frankly discuss it. I have never thought that breaking of windows and sporadic picayune violence is a good tactic. But, on the other hand, I cannot bring myself to become bitter and condemn young people who engage in it. In his book, Justice Douglas said that the Establishment, today, is the same as George III's. And he said if the Establishment does not stop its stampede toward oppression and repression, then the only honorable course is what men did in 1776.

Surprised to learn that Kunstler could cite a Supreme Court justice in support of violent protest, I later researched the book, which was titled *Points of Rebellion*. The passage he referred to reads as follows: "George III was the symbol against which our Founders made a revolution now considered bright and glorious. George III had not crossed the seas to fasten a foreign yoke on us. George III and his dynasty had established and nurtured us and all that he did was by no means oppressive. But a vast restructuring of laws and institutions was necessary if the people were to be content. That restructuring was not forthcoming and there was revolution. We must realize that today's Establishment is the new George III. Whether it will continue to adhere to his tactics, we do not know. If it does, the redress, honored in tradition, is also revolution." These were strong words coming from a Supreme Court Justice. Douglas' thin but potent volume drew rave reviews from those on the left while sounding alarm bells among those on the right. Many liberals regarded it as a better defense of civil protest than any expressed by its activist leaders. Kunstler then placed the strategies of intimidation and repression in the context of the Chicago trial.

Now the idea of this prosecution was to chill all of us. The idea of this prosecution was to set an example—to show you what could happen if you become involved in any social movement—to put fear where fervor was and to destroy fervor—to destroy involvement.

They selected eight people. They wanted the Panthers, as is now candidly admitted by the former United States Attorney for the Northern District of California. They wanted to get the Panthers by any means necessary. So, what better than to take Bobby Seale—who had replaced Kathleen Cleaver, who was a replacement for Eldridge Cleaver—and this last minute replacement, who gave a speech at Lincoln Park the Tuesday before nomination day—that's all that was needed.

Bobby Seale was cofounder of the Black Panther Party along with Eldridge Cleaver and Huey Newton. Raised in Texas, the son of a carpenter, he had an eclectic history: mechanic, musician, comedian, and ghetto street fighter.

> They wanted Dave Dellinger because he embodies the concept of the anti-war drive.

Dellinger was a Christian Socialist from Massachusetts and a hard core long time anti-war protester. He had spent time in jail for failing to register for the draft during World War II. He also protested the Korean War and the Bay of Pigs and was chairman of "the MOBE," the National Mobilization Committee to End the War in Vietnam—a coalition of many anti-war groups. He was regarded by the Chicago prosecution team as the primary architect of the demonstrations during the Democratic convention.

> They wanted Abbie and Jerry because they wanted to get what they considered all the freaked-out kids that are so "dangerous" to the stability of the United States.

Abbie Hoffman and Jerry Rubin were founders of the Youth International Party and had become famous for "yippie" street theater confrontation tactics. Hoffman, who regarded himself as an "orphan" and claimed to be the illegitimate son of the Judge Hoffman who presided over the trial, had a psychology degree from Brandeis and had been involved in the civil rights movement. Rubin was the son of a Teamsters official from Cincinnati and had been part of the Free Speech movement at Berkeley.

> They wanted Tom Hayden because he was one of the founders of SDS, he was deep in Newark during the period before the Newark riots, and he was a bridge, in a way, between mobilization [MOBE] and SDS.

Tom Hayden, as a founding member of the Students for a Democratic Society, had authored its most famous document—the Port Huron Statement. He was also a veteran of the civil rights movement and an activist in the Newark ghetto.

> They wanted Rennie Davis because he was working in the ghettos of Chicago and was the project director of the New MOBE and is

an extremely bright, articulate, intelligent young man who, if not stopped, might prove embarrassing at the least and dangerous to the system at the most.

Rennie Davis came from a farm community in Illinois, earned a Master's degree from the University of Illinois, and did further graduate work at Ann Arbor. He was also a founding member of SDS and had become active in the MOBE and was also a key organizer of the convention demonstrations.

> And then, they hadn't gotten what they really wanted, en toto. They wanted you, too. And there was one way to get you and that was to take some academic people and throw them in—to take away the faculty participation—just as they're trying to do with Bill Allen, right here.

Here Kunstler referred to John Froines and Lee Weiner. Froines was an assistant professor of chemistry from the University of Oregon who had done undergraduate work at Berkeley and had received his Ph.D. from Yale. He had been an organizer for SDS at New Haven and was a cofounder of the Radical Science Information Service—an organization credited with publishing journal articles on how to make stink bombs. Weiner was a teaching assistant in sociology working on a doctorate at Northwestern who claimed to be a "Government Certified Radical."

> I think that if there had been no Michigan and Balboa; if there had been no Berkeley; if there had been no indictments around this country, where their brutality—of the ruling class—was illustrated and exemplified, then I think young people would not feel the bitterness and frustration of the inability to reach responsible government.

The student demonstrations at the University of Michigan at Ann Arbor had precipitated the founding of SDS and the Port Huron gathering of radicals. Kunstler's mention of Berkeley was a reference to the Free Speech movement of 1964 and the police violence and arrests that accompanied it.

> This frustration is so bitter and deep that occasionally a few panes of glass are broken; occasionally some red paint lands against the Justice Department; occasionally these things happen. But they are so utterly picayune, compared to five minutes around Danang.

To get a broader angle, I climbed the stairs to the top of the stadium as Kunstler continued speaking.

> I hope government listens to what we say. I hope the informers in this audience report accurately what is said here so that government will learn. If someone had only gotten through to Marie Antoinette, she might have had an exemplary old age. The trouble is, it doesn't get through. Therefore, you have to fill the streets so they can see you.

Surveying the scene from the top of the stadium, I noticed Canova leaning against the railing a couple of sections away and went to join him.

> It is better to conspire to create a world where black and white can live together, where men and women are equal and poor people are abolished, perhaps by elimination of property as a private concept, than to destroy minds in the universities and beat heads with night sticks.
>
> We cannot just pick out these eight. They are symptomatic and representative, perhaps, but they are only eight and they are unimportant by themselves. The importance is all of us and we must all stand together. No trial must take place in the United States that embodies the threat to the soul of man without us being present.

Nodding at me as I came up to him, Canova pointed beyond the stadium toward El Colegio Road where we could see twelve police cruisers slowly moving along the road into Isla Vista.

> Trials are just one tool of organization. You must organize around the entire grasp of the Movement. The Movement makes lots of mistakes. We're disorganized. We sometimes bite each other's back. We sometimes malign and destroy each other. We make errors galore. They always tell us we're hurting our cause by what we do. But we are all united in one thing, and this I learned in Chicago: we all want the same type of decent world that we feel is possible. We're the greatest optimists in this country.
>
> This is no time to be frightened of Chicagos, frightened of prosecutions, frightened of your skin—even though fear is a legitimate emotion and we all have it. This is a time to make the Chicago Eight a symbol of something. This is a time to use that case to say, as they said in the courtroom: "This far and no further do we yield."

When I left them, I said I was coming here and I said, "If you wanted me to tell them one thing, what should I do, when I come to the end of what I have to say." And they thought for a minute and finally Rennie said "Just say 'Right ON!'" So, I want to add a few—just about five words to that, because I know that the missing one, the eighth, would have added a few more words. He would have said "All Power to the People! Right On!"

The crowd responded to Kunstler's speech with a thunderous ovation and howls of support. Attempting to ride the wave of that support, John Seeley—a local activist, former department chair of Sociology at Brandeis University, and, most recently, former Dean of the Center for the Study of Democratic Institutions—came to the podium and made a request for donations for the legal defense of the Chicago Eight and the Santa Barbara 19. In doing so, he made reference again to conspiracy and counter-conspiracy. His further reference to the possibility of violence beyond mere window breaking struck an even more ominous note.

Those of you who know which conspiracy you belong to; those of you who are with us, I now ask one thing at this time: before you are called upon—as you may well be—to spill the wine of your blood, because you are a student, because you are a member of a faculty, because you have an independent mind—before you are called upon to spill that wine, I ask you now, if it is there in your heart to bring your bread for the defense of the Chicago Eight and the Santa Barbara 19. People will pass among you with waste baskets, seeking such money as you have to give.

Seeley, along with members of the Radical Union, apparently had no intention of wasting any momentum Kunstler had generated. Phyllis Bennis and Geoff Wallace finished the event by announcing that a community rally and demonstration would take place immediately afterwards in Perfect Park.

On leaving the stadium, Canova and I separated as I lagged behind to take a few more photos. When I looked to rejoin him outside the stadium, commotion and shouting near Stadium Road suddenly drew everyone's attention. The density of the crowd made it impossible to see what was happening beyond the fact that two police cars had pulled alongside a third already parked. Making my way through the crowd toward the road, I found Canova. He explained what had happened before I could ask.

—The pigs ripped off Underwood, the same guy they jumped the first day of the Allen protests. He was carrying a bottle of wine in a paper bag and they thought it was a Molotov cocktail. He showed them what was in the bottle and they busted him anyway.

As he spoke we turned to see all three cop cars pulling away, followed by a hail of rocks from several in the crowd. A large group broke from the crowd and, continuing to throw rocks, chased the cars down Stadium Road. Canova turned to me, shaking his head.

—It's crazy—busting someone with all these people standing around. Why don't the pigs just send out invitations to riot?

—You got that right. It could be a long night.

*   *   *

Chapter 16

Canova and I returned along Ocean Road. He left to check his store while I went to my apartment. After tuning the radio to KCSB, I tossed together a scrambled egg sandwich. According to reports, a crowd of about seven hundred gathered at Perfect Park for the rally. But two blocks away a cruiser had already been smashed, overturned, and set afire.

Now about three to four dozen cops, clad in riot gear, moved on the crowd to clear the streets and prevent further rioting. But instead of dispersing, the crowd charged, advanced on the cops, and succeeded in driving them up Embarcadero del Norte. A reporter then commented on the scene around the bank.

—We've just heard the Bank of America has been broken into. Some reports are saying that fires have been started inside . . .

I wasn't expecting an attack on the bank. I grabbed the camera and bolted for the door with part of the sandwich in my hand.

—I'm going out there. If they're breaking into the bank, I need photos.

Matt supplied the voice of reason.

—Don't do it, man. You'll just get busted.

—Thanks, see you later.

The sun had set and it was now more difficult to see. Nearing the top of the loop, I heard angry yells and rocks bouncing off the pavement. At the Enco gas station on the corner, I approached a group that had just retreated from the street. The cops occupied the park. Another group collected to my left. Several among those in front of me gathered stones from behind the gas station. I stopped beside a few others who stood motionless in the background along the curb of El Embarcadero—watching and waiting.

The cops slowly advanced toward us as the group in front of me drew back, throwing rocks and taunting them. As I moved with the crowd south along El Embarcadero, the sound of broken glass rang piercingly from somewhere down del Mar. A couple of large rocks thudded and rolled in the street near where a group of cops in riot gear now stood at the southwest end of the park.

Suddenly a separate group of rioters, surprising everyone—especially the cops, charged from the direction of the Magic Lantern Theater. Throwing rocks and projectiles of every description, whooping, hollering, and howling like villagers in pursuit of a Frankenstein, this coiled mass thrust itself onto one side of the police line, breaking it apart and forcing a rapid retreat of its dismembered parts west across the park. The instant this group attacked, the group in front of me reversed direction and joined the onslaught with matching war cries and rock volleys. I froze, stupefied by the din they raised—banging sticks on metal garbage can lids, screaming like savages, and slinging bottles and rocks in javelin-throwing form across the park. Judging from the fury of their movements, they held nothing back.

Within seconds the combined attack of these two groups routed the cops, driving them in full retreat across the park toward del Mar. I noticed one cop knocked unconscious by a brick. Two others shouldered and dragged him along, straining to keep their shields toward in-coming volleys. Sensing weakness, the rioters intensified the attack. Several cops had by now received serious blows from the rocks. They limped on, retreating as fast as they could down Seville Road.

The rioters didn't let up. Here and there two or three stopped to pick up something to throw. Busting apart large rocks, tearing up loose chunks of asphalt, chipping off concrete from curbs—anything they could rip apart and lay their hands on got thrown at the cops as they retreated down the street.

In numb disbelief I staggered after them, glued to the scene like a witness to a train wreck. Following the riot as it coursed further down Seville, I saw where the crowd had broken out windows in two realty offices on the south side of the street. Further down I paused to attempt a photo of a few rioters passing under a streetlamp. My hands shook as adrenalin jacked my nerve endings. Over the blood thundering in my ears I heard another sound, an odd, out of place sound coming from my left. It was music. Barely audible, I couldn't make out what it was. Then the volume grew louder, much louder, until it was unmistakable. The Rolling Stones' "Street Fightin' Man" blasted from an open window filling the night air up and down the street. Some of the rioters cheered. The cops kept running until they were out of view, chased by rioters who turned the corner after them and disappeared in pursuit.

Everyone was out of range now. Feeling fastened to the middle of the street, I put down the camera, hands still shaking, listening to sounds from beyond the corner. Finally I stood and moved off in the direction the rioters had gone. But at the intersection I turned away from the rioting and went along Camino Pescadero toward the ocean. I wanted to walk. A current swarmed all around. In the air. In the rioters. In the cops. I felt it moving inside me.

After wandering the back blocks of Isla Vista for awhile, I came out at the top of the loop area again and approached the bank. A hundred or more people were gathered in front. Smoke rose from between pillars supporting the overhanging roof. Recessed lamps along the overhang emitted dim cones of light through the smoke leaving the entrance in a hazy, diffused glow. Remembering the camera, I snapped a picture, taking in most of the crowd and the bank.

Moving closer, I came to the edge of a bonfire fueled by an assortment of chairs, table tops, cartons, paneling, papers, and other paraphernalia taken from inside the bank and now mostly charred beyond recognition. Continuing left, I knelt down and worked the light meter. Tri X Pan was fast film but with no flash the shutter would be too slow for good definition. The light from the fire would help. I set the shutter at 1/15th and pressed off a shot. I reset the speed to

1/30th and aimed the camera a little more to the left across the flames and pressed off another. Moving slightly closer, I took two more shots while steadying the camera on my knee. As I stood up to get a better look, someone spoke from the left.

—What's with the camera, man? Taking pictures ain't cool.

—There's not enough light to get faces.

—All the same, point that somewhere else.

Having attracted unwanted attention, I headed toward the back of the building. On the way, I passed several small vertical windows. Through one rectangle flames could be seen leaping toward the ceiling. I stopped, pressed off a shot, and continued around back. As I turned the corner, two people  standing at the entrance slipped inside the bank. At the opening, pieces of glass from the broken doors lay strewn across the lobby floor. I peered inside for a few seconds. There was barely enough light to see to the far side of the room. Then, on impulse, I stepped through the hole in the door and plunged into the smoke-filled interior.

The two who came in before me scanned the damage from the middle of the lobby. When I appeared, they moved toward the door, glanced around, and left—perhaps because they noticed my camera. Now alone in the room, my eyes adjusted to the light and smoke, which wasn't yet thick enough where I stood to make breathing difficult. But I was too transfixed to breathe—gripped by an upheaval on the inside that matched what I saw in the room.

Directly in front of me, two large overturned lobby tables sprawled across the floor—one on its side, the other with legs straight up. Toward the far side of the room an L-shaped desk with a broken leg listed like a sinking ship in a sea of white papers strewn from ransacked files. Steel cabinets and drawers protruded like buoys through the surface of paper. A single ceiling lamp in the far corner dimly lit the lobby wreckage.

The main source of light came from the corner beyond the teller windows where something burned too brightly to see what it was. Flames reached halfway to the ceiling and silhouetted teller windows extending along the lobby to the far corner where it became difficult to see through the haze.

Alone in the burning room, the strangeness of the scene choked me as much as the pungent odor of smoke. I raised the camera, thinking it would record the unreality of it all. After quickly pressing off three shots at different angles into the room, I was about to take a fourth when two guys emerged through the broken door. They walked past me as if I weren't there. Surveying the destruction for a few seconds, one then picked up several booklets from among the papers beside a large desk and flung them across the room into the flames. The other did the same with a light-weight chair.

As they continued throwing debris into the fire, I stared at the flames through the camera lens. The current I felt earlier that night came over me again. Moving slowly, I bent down and picked up a bound booklet. It read: Bank of America Audit Report 1969. The current got stronger. I sailed it toward the fire, then picked up another and flung it. I grabbed another. But while raising my arm to throw it, an image flashed in my mind. I saw myself standing a few feet away, framing me in the viewfinder as I was about to throw the book. My arm stopped. As I lowered it, I noticed the other two in the room staring at me. Tossing the book aside, I turned and, almost running, crossed over the strewn glass and out the doors.

Several people now gathered at the back entrance. As I passed them I heard a voice. It was the last voice I wanted to hear at the moment.

—I'll be damned, Marleau! Is that gasoline I smell?

Canova grinned, obviously pleased to see me. For a second or two I stared at him with a face that conveyed God knows what. Groping for words, I mumbled a response.

—You should get out of here.

Pushing past him, I crossed the park in the direction of the beach. Surf pounded in the distance. I walked toward it until I felt the sand beneath my feet and salt air on my face. It cleared my head of the fumes, smoke, and bedlam that hung in the air over Isla Vista. Thoughts whirled: What madness! What was I thinking?

Walking and listening to the surf, I lost track of time. But when I started back, it must have been well past midnight. Returning along El Embarcadero, an unusual light radiated from the park area. When I reached the top of the loop, I stopped and stared in disbelief. Flames engulfed the bank and smoke rolled above the walls into the night. The roof and part of one wall had caved in.

When I'd left earlier I hadn't imagined fires inside would consume the whole building. The firemen and cops I had earlier expected to appear at any minute hadn't responded. Instead, the bank now succumbed entirely to flames and Isla Vistans controlled the streets. The scene was hard to fathom.

People gathered around the park area and along the street in front of the bank to watch. I walked around the loop toward the Magic Lantern Theater. Some stood quietly gazing into the fire. Others grouped together talking, laughing, and drinking from bottles of wine or beer. A few others leapt around the burning wreckage, occasionally letting out a yell and throwing something into the fire. I sat down on the sidewalk by a brick wall fencing a flower bed next to the theater and watched the fire. The pillars in front of the bank still held, but the front wall had caved inward when the roof collapsed. The brick walls on each side and in back framed the fire. It took the good part of an hour before the fire gutted most of the interior.

They had done it. They had really done it—whoever "they" were. Now all of us—whether residents of Isla Vista or students of the University—were sailing together, like it or not, into smoke-slickened, uncharted waters.

I stood up, tired and unable to stay any longer. As I started to walk away, I noticed three guys doing something near the front of the building where part of the fire smoldered. I approached to within a few yards to one side of them. They held refashioned coat hangers over what was left of the fire along the remains of the front wall. On the end of the hangers were several marshmallows. The one closest to me raised his hanger from the coals and with thumb and forefinger gingerly pulled at the end marshmallow. It had gotten a little too blackened and oozed off the hanger, slipping from his hand. He caught it before it hit the ground and raised it over his head. Then it disappeared into his mouth.

*   *   *

Chapter 17

Seeing the bank in the bright daylight the following morning felt like stepping

into a war zone in some other part of the world. It looked like a bomb had hit the building. Only parts of two walls and the concrete vault were left standing.

Steel beams and cross supports tilted into the charred and unrecognizable ruins piled in the center of what had been the lobby. In some areas ribbons of smoke still wafted into the air.

Two fire trucks were parked in front and several firemen rummaged through the the debris, apparently looking for something. To one side, near the vault

area, a portly middle-aged man, hat in hand as if in church, scanned the rubble in obvious disbelief. I later learned he was the bank manager.

Continually taking photos, I worked my way to the rear of the structure. A small crowd gathered there, a mix of adult locals and students engaged in heated talk about the bank burning. A middle-aged woman in sun glasses complained to one of the students.

—I look at this but I can't believe my eyes. It's so senseless. Why would they burn the bank? It's part of our community.

In shoulder-length long hair, the student defended the wreckage lying behind him.

—It's not senseless. Listen to me! The bank was targeted. It stands for everything wrong with this country and the damn war we're fighting. It's the only American bank with a branch in Vietnam. It's in bed with defense contractors. Litton, Douglas, Stanford Research Institute—they all share board members with the bank. On top of that, the bank's lawyers back the growers against the United Farm Workers . . .

—So just burn it down! That makes a lot of sense. I can't believe the police didn't stop this.

An older man standing next to her entered the fray.

—They tried to stop it. But they got the crap kicked out of 'em. There weren't enough of 'em. The damnedest skirmish I've seen outside of real war. But you can bet every cop in the state'll be showing up here tonight. There'll be a score to settle with those rioters.

He was right. In the aftermath of the bank disaster Sheriff Webster and his deputies had a lot at stake, including what was left of their pride. And no doubt they wanted to extract a price for their humiliation in the streets. Law and order had to be reaffirmed and no amount of talking would get that done.

The city and county of Santa Barbara combined did not have enough police to stem riots in Isla Vista. Webster had been shorthanded even for the Allen demonstrations. Taking control of Isla Vista required reinforcements from every county around Santa Barbara—from San Luis Obispo to Ventura and all the way to Los Angeles. Rumors circulated that these reinforcements would include the Los Angeles County Special Enforcement Bureau—a swat team of hard core "storm troopers," as the Radical Union referred to them, trained for every contingency from riots to hostage situations. Shortly before noon, Webster announced through local radio stations a dusk-to-dawn curfew imposed throughout Isla Vista.

The burning of the bank had moved the momentum of the Bill Allen demonstrations into the streets, beyond campus issues and into community, state, and national issues—especially the war and the financing of the war. The burning of the bank had upped the ante from demonstrations over the firing of a professor in a relatively obscure Anthropology Department to active resistance toward war policy and everything associated with it. No one knew exactly what was coming, but everyone felt the rising barometer of a looming bad storm.

Well aware of the general mood of confrontation, the limits of which no one could guess, I took up the camera and headed into the streets before sunset that evening. I had gotten too far into making a photo record of these events to stop now. The cops were coming to enforce a curfew and the mood in Isla Vista left no doubt that a good number of its residents would be saying "to hell with your curfew."

*   *   *

129

Chapter 18

My decision to hit the streets the night after the bank burning hadn't worked out well. Though I had sat in the cell for less than 24 hours, I was already sick of the place. Every hour the room seemed to get a little smaller. Since the cops hadn't yet granted anyone a phone call and weren't in a sharing mood, none of us knew anything about what was currently happening in Isla Vista.

As I reclined on an upper bunk, one particularly young-looking guy sat on the floor opposite me, leaning against the wall. Sometime around mid afternoon a cop came by—a short, stocky man with no neck and a head perched on massive shoulders. He stood across from our cell beyond the bars to the dining area and called out.

—Simpson?

The guy sitting on the floor answered.

—Sir?

The cop hitched up his pants and continued.

—You know that tape recorder of yours?

—Yes, sir.

—I listened to what was on it and that is the biggest piece of shit, messed up pile of garbage that I've ever heard in my life. I'm going to take that reel of tape and I'm not going to return it to you. Instead I'm going to flush it down the toilet. If you don't like that, you can sue me. And if you try that, good luck.

The cop turned and walked away. Simpson stared at the wall opposite him for a few seconds before responding.

—Asshole!

Curiosity roused me from my depression.

—What was that all about?

—I report for a campus paper down in the Valley. I was doing a taped commentary before I was busted.

—So what did you say?

—Something about how the cops were a total disgrace, abusing and beating up on people with no cause and how it was becoming clear why the students were referring to them as "pigs." Could be that was the part he didn't much like.

I couldn't resist a little sarcasm.

130

—Could be he wasn't thrilled with any of it.

Simpson laughed.

—Do you think so?

The fate of Simpson's tape reminded me of my camera. Clearly the cops couldn't be counted on to behave within the law. It had become a grudge match between them and street fighters. That meant I couldn't count on the cop who took my camera to turn it in. That might be good and bad. Bad, because I may never see my camera again. Good, because the film would stay out of official light. Or would it? Sooner or later, whoever had it would get around to emptying the film. Curiosity might lead to developing it. Then there was no telling what could happen. If they got their hands on someone they could prove was there, they would squeeze them for every last detail, squeeze them until they popped. I had seen a few people well enough I could identify them again. I didn't want to be in a position of getting pressured to do that. I had to find the camera. When were we going to get phone calls?

Dinner time rolled around. Macaroni, cheese, Wonder bread. The folks at Wonder must have had a deal with the county. I asked about phone calls. To my relief they said we would get calls later that evening. I didn't get to a phone until around nine o'clock.

I knew I would make one call, and that would be to Matt. I wanted to keep the folks out of this. I prayed he would be home. One ring. Then an answer.

—Hey Matt, it's Dan.

—You're at the county jail aren't you?

—How'd you know?

—You made the papers—with a long list of others. I figured you were busted when you didn't make it in last night. Then I saw your name in the *News Press*. You couldn't call sooner?

—No, it's been a disaster here. They don't know what they're doing. To make things worse we're the first ones in this place. They don't have the electronic doors working so they use these big manual keys—like an old West jail. What's happening out there? We hear rumors that all hell broke loose.

—Sure did. Reagan called in the National Guard. It's like a war zone. You can't get in or out without showing ID at guard stations. Every road has a check point. Helicopters fly overhead all the time. The cops tear-gassed several blocks last night. Probably more of the same tonight.

—Did they make any arrests on the bank burning?

—No. They indicted Bill Allen this morning, but not for the Bank. They've had their hands full just trying to keep a lid on this thing. I don't think they have much on who did it. They're asking anyone who has information to come forward. They say the Bank's going to put up some kind of reward.

—They got my camera.

—Your camera?

—Yeah. Listen, that's not going to be good.

—What do you mean?

—Can't explain that now. Just do me a favor and try to find out if there's some kind of evidence room where stuff they took from people might be gathered. I need to get it back.

—You can go to work on it yourself soon.

—Yeah, how's that?

—I called your folks. Your dad's on his way down here right now.

—What? Are you kidding me? You called them?

—Hey, I thought you would want me to. I don't have any money to bail you out. They set your bail at $3500.

—$3500? What the hell are they charging me with?

—Three counts: Curfew violation, failure to leave the scene of a riot, and inciting to riot.

—Inciting to riot? That's ridiculous!

—Well, it's pretty standard. They're hitting just about everyone they arrested with those charges.

—Swell. Still you didn't need to get my folks involved. We could have figured out something.

—What's the big deal? They can help. Sitting in that place isn't going to do you any good.

—You should've waited to talk to me. I'd prefer they didn't know about this. But what's done is done. I'll call home and find out what's happening. I gotta go now.

—Wait. I'm picking your dad up at the airport around eleven-thirty tonight. We're going straight to the jail. The cops said we can bail you out anytime. So we'll get you out of there in a few hours.

—All right. I'll see you then.

Since the cat was out of the bag, I made the call home. Mom must have been sitting by the phone. She picked up immediately. I told her I was fine and brought her up to date on the situation. She explained dad left about two hours ago to catch a night flight, but the weather was bad and there might be delays.

On the way back to the cell I fumed about Matt spilling the story to the folks. What was he thinking? I was on my own and wanted it to stay that way. Matt and Canova could have scraped together the money to pay a bondsman. That would get me out and the folks wouldn't have to be involved. Now everything was screwed up. No, *more* screwed up. I didn't want help from home and I especially didn't want help from the ol' man. Now he was on his way here.

Back in the cell, I hoisted myself into the upper bunk and stared at the ceiling, shutting out the others. The lights went out at ten o'clock. The cops believed in early to bed, early to rise. There wasn't much to do beyond brooding and sleeping. I decided to brood. Before the phone calls I hadn't let myself think much about when or how I would get out. Now that I knew dad was on the way, I had conflicting emotions—anxious to get out but not anxious to see him. I was also increasingly aware that being confined in a small space behind bars was not something I tolerated well. I had worked up some resentment toward the cops, but the sense of confinement now overshadowed that. All I could think about was getting out. I would go nuts if I had to stay in a cell for more than a few days. How did anyone adapt to jail time? The sense of not being in control of where I could move was a claustrophobic experience. Every minute I felt it more. Limitation of movement. Loss of control. For me these were more than irritating experiences.

Someone else I knew was like that too. He was probably somewhere overhead right now. He didn't like traveling by air even though he had been a pilot in WWII. I had always thought that was strange. How could he not like flying? Now I understood. He would probably feel fine about it if he were the pilot.

I finally let go of the brooding and dozed off. It seemed very late when I heard my name called. A cop opened the door to the cell. The others were trying to sleep so I didn't give them my parting regards. But I did stop at the doorway and nervously glance back, with a silent prayer that I wouldn't be seeing the likes of that place again—ever. Then the images of those photos of the bank crossed my mind.

We proceeded into the room through which I had entered the jail. The entire experience of the previous night seemed so alien it felt like it had happened years ago or in some vaguely remembered dream. Another cop sat at a chair on the opposite side of a long folding table covered with papers. I had to sign for the return of my wallet and a handful of change. I was then led into the next room where dad and Matt were waiting. They stood up as soon as I entered. Dad appeared tired but not angry. Instead, he had a concerned expression and gave me a nod. I was surprised at his first words.

—Did I wake you up?

It was his attempt at a small joke, but it was a good start. I built on it.

—Yeah, jeez, come back in the morning would you? After breakfast, because I wouldn't want to miss out on the food here.

He and Matt laughed and we all shook hands. I shifted to a more serious tone.

—I'm glad you're here. The sooner we're out of here the better.

Dad remembered the details.

—They give you back everything?

—Everything except my glasses and camera. I haven't seen those since I was arrested. But we can talk about that later.

Dad nodded. Matt opened the door leading outside. The rain pounded the pavement as we ran for the car. While driving back to the apartment, Matt did most of the talking—bringing us up to date on the situation in Isla Vista.

—Reagan called in the Guard early Friday morning. They have the place surrounded. Going in feels like visiting East Berlin. Coming out feels like an escape. The night you were busted was unbelievable. The cops grouped at Francisco Torres and San Rafael. The Highway Patrol and Santa Barbara Police were at San Rafael. They're probably the ones who busted you.

—Thanks. I'll keep that in mind.

—The heavy stuff started when the cops swept the streets between eight and nine o'clock. About 450 cops battled it out in the streets from about nine 'til midnight. That's about the time the rioters succeeded in beating the cops out of I.V. It was chaos. Tear gas, rocks, bottles, Molotov cocktails—there were even reports of the cops shooting at cars near San Rafael. Helicopters overhead. It was war. Total war. So when the cops got beat out of I.V., that was the last straw. Reagan pushed the panic button and called in the Guard.

Hearing all this wound dad up pretty tight.

—Good God! What's gotten into these kids?

Matt quickly moved on.

—Haven't heard for sure how many troops are here, but one guy told me at least 500 with about 2500 on standby. The same guy who was in command during the Watts riots is in charge here. It's freaky, seeing guys in full combat gear—with rifles and bayonets. Anyway, around one o'clock last night they moved in and advanced up Storke road to Francisco Torres to join the cops who had retreated there. It wasn't 'til about three or four in the morning when they cleared the streets and made it all the way to Perfect Park.

Dad broke in again.

—Good God! I can't believe they'd need the National Guard here. Who's working students up like that? Is it that Kunstler fellow?

Ever the pal, Matt shouldered the burden.

—Well, no, it's not really Kunstler. It's a lot of things. It'd take a while to explain it all. And I'm not sure I'd get it right. In fact, I'm sure I wouldn't. Situations like this, who can explain them?

I quickly threw in another question before Dad could work himself up any more.

—So what's going on tonight?

—Well, a helicopter flew over around six telling everybody a state of emergency had been declared. The streets had to be cleared. Anybody on the streets would be subject to arrest, etcetera. We can't go through the loop area. They have it all blocked off. So we'll have to circle all the way around through the west side of I.V. I heard they've already arrested more people tonight than they did last night. Probably because last night they couldn't catch anybody.

The last part slipped out before Matt realized what he had said. I was quick to correct him.

—Right! Anybody except me.

Dad looked back at me but didn't say anything, probably because he saw my eyes and the way they were waiting for him.

*   *   *

Chapter 19

We were up before eight the following morning. Dad wasn't especially comfortable on the small Danish couch in the living room and I had too many things on my mind to sleep. Dad made some phone calls and succeeded in getting in touch with a lawyer. We set up an appointment for Monday. Around ten o'clock some friends from our freshman dorm year dropped by to see what kind of radical hell-raiser I had become. I retold the story of my capture, arrest, and jail time—all to their great interest and amusement. Having them there reduced the tension that would have filled our small apartment with only Matt, dad, and I bouncing around. That afternoon dad and I spent the time in Santa Barbara finding me a new pair of glasses.

Sunday dad spent most of the day visiting a friend of his who lived in Santa Barbara whom he hadn't seen in several years. He wanted me to come along. I declined, having already formulated how the conversation would go. I imagined him responding to the question, "Hey Raymond, what brings you to town?" with "Hi Richard. Meet my son, Daniel. I was just passing through town bailing him out of jail and thought I would pay you a visit." The whole thing would go downhill from there.

While dad was visiting his friend in Santa Barbara, I went out to find Canova in search of advice about the camera situation. Matt suggested I let the lawyer do the work. But I wasn't sure yet how much to tell a lawyer in order for him to share my sense of urgency.

Canova was in the back of the bookstore. I found him holding a pan over a hot plate and pointed to the boiling water.

—Ramen for dinner again?

—The French revolutionary!

—You heard?

—Shit, way to go.

—You're the radical and I'm the one who gets busted.

—I talked to Matt. So when did your dad bail you out?

—Early Saturday morning. He flew down through the rainstorm. He's still here. We're seeing a lawyer on Monday.

—Hmmm. Expensive.

—Yeah, only that's not the worst of it. Aside from clubbing the crap out of me, stepping on my glasses, macing me in the eyes, calling me every name in the book, and using me as a human shield—aside from minor things like that—the cops stole my camera.

—That doesn't surprise me—freaking thugs.

—Well the thugs now have my camera and there's film on it—shots I took inside the bank the night before. As things stand, I could get suspended from the University, maybe even kicked out if they make inciting to riot stick. If I get kicked out, there goes the scholarship, there goes the student deferment. But if they find that film, it's worse. Even if they don't charge me with arson or something like that, they'll get me for just being there and that'll be bad enough.

Canova pushed the boiling water off the plate and sat on a chair in his makeshift kitchen-office-bedroom while I leaned against the wall. He ran his fingers through his hair—a habit whenever he was thinking through something.

—Look on the bright side. If you're in jail for arson you're not on your way to Nam. Come to think of it, though, I'm not sure which would be worse—fighting off Viet Cong in the jungle or fighting off big, hairy sex offenders in prison.

—Thanks. I knew I could count on you for a helpful thought.

—You know what? You're in a mess.

—Tell me about it. I need ideas. What am I going to do about the camera?

—I always said you shouldn't be messing with that damn thing. Are you sure the cops have it?

—What do you mean?

—Suppose they just tossed it aside after they busted you?

—Yeah, I thought about that. I already searched around where they busted me, but no luck. I'm sure they have it.

—So get it back.

—I'm putting the lawyer on it Monday, for all the good that'll do.

—You're probably worrying about nothing. Even if they have the camera, I bet they won't have enough sense to develop the film when they find it.

—I don't know. In the wake of a burned down bank, I'm not going to count on that.

—This would be a good time to know a cop, but sorry—I don't hang out with that crowd.

Canova's words "know a cop" sparked a neuron.

—Wait a minute. Melanie's dad is a cop!

—Well, there you go! What are you waiting for? Have her talk to him and find out what he might know.

With that thought, I left the bookstore and headed straight for Melanie's apartment. Canova hadn't strained himself to be helpful on the camera problem. But at least talking to him had gotten my brain working. How could I have spaced out about Melanie's dad?

She didn't have a phone, so the only way to contact her was to find her. Luckily she was home. I recounted my adventures with "law enforcement," including the loss of my camera and the trip to the County Jail. Then I pressed her to contact her father on my behalf to see what he might know or be able to find out regarding "lost" cameras. She wasn't as helpful as I had hoped.

—Look Marleau, things are a little strained between dad and me. You'd probably do better talking to him yourself.

—I see. So, let me think. I call him . . . What's his name?

—Scott. Officer Lampert to you.

—Right. I call him and say I'm a friend of Melanie's who was busted for inciting to riot the other night and I just wondered if you'd help get my camera back?

—Yeah, I know. It doesn't have a great ring to it, but, trust me, it's not going to sound any better coming from me. He may be a jerk about it, but you could give it a try. It may depend on the mood he's in and whether the image in front of him happens to be daddy's little girl or the bitchy daughter who never listens.

I nodded okay and she handed me his phone number before changing the subject.

—I know you've got a lot on your mind right now, Marleau, but what's going on with my photos? Didn't you say you could get into the lab this week? I'd really like to get something going on those.

—You're sure you want to follow through on that plan?

—Of course! My mind is made up.

—Suit yourself. The day before I got busted I scheduled space for Thursday afternoon at four. We can stay for as long as necessary.

—Thanks! That works for me. Let's do it.

I was glad to have Lampert's phone number but not excited about calling him. I decided to wait and see what the lawyer could do first.

*   *   *

Chapter 20

On Monday dad and I borrowed Matt's Volkswagen and went into Santa Barbara to meet with the lawyer whose name he had gotten from his brother-in-law. I didn't want dad's help, but after taking time off work, flying through a storm, bailing me out of jail at one o'clock in the morning with virtually all the money he had in savings, and finding a lawyer who might prove useful in fixing things, it would amount to little more than a spite-filled, up-current swim to say "no thanks."

Besides, he was being entirely too nice. Since his arrival, I had been on the lookout for any comment, put-down, or even annoyed look that could be used as an excuse for an argument—anything that would make it easier to tell him to go home. I liked the sense of freedom I had for the first time in my life—with my own place and my own income from the scholarship. This was the first time dad and I had been together on what I could call my turf. And for the first time I felt I could unload on him like he had unloaded on me in times past and not remain beholden to him by having to stay under his roof.

Living at home, I evolved a masterful degree of repression—not so much because he intimidated me but because I wanted not to be like him. He had a short fuse for anger and could turn into the Incredible Hulk in a flash, sometimes for reasons no one could understand. Consequently, I learned to stuff anger, perhaps too well. It wasn't an ideal adaptation, but the important thing was not to be like him.

But as I got older and experimented with a "controlled anger burn," I was seldom happy with the results. I seemed to have a talent for bad timing when it came to venting. Whenever I was worked up about something and ready to unload, the deserving person would not cooperate.

The most recent instance of this came with a woman—a typist who was helping me transcribe some recorded lectures for Macomber. If it was difficult for me to vent, it was especially so with women. My sense of fair play wouldn't allow it because it seemed too much of a mismatch. Over the phone, the typist had promised three times to have a manuscript ready only to tell me on the agreed date that it wasn't ready. The fourth time, I reached my limit and decided to pay her a visit. On the way over I rehearsed a dissection of her behavior. As soon as she opened the door, I walked in and began to inform her of the unprofessional and unacceptable nature of her procrastinating incompetence. I had gone on for no more than a couple of minutes before she broke into tears. Christ! Why couldn't she just stand up and take what she had coming? Between sobs she apologized for everything and went on and on, airing out a list of travails and misfortunes, including her mother being ill, that would have wrung sympathy out of Ebenezer Scrooge.

I could feel myself yielding to her emotional collapse and started to get angry at myself for that. So I told her I would find someone else to do the job and left as quickly as possible. Then I got even angrier. No doubt I had been suckered by the oldest of wily female tricks. I had fallen for her con just enough to derail my justifiable anger. In fact her con was so good I wasn't even sure it was a con. That's why I couldn't follow through and insist she finish the work. What if she really was going through hard times? I didn't know her well enough to be sure. It was really maddening. Why couldn't things be simple? Why couldn't a guy just get angry with someone who deserved it and have them stand up and take it like they ought to?

Now I was feeling a similar kind of outrage at dad. For the first time in my life all the switches were set for me to let him have it like he had given it to me on many occasions. Only now he was on his best behavior. In fact it was uncanny. I had never seen him treat me so well in a situation that so easily invited rebuke. Where was the Incredible Hulk when you wanted him? It occurred to me I could unload on him for no particular reason like he would sometimes do with my sister, mom, or I, but that would have meant becoming him. And that was not an option.

It was all too perfect—like everything had been set up to spite me. And now there was this lawyer business. After the beating I took from the cops, I felt increasingly wary toward the entire so-called "justice system." Cavalletto, Webster, Mullen, and McCaughey sounded all too proper. From the National Geographic magazines and potted plants in the reception area to the polished cherry wood desks, their offices in the heart of downtown Santa Barbara—on East Victoria Street—reeked of "oligarchy" as Canova would say. When our lawyer introduced himself, I felt I had walked into a trap.

—How do you do? I'm Ernest E. Pinkerton. Come into my office please.

Ernest E. Pinkerton! Could a name be any more established than that? I do nothing wrong. I get arrested and beat up by cops. And now I'm to be defended by a guy who looks and sounds like a cop. In fact he probably comes from a whole family of cops. I didn't trust him, but I found myself speaking like he was a regular guy.

—Hi, nice to meet you.

Pinkerton was dressed for success in blue suit and gold tie, looking fit and California tanned. He was all business. He reviewed the charges and asked for the circumstances of the arrest. I recounted the story, including the laundry list of police abuses. I mentioned the camera because I thought it might be useful in defense against the rioting charge, but I was nervous about it because I wasn't sure where talk of the camera would lead. If he asked about what was on the film I would have to lie because I wasn't going to break the news to dad or him about my being at the bank unless, for some reason, it became absolutely necessary. Pinkerton took a few notes and then leaned back in his chair.

—I'll contact the Sheriff's office to see if I can locate your camera. It should be in their possession, but it's hard to say what may have become of it given the unusual circumstances. We could press charges against the police on any number of counts and normally I would recommend that. But in your case, without witnesses, that won't be productive. The police will not testify against each other. To charge them with any offense and not be able to make it stick will only complicate your situation rather than help it. If we play the cards right, I think there is a chance we can get your charges dismissed. The only charges the D.A. may have success on are the misdemeanors, and, given the case load his office will be facing, I think they will only be interested in pursuing the extreme cases.

Dad looked hopeful.

—So you think you can keep this from going very far by talking to the D.A.?

—That's my hope, Mr. Marleau, but I can't guarantee anything right now. Dan is going to have to go to the arraignment, which I see has been rescheduled for tomorrow. We'll have him plead not guilty.

Pinkerton turned toward me.

—Dan, I need you to be here at nine tomorrow morning. We'll brief you on what to expect and what to say over at the courthouse. My colleague, John Niemand, will accompany you to the courthouse. After the arraignment, we'll see what we can negotiate with the D.A. It may take a few days to get his attention.

The meeting then wound down with some small talk about dad's bumpy ride through the storm in a prop-driven plane on the ride from San Francisco to the Santa Barbara Airport. We took business cards and a copy of the arrest report and left the office.

Since Pinkerton seemed to have the situation under control, dad decided to catch a flight back to San Francisco that afternoon. After picking up the few things he had left at the apartment, I drove him to the airport for a two o'clock flight. On the way there he surprised me.

—I was just thinking about the last time we were together out here, July of '67. I picked you up after the summer session. You shot that hole-in-one on number ten over at the Municipal course. We had a couple of beers even though you weren't old enough. I couldn't help thinking of that hole-in-one as a kind of omen—like you were meant to be here. Even though the place seems to have gone crazy now, I still believe things can work out for you here.

I was too amazed to say anything. I just nodded and smiled. At the airport I thanked him and we shook hands. The Hulk hadn't made the trip with him. I had no idea where he was. Now the opportunity was gone. I had really wanted to stick it to him. Now I felt frustrated and guilty—guilty for feeling frustrated over something as strange as not having gotten into a blow-out fight with him. Driving back to Isla Vista, I puzzled over what had just happened between us and couldn't make any sense of it.

*   *   *

Chapter 21

Aside from the long wait while the court worked its way through an endless line of the indicted, the arraignment the next morning went without incident. The judge read the charges. I pled not guilty. A date for trial was set. I began to think Pinkerton would prove right about the D.A. The charges would be dismissed against most of those indicted. There were too many and the cases too difficult to prove to bother putting through the system.

But the problem of the camera still had my full attention. I was in daily contact with Pinkerton's office about matters relating to my defense, but, for me, the calls had only one purpose: to find out if he had discovered anything about the camera. It took him a couple of days to discover that neither the Sheriff's Office nor the Santa Barbara Police had a Mamiya Sekor. In one respect that was good, but I still didn't know where the camera was. As long as it was still out there somewhere—in the hands of someone with a badge—it was a ticking time bomb for me. I figured that if a cop knew what was in it, he would love nothing better than to come forward and use it to nail one of those "rock throwing pukes." The fact that he wouldn't know whose camera it was could be solved with rudimentary police work on the serial number, since I had bought the camera at a local store.

Friday morning, with the problem of the camera and its film still percolating, I sat at the kitchen table with Matt sorting through our copies of the *El Gaucho*. The issue was especially thick with news items, commentaries, editorials, and letters to the editor. My sense of mission to find the camera and its film grew another tenfold after finding the following full page ad on the back page of the paper:

$25,000 REWARD

BANK OF AMERICA IS OFFERING $25,000 FOR INFORMATION LEADING TO THE ARREST AND CONVICTION OF THE LEADERS OF THE MOB VIOLENCE IN SANTA BARBARA

We are outraged by the wanton destruction of our premises in Isla Vista near Santa Barbara. The branch has been gutted by arson on the part of a destructive mob. This was no peaceful demonstration, nor was it a non-violent disruption used as a symbol to redress grievances. It was an outrageous act of violence. It was, in fact, an insurrection against the democratic process of the kind that leads to further violence, bloodshed and anarchy. We are deeply concerned, not only for ourselves, but for the physical and material welfare of our citizens.

As a preliminary response to the burning of our Isla Vista Branch and the further violence it portends, we are taking the following steps:

1. We are dispatching today an open letter to the Governor of the State and the mayors of the major municipalities, calling for prompt and effective measures to stop the wanton destruction that is defacing our land.

2. As a potential deterrent, we are filing civil "John Doe" suits against all participants in the burning and destruction of our Isla Vista Branch. We intend to seek and collect maximum civil damages from the participants.

3. We are asking the Grand Jury of Santa Barbara to convene as soon as possible and to issue criminal indictments for arson against all participants in the burning.

4. We are offering a reward, totaling $25,000 for information leading to the arrest and conviction of the leaders of the mob violence in Santa Barbara. The reward will be in the form of $1,000 for each participant conviction, up to a maximum payment of $25,000.

IF YOU HAVE ANY INFORMATION ABOUT ACTIVITIES SPECIFICALLY RELATING TO THIS DESTRUCTION OR THE NAMES OF PERSONS INVOLVED, CONTACT THE SANTA BARBARA POLICE DEPARTMENT IMMEDIATELY. THE TELEPHONE IS: (805) 965-5151.

The whirl of events since the Bank burning and my arrest had been so relentless I hadn't had time to register the effects much beyond my personal experience. The events had gained national attention. In the aftermath of the

144

National Guard occupation and departure, people all over the state and around the country argued about what had happened and why. Everybody had an opinion. Reading through the letters to the editor, Matt found one he had to share.

—Some girl says "Violence is stupid." What a dolt! What if her GI Joe dad believed that during World War II? Who would have stood up to the Germans? But at least she got one thing right. Listen to this:

> America does have a lot of grave problems, and maybe the system is jammed up. Maybe mass demonstrations are necessary to get anything moving. But if they are to have any positive effects they must have the support of many. To have this they have got to be visual, vocal, and rational, NOT violent. People have to use their heads, not their guts, if there is to be any rationality in this world. So think a little—you're supposed to know how.

Matt looked at me as he summed up.
—She's got a point. We're here to use our heads. Burning down a bank isn't a smart thing to do.
—Yeah? Listen to this.
I read from another letter.

> The recent violence in Isla Vista may certainly be 'deplorable,' 'condemnable,' and 'senseless,' as some students have taken great pains to point out. But while the news media and the Chancellor are applauding these students for their 'rational,' 'non-violent' approach, the *causes* of the violence have been left largely ignored. The I.V. rioting was not caused by the failure of the democratic process, but rather by the complete LACK of democratic process. Students have no voice in local decisions. Popular control is a complete fiction in I.V. The violence in I.V. had a definite clarifying effect. It enabled us to see the utter powerlessness of the community, a community forced to express itself in the streets; to that extent, the riots were beneficial.

Matt was not persuaded.
—That may seem to have a logic to it, but it really doesn't. Violence has a clarifying effect. Give me a break! It just puts everybody back in their own trenches and gets them digging deeper. But never mind that. Look at this. The Bank has taken out a whole page ad.

VIOLENCE IN AMERICA: ONE COMPANY'S POSITION

We believe the time has come for Americans to unite in one cause: a rejection, total and complete, of violence as a means of political dissent.

All of us, young and old, liberal or conservative, have for too long been silent on the issue of violence. We have been afraid of labels or slogans that would brand us as either arch conservatives or traitors to a liberal cause. Such sloganeering does all of us a grave injustice.

Let us, as a nation, find once again our ability to distinguish between protest and revolt; between dissent and chaos; between demonstration and destruction; between non-violence and violence.

Let us cease to condemn those who disagree with us, but let us also be prompt and resolute in putting an end to violence in our land.

To this end we applaud the courageous response of many dedicated public officials. They deserve the cooperation of all citizens. They will have ours.

Every American has a right to walk the streets in safety. No polemic should be allowed to obscure this right. Your wife or husband, son or daughter, ought to be safe in visiting a supermarket, a filling station or a bank—regardless of whether another may choose to reject that institution as an onerous symbol.

It is for these reasons that we plan to re-open our Isla Vista Branch on Monday, March 9. We realize that there is danger in this course of action. But we believe the greater danger to ourselves and to all of the people in this nation is to be intimidated by mob violence. We refuse to be so intimidated.

Is the branch worth this much? In monetary terms, the answer is no. It is not, and never has been particularly profitable. But it is there to serve the banking needs of the community and we refuse to be driven out of any community by a violent few.

Is this a bad business decision? Perhaps in a narrow sense it is. But we believe that at some time and in some place Americans must decide whether they intend to have their decisions, indeed their lives, ruled by a violent minority.

We are but one bank, but we have decided to take our stand in Isla Vista.

I turned to the page in my copy as Matt continued.

—I can see what they're saying about violence, but what are they thinking with this bullshit at the end?

He raised his voice to parody the melodramatic sentiment at the end of the text.

—We're but one bank, but we've decided to take our stand in Rio Bravo at high noon.

Then he lowered his voice to normal and continued in a tone of disgust.

—Hell, it's like some old time western with John Wayne circling the wagons and drawing a line in the sand, daring the bank-burners to try it again. The Bank won't be intimidated! No way! I'll tell you how well that'll play. There'll be more trouble. Do you really think the Cowboys and Indians can keep it inside the corral?

—Seems the Indians have taken out a full page of their own here in the back. Maybe they're ready for the Little Bighorn. They're even more long-winded than the bank.

I folded back the paper and began reading.

AN OPEN LETTER TO THE CITIZENS OF CALIFORNIA INCLUDING THE GOVERNOR OF OUR STATE. A paid advertisement from the UCSB Moratorium Committee against the Vietnam War.

Recently, a committee met on campus to collect signatures from students which would demonstrate that they, the students of the University of California, condemn the violence which has taken place here. Many students working on the Vietnam Moratorium Committee did not sign that declaration. We do not believe that a condemnation of violence necessarily shows an understanding of it. While the students who collected those signatures may mean well, they are lacking a far-sighted appraisal of our situation, including the symbols of the damaged buildings and the burned bank.

Could the students who signed that declaration be thinking in terms of results (that is, the damaged property) rather than the causes of those results? We ask this because the authors of that declaration neglected mentioning the frustrations of young Americans. For example, they did not choose to mention that an ending of the Vietnam War and an extension of the voting franchise would give young Americans under the age of 21 some way to decide their own destiny. The war is itself horrible and unjust. This unjust war

147

occasions the brutal deaths of both Americans and Vietnamese on a massive scale.

Five minutes of napalm bombing in a free strike zone is more horrible than all of the campus demonstrations, including those that will inevitably take place in the future. Many students would absolutely refuse to give value to one burned building when Americans and Vietnamese are forced by our politicians to shoot, burn, bomb, and torture each other to death. Americans under the age of 21 have no political leverage whatsoever to elect a leader who will bring an end to the Vietnam War now extending itself through the indiscriminate bombing of Laos. It is a matter of "taxation without representation" and, for this reason, some students hope that since the Bank of America building is already ruined, it will be remembered as an immediate symbol of social injustice.

Most students want peace. Most of us want peace in Vietnam and Laos, and we want peace here. This is the reason that many students could not participate in any of the violent acts which have taken place in Isla Vista. But may we remind you, indeed may we strongly remind you, that OUR peaceful demonstrations dating back to 1964 against the unjust laws binding young Americans have sometimes been ignored and sometimes been derided by immoral politicians. These politicians decide what is good for America solely in terms of their own economic gains and almost never in terms of a moral responsibility to our young nation. Need we remind you, for instance, that the San Francisco peace demonstration by 1/2 million Americans took place on November 15, 1969 without any incidents of violence. Tragically enough, it was ignored by our President and derided by our Vice-President, and our Governor was and still continues to be in accord with their opinions. Consequently, some young Americans—black, brown, white, yellow, and red—under 21 have shown their frustrations through violence.

But both the students and the politicians now use violence to achieve their ends. On the one hand, the students, who continually stress the rights of all individuals, destroy material things. The students hope that through their violent acts their society will allow human rights to supersede property rights. Yet, on the other hand, the politicians maintain that the only persecuted victims are the property holders. The politicians, themselves property holders, use enraged police officers to suppress the outraged students as a means

148

of protecting material things. Is it possible that many politicians believe that property rights are more valuable than human life? This conflict between property rights and human life that has met head on here will inevitably occur elsewhere in the future until our social injustices are corrected.

Matt could barely contain himself.

—So there you have it. Another line in the sand. The bank says they're taking a "stand" in Isla Vista. The radicals say violence is inevitable until their demands are met—how autocratic is that? As if they have some mandate to speak for the majority! With the Bank setting up shop again, this place is going to be a pressure cooker. The bank has managed to become the symbol of everything wrong with America, according to these wing-nuts. What brilliant reasoning!

—Don't you think the Bank deserves some bad press?

—I've heard the laundry list. The president of Litton sits on the bank board. Litton did almost half a billion in defense contracts in 1968. Then they borrowed about the same amount of money from the bank in '69. Wonder how they got the loans? Still that doesn't make me want to burn it down.

—What does it make you want to do?

—Well, it doesn't make me want to buy a camera, either. Look where that got you. And look where rioting has gotten the street radicals. And for what? Anything done to the Bank of America in podunk Isla Vista, California has as much impact as shooting BB's at a battleship. This war in Vietnam isn't coming to an end until politicians find a face-saving way out of it. If 100,000 people in San Francisco can't make them sick of it, anything we do here isn't going to get the job done. What they need is an exit strategy and I think Nixon's onto that.

—Not fast enough for me. And induction isn't all. Now there are other things.

—Like what?

—Someone's got to have my camera and whoever has it has the film. And that film could screw me. With the bank offering a reward, someone can make money turning that in. All the cops have to do is trace the serial number to me. The photos prove I'm in the bank. Then they tag me with something and push me to rat out others.

—You're thinking you would do some time?

—Who knows. Based on my visit to the county jail, I probably couldn't do a month of time.

—So has this Pinkerton guy found out anything?

—Not yet. But that reminds me. I should make my daily call.

I got Pinkerton on the phone. He said he was now sure the Santa Barbara offices had no camera like mine. He'd also contacted offices at San Louis Obispo, Ventura, Los Angeles, and the Highway Patrol. None of these offices had a Mamiya Sekor.

*   *   *

Chapter 22

I wasn't surprised Pinkerton came to a dead end on the camera. Recalling how the cops behaved the night of the arrest, I didn't get the feeling it would show up at a police station. But I also didn't believe whoever had it would toss the film. Curiosity, if nothing else, would prompt getting the film developed. Then potential reward money and the desire to bring the photos and the camera to the attention of the D. A. would trump any misgivings about having delayed turning it in. The time had come to contact Scott Lampert. After working on the approach, I called him early in the evening.

—Hello. Officer Lampert?

—Yeah?

—This is Dan Marleau. I'm a friend of Melanie's.

—You the guy she was with the night of that concert?

—Yes.

—I wish you hadn't taken her there.

—I gathered that.

—Why are you calling me?

—I've got a problem I thought you might be able to help me with.

—What would that be?

—I was busted the night after the bank burning. I was on the streets photographing the confrontations . . . part of a journalism class. Some police thought I was one of the rioters and jumped me. They took my camera and I haven't seen it since. I need to get it back. It's an expensive camera. I wondered if you saw anything or if you could ask around about it.

—Jesus! You know, son, you don't have a lick of sense. Anybody in their right mind would have stayed off the streets that night. And the same with that concert. I've got nothing against music, but that week any excuse for a crowd was an excuse for a riot. Now you've gotten yourself arrested and lost your camera. You don't have a lick of sense. And you expect me to solve these problems for you? Frankly, you don't deserve the time of day!

Silence.

—I've got to go.

—Wait! Listen, I know I'm not a genius in your book, but I didn't break any laws and I had a right to take photos.

—There was a curfew, son. You had no right to be out there past seven o'clock and we didn't even show up there until seven.

—Journalists have a right to be there.

—All right, just for laughs, suppose I think of you as a journalist. What would you have me do?

—I just need to know—did you see any confiscated cameras that night?

—No, I didn't.

—One of the officers who arrested me took my camera. Maybe it's sitting on the floor of a cruiser or a bus somewhere. There was a lot of confusion that night. If you could ask around, maybe somebody would remember seeing it.

—Fine. I'll ask around on one condition.

—What's that?

—Stay away from 'Lanie. You don't know what you're doing. You'll get her arrested in one of these so-called protests without even half trying. Do you get it?

—Yeah, I get it.

—All right. How do I reach you?

I gave him my phone number. He was my best hope for finding a lead on the camera. But I was already in a bind. I told him I wouldn't see Melanie, but I promised her we would be in the lab on Thursday. Since I planned to keep that date, I had already lied to him. Not a great beginning, but he was overstepping his parental authority. He had too much of the cop in him.

The next day I stopped at the bookstore to update Canova on the conversation with Lampert. As I spun out the details, he leaned back in his desk chair at the front of the store and listened. After I finished, he stared at me and said nothing.

—You're too quiet. What's up?

—This thing with your camera. I think you need to let go of it.

—Easy for you to say. It's not just the camera. It's the film.

—You're making too big a deal of it. Nothing's going to happen. You're too preoccupied with what might happen to *you*. It's easy to act when your ass is on the line. And it's so ironic considering you knocked Bill Allen for putting so much focus on himself.

—Is that right?

—Yes! You're too obsessed. Get out of your own funk and look around. There's a bigger picture.

—C'mon. Don't give me that!

—You're not the only one who got screwed by the cops. You're not the only one in line for Nam. You're not the only one getting shafted by the system. What you experienced validates what people like Kunstler are saying. The kind of abuses we see happening on campus, in Isla Vista, and in Vietnam are all of a piece. They're all part of the same mentality.

Canova got out of his chair and leaned toward me.

—Now we've got this situation with the bank in our back yard. Sure, some people didn't support that action. But even those who stayed out of it say they understand why it happened. They know the bank is involved in a lot of things they can't support—especially the war. It's clear the majority of students don't want the bank in their community. So what does the bank do? Just like the university, it ignores what students want, puts up a box, and continues operations. It wouldn't matter if we took a vote. It wouldn't matter if only five students wanted to use the damn bank. It would keep its doors open because it's on an enormous power trip. Nobody's going to push the Bank of America around. And it's the same with the University. We've got an opportunity here to get a point across. But you want to spend your energy looking for a camera that's probably in a dumpster somewhere. Think about what it takes to put your butt on the line to stop the Man from screwing everybody else, not just yourself.

As Canova vented, I fumed. Seeing my concerns as a selfish reflex didn't sit well.

—Look, damn it, I might be a little introverted here, but when my future is in the balance that's not exactly irrational, is it?

—The *fear* could be irrational. I'm not saying you should drop your own problems. Just put the bigger ones higher on your priorities. Think it over. That's all I'm asking.

With that he turned and sat in the desk chair again. Two customers walked through the door and I took the opportunity to leave with a parting comment.

—You're wrong about me.

*   *   *

153

Chapter 23

Thursday afternoon at the Devereaux lab with Melanie could have come at a better time, but lab hours were hard to get so I needed to keep the date. And it was easy convincing myself of that given the subject matter. We agreed to meet at her apartment and walk to the lab. On the way, a light rain began to fall. When we arrived, I fumbled with the combination padlock on the door for a few seconds before getting it open. Once inside we shook the water out of our jackets and hung them on a rack by the door. Melanie's hair had gotten wet so I grabbed a handful of paper towels. With a couple of towels in each hand, I gave her head a vigorous scrub.

—This'll give you a new do.

—Yeah, the egg-beater look. Why's it so cold in here?

As she said that, I sensed it was a spontaneous reaction to the clammy interior of the lab. But as I held her head between my hands and stared into her eyes we both realized how much like an invitation it sounded. We were motionless for a second, then I pulled her toward me and kissed her. When we came up for air, I dropped the paper towels, slid my hands down her waist, and began pulling her blouse from her jeans. She grabbed my hands and placed them on my waist.

—No you don't, especially in this refrigerator.

—We could go somewhere else.

She smiled and pushed me away.

—Thanks for taking the chill off.

—You're welcome. It's the only form of heat this place has, so . . .

—And you think I'm the sly one.

—Look. You're shivering again.

I reached for her, but she put her hand up.

—Stop it! I am not! We have things to do.

—And you think *those* photographs will keep my mind on business?

—I'm a good judge of character. I know you've got what it takes.

—Thanks. I think.

She was right. She knew I was no Romeo. She may not have trusted me with her film but she judged me well enough to let me take the shots and venture into a lab alone with me. Bold but not reckless, I assumed she was playing me every step of the way.

I grabbed the developing canister off a shelf and asked Melanie for the roll of film. While the negatives were processing, I set up two trays with chemicals for making the prints. In twenty minutes the negatives were ready to wash. But as I removed them from the canister, I couldn't believe my eyes. The entire roll was blank! There was nothing there!!

When unloading the film from the case, I noticed an inch of film sticking out but I assumed I hadn't wound the roll all the way into the case. Now I understood I had developed an unexposed roll. I stared at the film in disbelief. Melanie broke my trance.

—So, are they ready?

As I searched for an explanation, she sensed something was wrong.

—Is there a problem?

Panic lurched through me. I re-traced the handling of the film, but there were too many variables to sort it out on the spot. There was no alternative but to break the news to her.

—Listen. I don't know what happened. There's nothing on this film.

—What??

All at once her face broadcasted confusion, fear, and anger.

—What do you mean there's nothing on it?

—I don't know. I'm trying to think.

Now anger dominated her expression and tone.

—It's the film you gave me, Marleau. Why is there nothing on it?

—I don't know! I have to think it through.

I scrambled for a way out but could only come up with the truth, and that didn't reflect well on my so-called "character."

—Shit Marleau! I'm serious! What happened? Where are the photos?

—All right, look, I'm not proud of it but I didn't give you the actual roll.

I could have fried an egg on her forehead.

—What?? You fucking jerk!! What did you do that for?

—Calm down! I wasn't trying to rip you off. I thought you'd process it on your own. I kept the film as collateral.

—Jesus Christ! You couldn't trust me for a few dollars?

—Okay, it stinks, all right? I said I wasn't proud of it. It was a split second decision. You didn't trust me either.

Melanie wasn't cooling down.

—Yeah, but I had a little more at stake, okay? Now look what's happened thanks to your petty worries. What happened to the film?

—I don't know. Somehow in making the switch I must have mixed it up with a new roll.

—Well, Mr. Clever, I just gave you the roll you gave me. If you developed it, wouldn't you *expect* nothing to be on it?

—I'm not that much of a bungler! I brought the roll I thought was yours and developed that one—not the one you gave me.

—Well since now you don't know what roll is mine, don't you think it would be a good idea to check what's on the roll I just gave you?

I was in no position to argue. I prayed for a miracle, but when I developed her roll the results were the same. Now we had two rolls of developed, unexposed film. The initial shock had worn off and now I was angry with myself. I couldn't believe I'd screwed up so badly. I tried some reassurance.

—Let's not panic here. The roll has to be somewhere in my stuff. I'll find it. I promise you. I'm sorry about this.

Suddenly the reality that the photos were not at hand sank in. Melanie wilted, sat on the floor, and put her head in her hands. I thought she would start crying but she was too angry for that.

—I can't believe this, Marleau. You'd better not be lying to me.

—I've made a mess of this, but I'm not lying about it. I'll find the photos and make this right. C'mon, I'll walk you home. I'm sure I can get this sorted out.

Back at my apartment, I ransacked every square inch of the place. That turned up three rolls of new film and two rolls of exposed film. I knew what was on the exposed rolls—some beach shots I took in December—but now I wasn't sure. Somehow I had mixed things up, most likely after I had returned from the studio after the shoot. What a colossal blunder! But if that were true then one of the two exposed rolls I had must be hers. I called and was able to reserve half an hour of lab time the day after tomorrow.

*　　*　　*

156

Chapter 24

The following afternoon Canova and I met by accident crossing campus. At the bookstore the other day he had caught me by surprise criticizing my loner agenda. But some of what he said seeped through the cracks in my eggshell ego. I couldn't deny feeling a bit sealed in my personal funk. Grudgingly, I admitted my private crisis belonged to a bigger cause. When it came to bigger causes, the Vietnam War more than qualified, having already destroyed thousands of lives along with the political vitality of the nation.

I avoided the subject of my camera. Canova talked enthusiastically about a new group he had formed focused exclusively on hard core anti-war protest. Several in the new group had been busted by cops, so he had called a meeting to raise awareness about what the cops were doing and how to prepare for busts. Since I had first-hand experience with bust brutality, he wanted me to come. My story was relevant and my mood forgiving if not guilt-tinged, so I agreed to come to the meeting later that evening at his store.

By the time I arrived, the meeting had started. Twelve were gathered toward the back of the store. Canova sat on a stool in the far corner. I entered and sat on the floor as a guy sitting opposite me spoke.

—I was with my girlfriend in this small yard in front of my apartment. Suddenly, several cops came around the corner and yelled, "Get those pukes," along with other obscenities. We ducked into the apartment and they stopped at the door. One of them shouted, "Come out of there, or we're coming in, you little shits." Then they busted the door open and came in. We didn't put up any resistance but they beat us with their clubs anyway. They grabbed me by the hair and dragged me to the ground outside. They hit my girlfriend on the legs until she could hardly walk. After handcuffing us, they used us as shields when they took us to the Bank. Then at the fire station, they shoved us against the wall. I had hardly any sensation in my hands because of the cuffs. When I complained about it, they tightened them more.

A voice from behind summarized in a word.

—Assholes.

A guy leaning against the bookshelves near Canova spoke next.

—I was arrested early Thursday morning in Perfect Park. Some pigs chased us from the park and caught up with me and pushed me over a picnic table. Then a bunch of them beat the crap out me with nightsticks—all over my body, including my head and groin. I was bleeding from the mouth but one of them said, "You're not bloody enough yet." There were several others they'd busted and they used us all as shields when they marched us over to the Bank. From there they took us to the San Rafael parking lot, where they kept us standing for two hours. They said stuff like we'd be shot if anyone tried to rescue us. Then we got bussed to the fire station. I had those fucking plastic handcuffs on for over five hours before they took them off. I still have partial paralysis in my right hand. Oh, and I forgot. On the way to the fire station they maced a bunch of us who were crammed into the back of the bus.

For the next half hour others told similar stories about themselves or friends who had received rough treatment from the cops. Canova then pointed to me.

—For those who don't know him, this is Dan Marleau. Glad you could join us, Dan. You had a similar experience?

—Yeah, I'd say so. The night after the bank burning I got clubbed and maced in the face and eyes. They also took my camera, stripped my glasses and stepped on them, handcuffed me, and used me and two others as shields as they moved up Seville. But, you know, we could go on talking about all the garbage the cops have been pulling, but what's the point? I mean it's obvious they don't give a crap about . . .

Canova cut me off.

—Right. We could spend all night making the cops and their pig behavior the center of attention—and the outrages they've committed certainly merit attention. We all need to be aware of it to protect ourselves. Their actions show no interest in justice or even the law. But what we need to do now is keep the absurdity of their violence from creating fear and panic. We need to stay focused on the goal—and that's stopping the war. With all the media attention on the bank burning, we have a big opportunity. The bank has now become *the* symbol of the war. We can use that symbol to our advantage. In fact, the bank is making it incredibly easy for us by re-opening in a cracker box pre-fab trailer. By shutting them down again we can make our strongest anti-war statement yet and keep getting national press. In light of what's already happened, we have a blueprint for how to do that. The cops can't defend the bank without building a fort and putting a garrison around it. And, so far, they haven't had the wherewithal to do that. That gives us an opening. Without a steady presence at the bank they have to respond to threats. And response takes time. That time lag may be enough to get a fire going they can't stop. My sense is we'll need to act soon before they wise up.

Canova fielded questions and a more specific plan took shape. Then the meeting broke up with the word that everyone would stay in daily contact. After the meeting I waited until only Canova and I were left in the room. For me, he had more explaining to do.

—You brought me in on a plan to burn down the temporary bank?

Canova looked me in the eye but said nothing.

—You see that as the way to protest?

He moved a stack of paperback books into a corner before answering.

—Torching that bank? Think of it as *tactical publicity*.

—Christ! Burning a bank is more than a publicity stunt. Getting busted for a prank like that could mean doing serious time.

—True. So if you're playing with fire, you make sure the stakes are worth the risk.

—What about making sure it's the *right* play. That's how we got into Nam. People not making the right play. Now you want to burn down the bank again? Where does it all stop?

—Nothing happens in this country without taking risks. Change is dangerous work.

—It doesn't have to be violent work.

—In your dreams.

—I'm no dreamer!

—You're right. You're a spectator. Enjoy the show.

—I'm the one who got busted, remember?

—From behind a camera.

—I don't have it any more, remember?

—Yeah, but you're still behind it.

—What I saw that night I didn't want to be part of.

—Don't give me that!

—What do you mean?

Canova broke into a knowing smile.

—I saw your face the night you came out of the bank. Don't tell me you weren't into it.

That remark stalled me. As I faltered, Canova pressed the advantage.

—Yes, that craziness had a truth in it. Don't tell me you didn't hear it—that little voice saying "Yes!"

A spark of the feeling I had as I threw the audit report into the fire came back to me. I remembered the voltage that went though me—as if I were the ape with the jawbone in *Space Odyssey*. Canova saw through me. I struggled to explain.

—I had the camera. But I wasn't *behind* it. It was like I *was* a camera—trying to frame what was happening in my head. But I got confused . . .

Canova looked down and let out a sigh of weary disgust.

—The point is to do something more than look.

—I'd just like to see it . . . real clear.

—Bra—vo. By the time you get clear we'll all be dead.

I was beginning to get very unclear. Canova didn't let up.

—What's it going to take before you realize you're getting screwed? When do you wake up? Is it when they arrest you for stuff you didn't do? Is it when they beat and mace you, rip off your camera, and break your glasses? No, that's not enough. Is it when they use you as a human shield? Or when they accuse you of crimes you didn't commit? Or when they take away your scholarship and throw you out of the University? Or when they find those photos and indict you for burning the bank? Or maybe it won't be until they send you over to Nam. Maybe that's when you'll wake up.

He pressed onward as I floundered.

—You're the one who told me you didn't want to risk your life for nothing, remember? Remember the ride in that candy-coated Charger? Well, think of it this way. Now you're sitting in a bigger car with a bigger drunk at the wheel and guess what? Just like then, *you're doing nothing about it!*

He really pushed a button with that one. I put my hands behind my head and stared at the ceiling.

—You need to do something before it's too late—for you and a lot of others. That bank is the symbol of an ugly reality—the reality created by goons who see fit to finance a war that sends people like us into meat grinders—and for what? The cause is worth the risk. Don't you see that?

I turned around and walked away.

—In a few days Jerry Rubin is coming to campus to speak. Afterwards there'll be a rally in Perfect Park. We can make use of the crowd and barricades to put a buffer between the cops and the bank. It'll slow response time. There'll be a good chance to keep a fire going long enough to destroy that cardboard box before they can put it out. It'll be a piece of cake. I'd like you with me on this. What do you say?

I turned around and stared at him. Amazing myself, I walked up to him and placed all the fingers of my right hand on his chest.

—All right. I'll surprise you. I'm in.

Canova eyed me closely, searching for signs of jest as I continued.

—We'll try it your way. I hope you're right about it making a difference because I need for that part to be right.

—It will make a difference, you'll see. We'll take it a step at a time. But if the cops show too soon, we get the hell out.

—Right. I've seen what happens when people stick around too long.

*   *   *

Chapter 25

The next morning I didn't wake up until I heard a knock on the door. Matt had already left for class, so I rolled over thinking whoever it was could come back some other time. But the knocking continued. Finally I got curious about who was being so damn persistent and answered the door. A guy in a coat and tie stood at the entry.

—You Dan Marleau?

—Yeah. What's up?

—I'm Detective John Newberry, Santa Barbara County Sheriff's Office.

He held up a piece of paper for me to see.

—Subpoena.

He took off his sunglasses and flashed a badge as he walked past me into the living room.

—Subpoena? You're kidding. What for?

—We're collecting evidence connected to various violations of the law committed on and off campus during the months of January and February. We understand you own a camera and may have photographs that would assist in the identification of perpetrators. I need you to turn over to me all photographs and negatives in your possession.

Immediately Lampert crossed my mind. That son of a bitch! He put his cop friends onto me.

—Christ! That's absurd. I don't have anything that would interest you guys.

Newberry smiled condescendingly.

—We'll have to be the ones to determine that.

I stood glaring at him, trying to think. But I wasn't good at thinking under pressure. To give myself a little more time I told him I wanted to see the subpoena. I stared at it, pretending to read while paranoid thoughts pumped through my head. Why was this happening? Was it really Lampert who put them onto me or did they find my camera and now wanted the rest of what I might have? I tried to recall if any of my photos could cause me or anyone else trouble. What that guy, Nolan, from the Radical Union had said came back to me. Maybe I should have listened to him. Newberry grew impatient.

—C'mon. Everything's in order.

Unable to stall any longer, I motioned to a cardboard box sitting beside my desk at the corner of the living room.

—Everything's in there.

Newberry picked up the box, placed it on the kitchen table, and examined the contents.

—When can I get this stuff back? I need some of it for a class I'm taking.

—Can't tell you that for sure. Could be a while.

—I know exactly what's in there and I want it all back. I have an attorney and I'll be contacting him to make sure I get it all back.

—I'll have to take those as well.

Newberry pointed to two rolls of film sitting on the edge of my desk. A new wave of panic hit me.

—That's nothing—just some beach photos I haven't processed yet.

They were the two exposed rolls I wanted to check for Melanie's photos. Newberry nodded but took the rolls. Then he tossed them in the box, picked it up from the kitchen table, and headed for the door.

—As for your lawyer, have him contact the D.A.

These last words carried a menacing tone as he closed the door behind him. I sat down on the couch and tried to sort through the situation. It looked ugly and my imagination made it uglier. He had the rolls that might have Melanie's photos on them. If they developed those . . . It wasn't even a question of "if." It was a question of "when." He wouldn't have taken the rolls if he didn't intend to process them. Was one of those rolls hers? I thought it had to be there but now I was praying it wasn't. Melanie was already hot enough about it, but I'd be better off in Nam if her photos surfaced in someone else's hands—not to mention the police.

And that was just for starters. What about the other photos? What could they be used for? Would they lead to other arrests? Would my name get associated with all that? Could they use the photos to indict me for something? Could I somehow force them to give me back the photos? These were questions I couldn't answer.

I immediately got on the phone to Pinkerton's office. He wasn't in, but I told his secretary about the subpoena and that it raised issues I'd like to discuss with him in a personal meeting. She said he was out of town and wouldn't be able to see anyone until Friday. The earliest time she could schedule was late Friday afternoon.

After hanging up the phone I grew angrier by the minute as I stewed in the mess. I felt helpless and victimized all over again by the cops. This time it felt even worse. Since the arrest, concern about my student status and precious deferment receded daily against mounting outrage about the loss of my camera and film and being treated like a petty criminal. This subpoena business was too much. Visions of payback steadily acquired a more seductive glow. The cops, the bank, the university—it all began to feel like some Kafka nightmare of insane violations and oppressions.

When Matt came back from his class, I told him what had happened. He volunteered the use of his Volkswagen for the trip to Pinkerton's on Friday—but not without special commentary.

—You know, you're a great roommate. Who needs television with you providing so much entertainment?

—Glad you're benefiting from my calamities, good buddy. I'll try to keep the streak of misfortunes going for your amusement.

Then he surprised me as his tone changed from chiding to serious.

—Are they going to find anything damaging to you in those photos?

—Most of them are from the Allen demonstrations. I'm more worried about what they might find to indict someone else for God knows what. Then my already huge popularity will really soar!

I wasn't going to let on about Melanie's photos. I wondered how much I should tell Pinkerton. And even if I told him everything, what were the chances he could do anything about it?

*   *   *

Chapter 26

Early in the week protest momentum swelled again on campus in anticipation of the visit by Jerry Rubin on Friday. A report in the *El Gaucho* aroused more student outrage toward the administration. Governor Reagan requested the Regents launch a thorough investigation of four professors: Angela Davis and Michael Tigar of UCLA and Richard Flacks and Bill Allen of UCSB. In a letter to the Regents, prodding them into action, Reagan accused the four of using "inflammatory speech" and "militant activism." In a speech earlier in April, given to the California Growers Convention held at Yosemite National Park, Reagan further clarified his message to campus administrations. He would tolerate no more coddling of violent protesters or acquiescence toward demands made through violent protest. Reagan's speech contained several memorable lines.

> Appeasement is not the answer . . . If it's to be a bloodbath, let it be now . . . There are growing signs that the good kids have had it up to here. They are losing patience. Any way you can shorten their patience, do it . . . There comes a moment when we must "bite the bullet" so to speak, or take action when it is necessary to do so. Alumni of embroiled campuses should urge administrators to "bite the bullet" now.

Reagan clearly wanted the Regents to mobilize in an effort to weed out campus radical leadership—whether student or faculty. By Tuesday it became clear this weeding included *visiting* radical leadership. Chancellor Cheadle rescinded permission for Jerry Rubin to speak on campus. The Santa Barbara County Board of Supervisors then denied him permission to speak in Isla Vista. The Board then denied him permission to speak anywhere in the county.

Refusing to allow the university and county officials a complete victory, the Associated Students Lectures Committee and the Radical Union agreed on a plan to have Nancy Rubin and Stu Albert—a close friend of Jerry Rubin's—speak in his place. Editorials and letters in the *El Gaucho* fueled more outrage by calling the refusal to allow Rubin to speak a flagrant violation of freedom of speech and further confirmation of George III style oppression by the University and the County. Not since the day after the burning of the bank had there been such anticipation of violence.

By the time Nancy Rubin and Stu Albert arrived Friday afternoon, the administration had designated the lawn area behind the UCEN for them to speak. This choice kept the crowd on the opposite side of campus from the Administration Building.

Canova and I met at the UCEN and took a position on the lawn that sloped down to the lagoon behind the building. Nancy Rubin spoke first from a platform installed near the lagoon. Jerry had given her a message for the students at UCSB which she proceeded to read from a sheet of legal paper she held in both hands.

> Once upon a time we thought we could end poverty, racism, and war by non-violent sit-ins and moral pleas. Those days of innocence are over. Four years of fighting experience have taught us bitter lessons. We live in a land which has declared war on its own children, on the future. We live in the midst of a dying beast that will kill anything that moves. To be young is a crime. Any crowd of kids automatically constitutes a riot. The Law has become illegal.
>
> Our bravest brothers are beaten and killed in the streets, exiled into strange lands, or thrown into detention camps called jails. Everything beautiful we build is smashed by pigs' clubs. We get our education in courtrooms, not classrooms. We are faced with two choices: OBEY or PERISH. We are fighting for our very survival as a generation.
>
> Can the beast be tamed within her own rules and regulations? Within the electoral system, within law and order, within police permits and regulations, within the boundaries of middle-class Amerika?
>
> Can a society which makes distinctions between rich and poor, white and black, employers and employees, landlords and tenants, teachers and students, reform itself? Is it interested in reform, or just interested in eliminating nuisances? What's needed is a new generation of nuisances—a new generation of people who are freaky, crazy, irrational, sexy, angry, irreligious, childish, and mad.

Wild applause erupted from the crowd. Nancy went on to complain that authorities consistently violated basic rights of activists and demonstrators all over the country and that the Bill of Rights had become a mockery. The refusal to let Jerry Rubin speak at UCSB counted as the latest example of the violation of freedom of speech and the right to assembly. She explained Rubin's response.

166

Jerry would have come to speak anyway, but he received threats from federal agents that if he did he would be immediately arrested and returned to Cook County Jail. They would love to get Jerry back in Cook County Jail. We decided that he can do more by staying out of jail.

She then congratulated the crowd on the burning of the Bank of America.

It's good to see the people of Santa Barbara fighting capitalist institutions like the bank. We all know that property is the real theft and the real violence.

She then suggested that the bank burning had been a factor in Judge Hoffman's decision to allow members of the Chicago trial out on bail in February when, following the verdicts, five of the members were waiting for an appeal on convictions for crossing state lines to incite a riot.

We thank you for your contribution in the struggle. We've got to fight for everything. And that's the reason we're here today—to thank you all—and to keep the tide moving.

Nancy then handed the microphone to Stu Albert—Rubin's friend and the Yippie candidate for Sheriff in Alameda County. Albert began by also congratulating the crowd on the bank burning, saying they were one with the spirit that created "People's Park" in Berkeley. He picked up Nancy's tone of rebellion and amplified it further.

Those of us in the revolution should have no reservations about using the tactics of the Latin American revolutionaries such as kidnapping the pigs to gain the release of our prisoners of war. I have personally pledged that Bobby Seale will not go to the electric chair. And I will make sure of that by any means necessary—including the rip-off of pigs.

But with these remarks Albert began losing part of the crowd—for whom property damage was one thing and kidnapping something entirely different. Several booed while someone stood up and shouted that it was hypocritical for Albert to speak of kidnapping or killing "pigs"—because that would be stooping

167

to their level. Two more yelled out similar complaints. Visibly subdued, Albert shifted into talking about the injustices of the Chicago Seven trial in an effort to defend his "exchange of prisoners of war" plan for responding to "political" arrests. But sensing he had lost much of the crowd, he wound his speech down quickly.

Someone from the group of organizers then came to the microphone and announced that the Jerry Rubin Navy, with a contingent of the National Liberation Front, would be landing within the hour at the Isla Vista beach. Following the landing there would be another rally at Perfect Park.

Canova and I walked down to the Isla Vista beach to see the landing. It turned out to be a surrealistic display of guerrilla theater performed by a group of Rubin supporters. Somehow they had commandeered a small military-style beach assault craft complete with hinged landing ramp. Where they had launched from or how they had gotten the craft, no one knew. Nevertheless, it made for an impressive stunt. The landing craft was loaded with about twenty-five, screaming, arm-waving protesters, ready to carry the cause into the streets of Isla Vista and Perfect Park. Most wore Indian costumes and carried toy bows and arrows and rifles.

We followed the mock assault team up the beach and into Isla Vista. At Perfect Park someone started a rumor that Rubin would, after all, make an appearance and speak to everyone in the park. Another reported that Rubin had been in hiding, disguised as an Indian, among those in the landing craft. But these rumors turned out to be propaganda for stimulating the crowd. Then a more restrained Stu Albert spoke again for a few minutes after which everyone stood around for awhile expecting something else to happen. Something else did happen, but it wasn't what anyone expected.

Inexplicably, Dean of Students Lyle Reynolds had walked into Isla Vista and now stood at the edge of Perfect Park. The Dean wasn't aware he had chosen to stand near two guys who were sharing a joint. Noticing the Dean, they walked over to him and the one wearing a leather vest with no shirt took a big drag from the joint, blew the smoke in Reynolds' face, and then held out the joint to him.

—Hey, would you like a toke, man?

Dressed in slacks and a sport coat, Reynolds looked like a tax accountant finding himself in the middle of a Hell's Angels convention. Clumsily attempting to appear cool, he declined the joint.

—I've already tried it.

Others noticed Reynolds and a crowd formed around him. As the crowd grew, he became more uptight. The friend of the guy in the leather vest wore a red bandana headband. He took off the headband, put it on Reynolds' head, and tried to coax him into joining a chant.

—C'mon Dean, chant with us. You know where it's at. Fuck Reagan, fuck Reagan!

Then the whole crowd began chanting.

—Fuck Reagan, fuck Reagan!

Many raised their arms in rhythm and gestured for Reynolds to join them.—C'mon Dean, Fuck Reagan, fuck Reagan!

Overwhelmed and apparently paralyzed by the situation, Reynolds clearly had no idea what to do. Robotically, he made a fist and, still wearing the headband, raised his arm in the radical—power to the people—salute. He seemed unable to speak but pumped his arm in time with the crowd's chant.

—Fuck Reagan, fuck Reagan!

Sensing Reynolds to be completely in their power, a few in the crowd altered the chant.

—Fuck Reynolds, fuck Reynolds!

Before long the chant shifted and the entire crowd yelled in unison.

—Fuck Reynolds, fuck Reynolds!

Incredibly, Reynolds continued pumping his fist in the air—again and again. Canova and I approached the edge of the spectacle. While chanting, a few in the crowd began to push Reynolds around the circle. Apparently having begun to sense the weight of the ridicule, he struggled through the circle and wandered off in a daze. The crowd then broke off the chant with laughter as the Dean made his way down the street. I stood motionless, watching him disappear around a corner. Canova reacted to the stunned look on my face.

—Rally's like this bring out all kinds of people. You can't fight that battle for him. If he's going to come out here, he has to know how to handle that. It'll give him a taste of what it feels like to be powerless and get no respect.

My appointment with Pinkerton was at four o'clock. I thought about not going but Canova persuaded me there was time to meet with him and return.

The temporary bank was located on the southwest corner of the parking lot on the south side of the destroyed bank. Chain link fence bordered all but the entrance to the lot.

We weren't certain on the timing of events other than waiting until conditions were right well after dark. This required the absence of police in the area, continued presence of a sizable crowd near the bank and in the lot, and the maneuvering of dumpsters into strategic locations to block easy access to entrance to the lot.

According to Canova, given the right conditions, the assault on the bank would be coordinated in two waves. A first wave would consist of two runners breaking the front doors and throwing Molotov cocktails inside. In the second wave, three others, armed with cartons filled with gasoline, would run to the front doors and add more fuel to the fire. Canova and I and several others would monitor the approaches to the bank and attempt to keep access blocked through use of dumpsters, vehicles, and whatever other obstacles could be commandeered.

*　　*　　*

Chapter 27

I arrived at Pinkerton's office several minutes late, but found it unnecessary to apologize. He kept me waiting among the peace lilies and the cherry wood until almost five o'clock before calling me in. I informed him of Detective Newberry's visit and the confiscation of all my photos.

—Is there anything I can do to squash this subpoena and get them back?

—Not likely. We would need some basis for an injunction.

—There were two rolls of undeveloped film. They have nothing to do with the demonstrations or riots.

—What's on them?

—Well . . . I'm not sure. There was a mix up with some rolls. Isn't it an invasion of privacy, though? I guess they can take the prints, but wouldn't they need a search warrant to process those rolls?

—A search warrant becomes necessary if they seek evidence to indict you.

—Does that mean they can't use any of the photos against me?

—That gets complicated. Is there something on those rolls that could be of concern?

—Not for me.

—Do you want to explain that?

—Ah . . . well, you see, there was this woman, a student. She wanted some pictures to use in her portfolio. The pictures are a bit sensitive. Some of them are nude shots. I'm not sure what the cops will do with them but I know what she'll do to me if she finds out they have them.

—I see. Is she 18?

—I think so. I didn't ask her.

—It's just her in the photos?

—Yes.

—But you don't know if these photos are among those Detective Newberry took?

—No, because there was this mix up.

Pinkerton smiled and leaned back in his chair.

—I understand your concern. We could seek an injunction. I could demand that a judge return those photos as private and beyond the scope of the subpoena. That would, however, take a significant piece of work that, since we are near its limits already, would exceed your father's retainer. Perhaps, if you feel it's important enough, you could speak with him about increasing the retainer.

—Maybe it wouldn't take an injunction. Maybe you could try a phone call? If they do have those photos, they'll see they're not relevant to riots or demonstrations.

—You can see that, but it may not be perfectly obvious to them. They may want to contact the subject, ask more questions of you, probe a little further. It's hard to say what kinds of connections might go through their minds—especially if we start drawing attention to the photos. Given a goal of minimizing costs, I would advise holding steady. My guess is the nude photos, if they come to light, will be put aside and kept out of the investigation. If we don't make a fuss, I doubt you need to worry.

I paused, sinking into frustration, but only briefly. I needed to get clearer on another point.

—So is the same thing true with the camera film? They don't need a warrant to process that roll?

—No. The camera wasn't acquired through a search of private property.

—Can they use that film against me?

—Is there something on that roll that might interest them?

—I was on the streets with my camera the night before the arrest, the night of the bank burning. I took some shots of a few clashes between the rioters and the police. Late in the evening, I found myself near the bank and noticed flames coming out a side window. Moving closer, I saw the door on the west side broken open. I went inside and took several more shots. Later that night, I took more shots from the outside when flames took the whole building.

Pinkerton leaned back in his chair.

—You're right. They might be interested in those. Did you participate in any way?

Here, I couldn't manage the whole truth.

—No. But I can't prove that.

—Did anyone see you there who might be able to identify you?

Again I held back. I couldn't implicate Canova.

—A lot of people saw me there. Any of them might remember me. I stood out because of my camera.

—Photos alone won't convict you of anything. The police would have to prove you took the photos to place you there. That would require a witness or two. My colleague Mr. Niemand tells me that David Minier, the D. A., is preparing indictments on the bank burning and related street rioting. The basis for some of these indictments includes photographs that place suspects at the scene. Once they arrest a few suspects they'll use various plea bargains to help identify others. Minier would definitely be interested in your film for that purpose. With witnesses placing you there along with your film, the fact that you aren't in the pictures wouldn't preclude going after you. The police are hot as hornets about the bank burning. If they can make a charge stick, they'll pursue it. Are you continuing to look for your camera?

—Yeah, but it seems whoever has it just wants to keep it.

—That's possible, but remember the bank is offering reward money to anyone who provides information leading to conviction. Whoever has your camera will find the film. What would you do you in that person's shoes?

—I'd go for reward money.

—Well, your course of action is clear. Keep trying to find your camera. Have you tried looking in the classifieds? Someone might have found it near where you were caught and run an ad to locate the owner.

—Yeah, I've been watching the papers. No such luck.

—You could also run you own ad.

I nodded and stood, ready to leave.

—My trial date isn't for another couple of weeks?

—Yes. April 30th. But I think the D. A. will go ahead and drop most of these cases. They don't have proper evidence on the circumstances of arrest, other than for curfew violation. And that's not worth the county expense to take to trial on a not-guilty plea. By the way, for what it's worth, I just learned that Patrick McKinley, one of Minier's new prosecutors, was arrested while observing the situation in Isla Vista one of those evenings. He spent eight hours in county jail before they wised up enough to release him.

—The right hand doesn't know what the left is doing.

At the door I thanked him as he offered a parting piece of advice.

—Given what we know, it would be a good idea to stay off the streets.

I left Pinkerton's and thrust the Volkswagen back on the freeway. My course was now clear and it didn't include spending more time looking for the camera or staying off the streets. Thinking about the camera just made me angry. And finding it now seemed irrelevant if not a lost cause.

Searching for news on the situation in Isla Vista, I tuned the car radio to KCSB. Bill James—President of the Associated Students and an opponent of the Radical Union—came on the station for an interview. When asked about

173

the threat of more violence in the streets, he made a surprising admission about the potential for violence.

> It may have to come to fighting in the end. But I think we are far from the time when we actually have to pick up a gun. There are so many other things that we have not done. And I don't mean sitting down in front of buildings. We can run the same mental or psychological game the Bank of America ran when it placed those ads—and we have the funds here to do it—and we can send students out to speak. This is the type of education that should be undertaken. This is the type of program to put forth—all within the law.

James, like Tom Hayden, also drew a lesson from the film *Z*, but a very different lesson.

> This was the major point made in *Z*—you can do it within the law if you organize yourselves. Keep yourself calm and rational.

James' next words gave a voice to growing division within the student community. He called for a spirited backlash against the faction of students supporting militant activism.

> I think the students who live in this community must take a stand against groups of people—whether they be students or otherwise—who are involved in something that will endanger the lives of the students who are here. I ask you: who are you fighting? I think that students should either stay in their homes, don't go out in the streets, or—those of you who want to protect your community from people destroying it should get out in the streets. Those who want to go out should do what they can to stop this sort of action from taking place. I think that at some point we have to take a stand, no matter how unpopular it might be. I don't think our administrators—who are supposed to be our leaders—have taken a significant stand. Neither have our government officials. And, least of all, the faculty—they are not taking a stand to correct the ills of this community. I'm unhappy about the way things are going.

According to a KCSB reporter at Borsodi's, a sizable number of people—300 to 400 strong—already roamed the streets near the loop in violation of the curfew.

174

But, thus far, the police remained out of the area. Canova's information was apparently correct. But James' call for help would make action in the streets more complicated. Defenders could definitely obstruct the operation. I pushed the pedal to the floor of the Volkswagen, but that didn't increase the speed much. In fact, the car slowly began decelerating. I pumped the pedal again. No change. The car continued slowing. I pulled to the side of the freeway. The gauge was on empty.

Great timing! I jumped out of the car and jogged to the nearest exit. At the top of the La Cumbre exit, I noticed a gas station across the parking lot on the far side of the Plaza. But when I reached the station, I realized I had no money—not even a coin. The lone person working wasn't sympathetic. Even though I promised I'd repay him the next day, he refused to give me any gas. As I debated what to do next I noticed he had a small radio tuned to KCSB. Someone introduced as Curry Davis repeated the plea Bill James had made earlier.

> All we're doing is trying to interpose some of the people against some of the other people in front of the bank to say that burning the bank, again, would be counter-productive. It would allow people in Santa Barbara to be proud of themselves when they send more cops out here, instead of making them ashamed of themselves for the kinds of things that the Bank of America stands for. Maybe the first time it was productive. I don't think so the second time.

Canova's plan had not anticipated a crowd divided in sympathies. I needed to get back to Isla Vista. That didn't leave many choices other than my least favorite transport—hitching a ride. The La Cumbre on-ramp was well lit, but it took a long time before a guy in an old Corvair finally pulled over to offer a ride. He said he owned a print shop in Goleta where he needed to check on the crew working an overnight job. He could take me to Hollister where I could hitch another ride to campus. With his car radio tuned to the campus station, we both listened to accounts of the street rioting. Like everyone, he had an opinion.

—Hey, dig this, I used to think UCSB was more conservative than UCLA. I went to school there and got to know the place. But I can't imagine stuff like this happening at UCLA. UCSB has become more like Berkeley. Hell, it's worse than Berkeley.

—Yeah, I've heard people say activists from Berkeley come here for the action. But I haven't met up with any.

—What's this now?

He reached over and turned up the radio. Bill James was on again.

We need as many people who can to come out and help. We need you to come out and help put out fires that have been started in some of the dumpsters and to help protect the community. No one should go out just to be a sightseer or an on-looker. You should stay in your apartments, stay in your homes. Don't come out here unless you're trying to help to protect the community. And if you do, leave your firearms at home.

My driver reacted in disbelief.

—Did you hear that? Can you believe what he said? "Leave your firearms at home?" Now there's some good advice! Do you hear how crazy that sounds? People taking to the streets with guns—nine miles outside of Santa Barbara! I can't believe he said that. And the worst of it is he's probably right to say it. That's how crazy things are getting out there. The way it's going, we'll see gun warfare between those students—speaking loosely—and the cops.

—I've heard the cops have already used shotguns loaded with birdshot.

—Well, there you go, then.

—But students don't have guns.

—Who says?

We reached Hollister and he let me off near the entrance to Ward Memorial Highway. With the sparse night traffic to campus, it took thirty minutes to catch another ride—this time from an engineering student. His car radio brought us another update on the situation in I. V.

A number of people responded to Bill James' call for help a little earlier this evening. These people have shown a lot of courage and it appeared the situation would remain under control. But in the last half hour the situation has worsened. The militant members of the crowd appear to be far outnumbering the peace keepers and the situation is deteriorating. We are no longer recommending that people come out. It's better to reduce the number of people on the streets because it's becoming clear the situation is becoming more aggressive and dangerous.

The engineering student dropped me off on the east side near his dorm residence. The air had cooled as an approaching mist, laden with salt, oil, and eucalyptus scents crept between the buildings. I quickly crossed campus. Christ it was late! I'd squandered much of the evening because of the gas problem. Shit! Canova would be thinking I'd changed my mind. Since my apartment on

176

El Nido sat directly on the way to the loop, I pulled in quickly to get a jacket. But when I opened the door, I stopped, stunned by the person sitting on my living room couch.

*   *   *

Chapter 28

—Melanie!

—Dan! Where've you been? Matt said you'd be back a long time ago.

—I ran overtime with my lawyer, and then Matt's car ran out of gas on the ride back. Why are you here? And where's Matt?

—He's out there. He had the radio on when Bill James called for help, so he went out. They started fires and were threatening the bank again. He said I could stay here and wait for you.

—Christ! He doesn't know what he's getting into.

—I tried to stop him.

—I need to go.

—No! Now they're saying to stay away. It's gotten out of control. The police will be there any time now.

—All the more reason to warn him. The cops are more dangerous than the rioters.

—You'll just get *yourself* busted again.

In a hurry to leave, I opened the door.

—Relax. I'll be back before you know it.

—Wait. There's something else.

—Now's not a good time.

—Dad might have found who has your camera.

—What?

—He found out about a cop who kept a camera the night you were arrested. It could be yours. He tried to call you yesterday.

I closed the door.

—Who is this guy?

—His name is Caldwell. Like dad, he's part of the Santa Barbara force. That's all I know. He said you should call him at this number between nine and nine-thirty tomorrow morning.

—Call who? This guy Caldwell?

—No, dad. I don't have Caldwell's number.

She handed me a slip of paper.

—That's good. Thanks for waiting. You could have left a note.

—I know. But I wanted to talk to you about the photos. I need to go over it with you and figure out where they are. It's driving me crazy, Marleau.

—Okay. We'll do that. But not now. I really have to go. We'll talk later.

I opened the door again before she could say anything more and bolted down El Nido to El Embarcadero and over to the loop. Perfect Park came into view. A crowd of maybe three hundred or more, dispersed in groups of various sizes, filled the park. Across the park to the right several people stoked a fire in a dumpster that had been rolled near the entrance to the bank parking lot. I crossed the park and searched through the crowd around the burning dumpster. Beyond the dumpster I passed a burning car, checking every face reflected in the light of the fire. Then a voice called out behind me.

—Where the hell have you been?

I turned to face Canova.

—Hey, Paul! Matt's car ran out of gas. I'll explain later. What's the status?

—According to plan, except for you—and these Boy Scout defenders staying up past bedtime. The first wave moves soon. We've got this car and dumpster in the way but we need more barricades. C'mon, let's find another dumpster we can push out.

The two of us went behind the building housing Borsodi's Coffee Shop, found a dumpster, and pushed it toward Embarcadero del Norte. As we moved the dumpster into the street, the sound of broken glass suddenly penetrated the crowd noise. I could see something large had been thrown through the glass front doors of the bank. Seconds later two figures ran to the front steps and each threw a flaming object into the bank lobby. Immediately the inside lit up as the two disappeared around the side of the bank. I stood watching the flames grow inside the lobby as an alarm bell sounded a steady ring. But as we were positioning the dumpster, Canova froze.

—What the hell?

He pointed toward the bank.

—We need to move. They're putting out the fire!

He pushed his way past me. I followed him, running through the crowd toward the bank. Two figures emerged through the broken front doors. They had already put out the fire. Five others joined them and all stood on the porch and yelled at the crowd to stop as they ducked volleys of small rocks and dirt clods thrown at them. When we were within a few yards of the bank steps, I grabbed Canova by the shirt and pulled him to the ground. He sat up and glared at me.

—What the fuck are you doing?

—Matt is up there!

He glanced toward the bank.

—Matt?! What the hell!!

Someone yelled from behind us.

—Cops are coming!

Before Canova and I could move, a small dump truck with plywood extensions on the side smashed aside one of the burning dumpsters and rolled into the bank parking lot. Cops lined the sides of the truck. Pinned by the chain link fencing on the sides of the lot, the crowd squeezed past the truck at the entrance and scattered wildly. Those on the bank porch stood waving their arms in the air and shouting at the cops that they were defending the bank. We scrambled to our feet. Headlights from the truck now illuminated the bank. We had taken only a couple of paces toward the north fence line, when an explosive boom pierced through the crowd noise and police commotion. We both hit the ground again. I shouted to Canova.

—What was that?

Cops had exited from the bed and taken positions around the truck. Another truck had pulled beside it and now another rolled forward across the lot at the edge of Perfect Park. Someone called out from the bank porch.

—Look! He's been shot!

Everyone near the front of the bank had flattened themselves on the deck of the porch. One of them called out again.

—Hold your fire! Don't shoot! We're defending the bank! Help us! Someone's been shot!

A cop from the first parked truck slowly walked toward the bank, then stopped and looked around before continuing toward the porch. He spoke defensively.

—We want you to understand right now that no policeman fired. This was not a policeman!

I could hear another cop using a radio to call for an ambulance. Someone leaning over the body on the porch cried out.

—Why did you shoot him?

With everyone crouched or flattened on the bank deck, I couldn't tell who had been shot. Thinking it was Matt, I ran to the steps of the bank. Then I saw Matt kneeling over the body along with two others. A guy opposite Matt spoke to the victim.

—Don't try to move.

Agitated but insistent, the cop near the bank porch continued defending his men.

—None of my officers has fired, we didn't shoot. I've checked with all my officers. None of their weapons have been fired.

The guy opposite Matt yelled at the cop.

—This guy's got a bullet hole in him. Where did that come from?

—We've heard reports about snipers.

A siren wailed a few blocks in the distance. The victim's shirt had been opened and his pants unbuckled. There was a small hole low on the abdomen from which a part of the intestine protruded. Oddly, there was no blood. Matt spoke to him.

—You've been shot, but it doesn't look bad. Relax, you'll be okay. There's an ambulance on the way.

Shortly after Matt spoke, the victim's eyes rolled. Matt suggested he might have gone into shock. The guy opposite him tried to rouse him.

—Can you hear me? God! He's lost consciousness.

For a long couple of minutes everyone near the bank stood or knelt in silence. Finally, an ambulance marked "Goleta Valley Hospital" wheeled into the parking lot beside the bank. Medics exited quickly, joined by two cops who followed them to the bank porch. The medics carefully moved the victim onto a stretcher and loaded him into the ambulance. As the ambulance moved out of the lot Matt turned his attention to Canova and me for the first time. His mind reeling, he glared at us for several seconds until finally spitting dart-like words toward me.

—What are you doing here with him?

Dazed, I couldn't think how to account for being there. Before I could reply, Matt turned to Canova.

—You can thank him for this. It's all a big game for you, isn't it? Now someone's been shot!

With cops milling around and clearing the perimeter of the bank, Canova sensed it was no place to be tossing accusations. He stepped toward Matt and spoke in a hostile, choked whisper.

—Shut the fuck up!! You don't know anything!!

Then he whispered to me.

—C'mon, let's get out of here.

At first unable to speak, now I couldn't move. Canova took only a step before being stopped by a cop who ordered everyone to stay put.

Matt continued glaring at me. Averting his gaze, I looked past him and noticed Melanie standing a few feet away.

—Melanie! What are you doing?

Before she could answer, another cop approached the bank porch.

—We need you all over by the truck. There could still be a shooter in the area. Before anyone can leave we need your name and contact information. You're witnesses to a shooting and there'll need to be an investigation.

We all gathered by the first truck. Canova eyed Matt uneasily, but Matt gave the cops nothing more than his contact information. When everyone had reported, we were told to return home as quickly as possible. Matt headed for the apartment and Canova for his store while I walked Melanie to her place.

It all happened so quickly and violently Melanie and I were struck dumb. We passed two blocks in silence until I began to drift out of numbness. Finally I couldn't bear the silence any longer.

—What happened? When did you leave the apartment?

—After you left, I was done reading and sitting there by myself. On the way back, I got curious and passed through the loop. I saw you and Canova talking.

She paused for a few paces while I said nothing.

—You were helping him, weren't you?

There was no use hiding anything. I didn't answer, but that didn't stop her.

—You thought that was the right thing?

—I don't know what I thought.

—God, I hope that guy is okay. It makes me sick thinking about it.

We said nothing more until we came to her door. I told her I'd be in touch and left. When I got back to the apartment, I was relieved to find Matt wasn't there. He didn't have his car so I assumed he must be walking off the shock. I sat on my bed, held my head in my hands, and rubbed my face. I was beat to the bone but sleep seemed impossible.

*　　*　　*

Chapter 29

Sometime in the early morning I finally dozed off for a while. When I woke up and walked out of the bedroom, Matt sat at the kitchen table slowly circling a spoon in a cup of coffee. He looked like he hadn't slept all night. I took a seat opposite him at the table. After a minute or two he broke the silence.

—He's dead. I phoned the hospital.

Stunned by the news, I was slow to react.

—Dead? How is that possible?

—They said he died in the ambulance. Kevin Moran—that's his name. A student.

—The wound was small. There was hardly any bleeding.

—The bullet hit a major artery. All the bleeding was internal.

—God! What a bad break!

—For him. A lucky break for me. I was standing next to him. Look at this.

He tossed a long-sleeve Navy blue wool shirt at me. I recognized it as the over-shirt he was wearing last night. Rising from the table, he came around in front of me, took the shirt, and slowly put it on. Then he stood with his left side next to me, gathered the shirt at the side, and put his end finger through two small holes in the shirt.

—I was standing to the side and in front of him. The bullet passed through my shirt before it hit him. Here, put your finger through it.

—I can see.

The bullet couldn't have come any closer to him without hitting him. The thought of it startled me. I could only imagine what it did to him. His absence all night now made even more sense. Searching for words, I could only say the obvious.

—Jesus, that's a close call.

—No shit. Why him and not me?

—Why anyone?

—Yeah. Gives you a strong hit on how senseless things get when people do things that don't need to happen.

I knew he wasn't referring to himself, but I turned it toward him anyway.

—How did you end up at the front of the bank?

—I was listening to the radio. Bill James came on and asked for people to help control the streets. I was still angry about what had happened in February and I didn't want more violence and more cops coming into Isla Vista again. So I went to the loop. I was out there for about half an hour. While standing on the east side of del Norte, I noticed two people around flames inside the bank. I thought they were starting the fire but then I saw them beating it out with their coats. After the fire was out, they came onto the porch and stood there facing the crowd. That's when I knew where I was supposed to be. I joined Kevin and the others on the porch. We held off the crowd for a while until the cops pulled into the parking lot. We knew they might mistake us for bank burners but we had no place to run with the fence on either side and the cops shining headlights on us. So we waived our arms in the air and said we were defending the bank. Then I felt a gust of wind at my side and someone spoke to my left. I turned around to find Kevin on his back on the deck. One of the other guys had already figured out he had been shot and was pulling his shirt up to find the wound.

—Any idea where the shot came from?

—Not really. But they'll have ballistics. There was no exit wound on Kevin, so they'll have the bullet too.

Matt sat down at the table again. The way he looked at me I could tell he was finished talking about himself.

—You and Canova read any good books last night?

I didn't feel like getting into it with him. To distract myself, I searched my pocket for the note paper Melanie had given me with the phone number on it. Matt wasn't letting up.

—Listen to me. I know you were with him and he sure as hell wasn't minding his store. How can you allow yourself to be part of that shit? Now somebody's dead—and for what?

—We don't know who's responsible.

—Yeah, we do. He'd still be alive if people wouldn't confuse political protest with senseless destruction of property. That kind of thing is anarchy not protest.

—I know your thinking on this. But you don't have to use a match to destroy property and lives. There's bloodless violence, too. And banks know a little about that. What happened to Kevin was not part of anyone's plan.

—Plan? That's just it. You start burning things down, don't pretend you can control the outcome. There was no cause for taking risks like that. It's worse than manslaughter.

—Look, I'm not doing this with you right now. Think what you like about me. I need to make a phone call, so let's just drop it!

Matt pushed his half empty cup away and stood up.

—Fine. I've got to go and give the cops this shirt. They need it for their investigation. Meanwhile, stew in your own juice.

He left the table and walked to the door. Then I thought of his car.

—Oh shit! That reminds me.

—What?

I explained what happened to his car and that I had to leave it because I had no money on me. To him it looked as though I chose to make participation in street rioting more of a priority than getting his car off the freeway. He stormed out of the apartment with a parting demand that his car be in his parking space by noon. I didn't feel like dwelling on his car, but I would have to deal with it soon. It was past nine. I would call Lampert—more to find out what he knew about last night than about my camera.

After two rings he picked up.

—Officer Lampert? This is Dan Marleau.

—Okay, listen. I didn't work last night and this morning I find a student's been killed, so I don't have much time for this now, understand? Here's what I have. By sheer accident I found out about someone who might have your camera. There's not a damn thing I'm going to do about it. But if you want, you can contact him—for all the good it might do, which may not be much. If it's your camera, maybe you'll get lucky and he'll give it back to you if you approach it right. Say you're contacting different officers who were on duty the night of your arrest. Say you're looking for your camera. Describe it to him and see what he says. If he isn't forthcoming, you're screwed. It's the best I can do for you.

—I get it. Thanks.

—His name is Caldwell, Ben Caldwell. He's in the phone book. Lives on Garden Street. Call him at home. Don't mention my name. I don't know a good time to reach him. Everyone's on overtime these days.

—Thanks. I'll check it out.

—I've got to go.

—Wait! Just one more thing. Did you ever say anything to anyone about me taking photos at the Bill Allen protest?

—I've never said crap about you to anyone. Why do you ask?

—A guy named Newberry came by my place with a subpoena and took all my photos. I don't know why that happened.

—I don't know a thing about it. I've got to go now.

185

I looked up Caldwell in the phone book and dialed his number. I thought I might get lucky and catch him at home, but no one answered. Then I left to find Canova. I wasn't in a hurry to see him, but he knew the guy who owned the record shop next to his bookstore and he had a car. Maybe I could persuade him to give me a lift to Matt's car with a can of gas.

When I arrived, Canova was alone in the store, stacking books in the far corner. I sat in a chair near where he was working and stared at the bookshelves. He spoke without even looking at me.

—Don't start with me about it. What happened was insane. It wasn't something we caused.

—That's convenient. I could take a long shower and not feel any cleaner.

—You feel that way because you frame it wrong. It was the cops who did it. They don't really give a shit about what they do to take back Isla Vista.

—Nobody knows what happened yet. Maybe we'll never know. But whoever's responsible, I can't get myself as clear about it as you are.

Canova said nothing and continued sorting through books.

—But I didn't come here to talk about that.

—Yeah? What's on your mind? You back to your self-absorption?

This remark drew hackles, but I refused the bait. I explained to him the petty problem of getting Matt's bug off the freeway where I had to leave it. After saying he hoped it got sideswiped by an eighteen wheeler, he grudgingly agreed to borrow the car and drive me to Santa Barbara, since the owner didn't let just anyone drive it.

On the way into town I brought Canova up to date on the developments with the subpoena and Lampert's news about Officer Caldwell. Despite a return to the subject of the camera, the Caldwell news seemed to interest him.

—So have you contacted this guy Caldwell yet?

—I phoned him a couple of times but no answer.

—If he's in the phone book, maybe you should stop at his house. He might have left the door open and you can walk in and get your camera.

Canova was joking but he gave me an idea.

—Come to think of it, I do have his address. Would you mind swinging by there? If I could catch him at home, it'd be better than talking on the phone. I'd like to see his face when I ask him about the camera.

—What are you going to say to him? Hey, I'm the guy you busted the night you all were having such fun getting rocks thrown at you and I just wondered if you'd give me back the camera you stole from me?

—Yeah. Something like that.

—Maybe you should have your lawyer call the guy. He could tell him he's working on a case, that there's a missing camera, and his client, the son of the mayor, is attempting to recover it.

I thanked him for the great advice. When we arrived at Caldwell's house, Canova stayed in the car while I went to the door. There was no doorbell, but repeated knocking brought no answer. I walked to a fence at the side of the house and peered through the crack between the fence and a gate. No sign of anyone. On impulse, I went to the front door again and tried the knob. It was locked. Then I returned to the car. Canova noticed the attempt to open the door.

—You should've tried the back door or a window.

—C'mon, let's get out of here before you get me busted for breaking and entering.

Canova grinned as we pulled away. We found Matt's car on the side of the freeway where I had left it the night before. After pouring a can of gas in it, I thanked Canova for the lift and returned to Isla Vista shortly before noon.

The return of his car on schedule placated Matt, but it was clear I wouldn't be borrowing it again. The events of yesterday put a huge strain on our relationship. It wasn't easy for either of us to be in the same space anymore, but we didn't have many options. Sleeping on the floor of Canova's store might work in an emergency but not on a daily basis. Melanie might have been persuaded to lend me her living room couch, but after the fiasco with her photos I couldn't contemplate asking her. Other buddies I might impose on were either in tiny dorm rooms or stacked three or four deep in seedy I.V. apartments. Everything about my current situation felt cramped, uncomfortable, and worsening.

*   *   *

Chapter 30

The Moran shooting had thoroughly stunned the Isla Vista and campus community. Although a limited police presence continued in the streets at night, no major protests or confrontations with police occurred through the weekend. Monday morning a Memorial Service for Kevin Moran at the Isla Vista Beach drew a large number of local residents. It was the first time in months a crowd had gathered on or off campus where the mood was somber and the threat of violence distant. The rhythm of the surf mixed with subdued voices from conversations among groups arrayed along the cliff. Matt had left early for the service. I wanted to attend but did not look forward to it. By the time I arrived at the beach the minister from an Isla Vista church who had been appointed to deliver a brief eulogy had just begun to speak.

> We are gathered here today to honor Kevin Patrick Moran, a student who in an act of courage and bravery has given his life while defending this community. Kevin was a UCSB senior who had come out of his apartment to help put out fires in Isla Vista. He was shot and killed early Saturday morning as he stood on the front porch of the Bank of America.
>
> The exact circumstances surrounding his death are not yet entirely clear, due in part to the turmoil immediately following the killing and in part to the lack of information from the Santa Barbara Sheriff's Department. But I'd like to recite what is known of the events to show Kevin's integrity and to pay homage to his honorable actions.
>
> Kevin left his apartment a little before midnight with two other friends in answer to an appeal made earlier by Associated Students' President Bill James on KCSB radio. James called for students to help keep order and to put out fires in the streets of Isla Vista. According to Thomas Thomaides, Kevin's roommate, they helped to put out two fires near the Bank and then they urged the crowd not to burn the bank.
>
> But eventually an attempt was made to burn the bank and the police moved in. One truck pulled into the bank's parking lot and

188

shortly after that they heard a shot. Then Kevin fell down saying "I think I'm shot!" A war veteran from Vietnam, who was also on the balcony, attempted to give Kevin first aid, but within two or three minutes after the shot, Kevin was unconscious.

About this time, a policeman reached the balcony and radioed for an ambulance. Kevin was pronounced dead on arrival at Goleta Valley Hospital. We don't yet know how this shooting happened or who is responsible. But needless to say, it's a great loss and one that could have been prevented had many residents of Isla Vista chosen a nonviolent means of protest.

Kevin, his roommate Thomas Thomaides, and several others who joined them on the porch of the bank stand as role models for all of us. In light of their actions and the tragic consequences for one of them, all who have participated in Isla Vista street riots the past several months will hopefully reflect on the wisdom or necessity for violent street protests.

The minister continued speaking for a few more minutes, then concluded by announcing that, in memory of Kevin, donations could be made to The Kevin Moran Memorial Fund where all proceeds would go to the campus anti-war committee.

As I walked toward the ramp to Isla Vista, Canova came up to me from out of the crowd.

—Did you hear the news?

Having had enough bad news, I said I hadn't with an edge of apprehension.

—Webster just held a press conference about the shooting. Some cop with a rifle owned up to discharging a 30.06—same caliber they took out of Moran.

—Jesus!

—They sent it to ballistics in Sacramento. He said the slug was so deformed they might not make positive identification. But that seems like hedging because he also said the cop admitted the gun went off by accident. They even have the spent cartridge. He claims there was a problem with the safety.

—People will say he did it on purpose.

—Well, he's also claiming it was a ricochet because of the deformity of the slug and a piece of it was missing. If that holds up, it would support the cop's story it was an accident. There's also the faulty safety mechanism. But who knows what to believe when you're dealing with these guys. I hate to say I told you so, but the cops are really out of control.

189

—Can't argue with that. But I'm thinking they're not the only ones.

—C'mon, you're not going to blame what happened on what we did?

—I'm not blaming anybody but I'm not feeling innocent either. The truth is I don't know what to feel and that's a creepy feeling, if that makes any sense.

I left Canova standing on the beach and walked back into Isla Vista. That afternoon, feeling the need for a break from Isla Vista and the campus scene, I went for a walk along the sandstone cliff overlooking the beach. I jogged the half mile or so to Goleta point. On the return trip I stopped where Ocean Road ends at the edge of the cliff and leaned against the chain link fence to take in the view. The sky was clear but a thin haze made the outline of the Channel Islands barely visible in the distance. Gazing toward the edge of the surf, I noticed two people casually walking. They were close enough to my vantage point that I quickly recognized the profiles of Kyle and Melanie. What were they doing together? Given the way she introduced herself to me, it shouldn't come as a shock to find her flirting around. I should have expected it. But Kyle—that was something else. I couldn't believe he would hit on my girlfriend.

Girlfriend? I hadn't thought that way about Melanie until now. She was more like a friend who happened to be a girl. We'd been on a couple of dates, that's all. I watched them closely as they walked along the stretch of sand toward Isla Vista. They seemed to be having a very friendly conversation.

*   *   *

Chapter 31

In the waning days of April, the weeks of protests, violence, police crackdowns, and the death of a student weighed heavily on the campus and Isla Vista community. During the last week of April, the curfew had finally been pushed back to 11pm. Two dorm buddies of mine from freshman year now living in Isla Vista saw that as an opportunity for a much needed "time-out." They didn't use the word "party" because that seemed too cavalier to fit the sober circumstances. A small spate of escapism had its attractions for anyone living in Isla Vista over the last several months. So Saturday night I forced myself out the door of my apartment.

The time-out hosts, Ted and Rob, lived in a two bedroom corner apartment on the lower level of a complex near Pasado and Camino Pescadero. Well before I got to their door, I could hear the stereo blasting out the sounds of Van Morrison's "Moondance" through the open windows.

A cloud of incense and herb met me as I opened the door. Only a light from the kitchen stove to the left and another lamp in the corner of the living room to the right lit the interior. The time-out didn't lack attendance. People stood talking in the kitchen and covered the floor in seated groups around the living room. Standing by the keg in the kitchen, Ted saw me first as I walked in.

—Hey, Marleau—the famous French revolutionary! What's happening in the streets? You set fire to any cop cars on the way over?

—Very funny, blockhead.

—Right. I forgot. Only banks for you. But hey, you know what they say about revolution.

—What's that?

—Better free your mind instead.

—That's heavy, Ted. I'm hungry. You got anything to eat here?

—Sure. We've got some pizzas coming. Should be here any time now.

Someone called to Ted from the hallway and he wandered off. Knowing Ted's odd sense of humor, I figured the pizza thing for one of his jokes, making everyone think pizza was coming so he could laugh his head off whenever someone asked about it. So I sneaked a look in the refrigerator. A jar with two pickles, a carton of eggs, chocolate syrup, half a carton of milk, and a moldy slab of cheese. I checked the cupboard to the left of the fridge. A large jar of peanut butter and a box of Ritzes. That would do. As I closed the cupboard door, I noticed something wrapped in wax paper on the second shelf. Four brownies. Downing one of those held off starvation as I spread peanut butter on several Ritzes.

A beer from the keg washed down the peanut butter and I went off to check out who was in the living room. After making the rounds for about half an hour I wandered off into the back bedroom looking for Rob. I found him engrossed in a conversation with several others, one of whom was another member of our freshman dorm year. They were in the middle of an argument about a movie they had recently seen—*Women in Love*. Rob was explaining something to the rest of the group.

—And the oppressed becomes the oppressor and he evolves into the syndrome of classic sadomasochism. Look how he treats the workers in the mines. And then there's that scene with the horse. Remember the horse? Gudrun and Ursula are out for a walk near the railroad tracks and Gerald is on a morning gallop with his horse . . .

Rob broke off in mid sentence when he looked over at me.

—What's up with you?

—What?

—You look kind of out of it.

Before he could continue the interrogation, Ted burst into the room.

—I turn my back for a few seconds and you guys are all crammed in here making with the mental masturbation. Rob, there's some woman looking for you and we need some new music. Let's get with it men.

Everyone filed out except me and the other dorm member whose name I couldn't remember at the moment. He picked up a plastic pitcher sitting on the floor next to him, poured out half a glass of what looked like iced tea, and handed it to me.

—Here. We've all done some.

—What's this?

—Spiked tea. It'll give a little buzz.

—I don't know. I'm not thinking too straight already.

—Please. The problem is you're thinking too straight.

He snickered at his little joke. I raised the glass, drank it down in three swallows, and chased it with beer. Then we joined the rest of the party in the living room. After attempting sporadic conversation, I gave up talking as my head began to spin. Sitting with my back against the living room wall, staring at eyelid lights, listening to "Paper Sun"—these were the last things I remembered before I timed out.

* * *

192

Chapter 32

—Marleau?

Someone calling me.

—Marleau!

I strained to see who it was.

—Marleau! What are you doing here?

I opened my eyes again slightly but quickly shut them again. Someone stood over me, but I couldn't see who it was. Raising myself, I discovered sand covering the length of my legs. Sand also clung to my hair and the left side of my face. I shook what I could out of my hair and brushed off my face. With eyes better adjusted to the light, I looked up again.

—Kyle? What are you doing?

—You look like something the tide tossed up. The little lady put you out last night?

—What are you saying?

I didn't know which felt worse—my head or my stomach. The more conscious I became the more my entire body felt like it had passed through the spin cycle of an industrial strength washer. Kyle answered with a bemused look.

—I'm saying what're you doing here covered with sand?

I was slowly getting my bearings. Sun breaking on the horizon. Air cool. Signs of early morning on the beach. I couldn't recall how I got there. Put out by the little lady? I thought of Melanie. Then it came back to me. The image of Melanie and Kyle on the beach together last week.

—Speaking of the little lady, what were you doing walking with Melanie here the other day?

—Oh that. Well, let's see.

Kyle sat down beside me on the sand.

—I was telling her how nice it would be on the beach at sunset, just her and me.

—Crap!

—Truth is, we ran into each other walking the beach. So we started talking. In fact we talked about you.

—About me?

193

—Yeah, she wanted to know if you were from another planet. Naturally, I had to set her straight. Told her it was just the opposite.

—Huh?

—That you were the man from underground. Seeing you this morning, I'm convinced of it.

—No, I'm the creature of the tide, remember?

Kyle was making light of it, but I pressed him further.

—She seemed to be smiling at you a lot.

—So you were spying, huh? Why didn't you say something to us?

Realizing I should have called out to them, I explained defensively.

—Well, I was up on the cliff over there and you two were clear over here walking away from me.

I pointed out the positions as I spoke.

—A little worried about her, are you?

—Worried? I don't know. Ugh! My head is killing me.

I flopped back into the sand and stared at the sky.

—What's the matter with you? You're paranoid and you look sick as hell.

—I went to a party last night. I don't even remember how I got here.

—What kind of drugs?

—I didn't do any drugs.

—You could fool me.

—Come to think of it, I did drink some stuff. Don't know what was in it.

—First time tripping?

—You think it was acid?

—From the looks of you.

—That explains it. Just leave me for the tide to pick up.

—You always drink strange stuff at parties?

—What's the big deal? You do stuff don't you?

—I've messed around some. Not anymore—other than occasional weed.

—Why not?

—Better question is "why?"

—So why did you?

—I put drug use in two categories—pain killers and time killers. Aspirin is a pain killer and the heavy stuff—that's all time killing.

—Something wrong with killing a little time?

—I don't mean passing time. I mean *slaying* time. Time killing drugs are "now" enhancers. They amplify the immediate and fade out the past and future—along with most feelings of loss and worry.

—So what's the problem with that?

—Killing time has a price. I like feeling stretched—across a past, present, and future. It gives a sense of action, of reaching I can't stand to be without anymore. When you're merged, when you're lost in the moment, you're shaped but you lose all sense of shaping. You need the sense of time for that.

—What about creative visions?

—You might see things on a drug that seem far out, but in my experience those leaps are never as great as they looked when you were high. When you come down, they don't look nearly as brilliant. No, I'm hooked on time. And I don't like it watered down much. But when I do take a holiday from it, the better way is sex.

—Sex? So drugs are a sex substitute?

—Not quite. Sex and drugs are both time killers. But a chemical you put in your mouth can't compare to a woman.

—A drug might be more prudent.

—Right. Old man time and women—they expect things from you.

—People talk about psychedelics like they challenge you, like they're a kind of test, how they open you to something bigger, toss you into a current where you're not in control.

—There's some truth in that, but there are better tests. It's too easy to put stuff in your mouth and think you've done something.

—But what about the trip, the place where it takes you? Doesn't that show you something about yourself?

—It trades on illusion—a magician pulls a rabbit out of a hat because there's already a rabbit in it.

Kyle leaned over and picked up a piece of driftwood as he spoke.

—If drugs give you anything, they give you what you've already got. But they can't get to the deepest layers. There's no chemical shortcut for that. The harder something is to do, the more it can show you about who you are. A drug is too easy. But suppose you tell me. Was it worth it?

—Can't say. Haven't digested it yet.

—Why'd you drink that stuff? You don't strike me as the gullible type.

—I don't know. Maybe I wanted a new slant on things. I'm not seeing so good right now.

—Why's that?

—All I see is lies, lies all around.

—So where are the lies?

—Where aren't they? The government lies about a war it wants you to fight. The University lies about why they're firing a prof. The bank lies about its corporate motives. The church lies about the meaning of it all. Communities

195

prop up all the lies. And my best friend thinks I lie to myself. Worst is, I think he's right.

—You left out Santa Claus.

—Don't get me started.

—Everything begins with a lie.

—How do you figure?

—We all start off with what someone else tells us.

—And it goes downhill from there.

I stared up at the sky. Kyle tossed a piece of driftwood toward the surf.

—You trust yourself?

—Like I said, I'm not seeing so good right now.

—So you thought you'd trust a drug?

—What the hell.

—Why not trust your confusion?

I sat up and tossed another piece of driftwood toward the one Kyle had thrown.

—Wouldn't that be a little like trusting the inmates at the asylum?

—Confusion isn't insanity.

—Feels like it.

—Listening to your own confusion might be better than listening to lies.

—Sure, but one voice says "See it this way." Another says "What about this and that?" Back and forth it goes. There's no clarity, no good move. Feels like I should do something, but every play feels wrong.

I tossed out another piece of driftwood. It hit the surf and got sucked into a wave.

—Feels like you should do something?

—You know. With all this stuff going on. Do you burn a bank to stop a war? And if people get killed in the process? What if the means of protest match the means of war? What sense does that make?

A large wave climbed the sand toward us.

—You know that camera of yours? Sometimes the more you focus, the fuzzier things get—not because there's something wrong with the lens but because things are really fuzzy. The thing that bothers you is the fuzziness. You mistake it for confusion. But that fuzziness may be the thing to trust. Take the horizon out there. Does it resolve into a line?

—C'mon.

—Confusion may mean you're seeing better not worse.

—So where's the consolation in that?

—Having to act when you can't bring everything into focus is tough. But we can't choose not to act. Even sitting still is an act. That's why we like to stop time. Things can get awkward. You can see why people find drugs tempting—or why it's tempting to insist on having been right even with the constant likelihood of being wrong.

Kyle threw another stick of driftwood.

—Hey, I've got to go.

—Meetin' someone?

—Yeah, Melanie.

—You jerk.

He plodded away through the heavy sand. I shouted after him.

—Hey, thanks for the confusion.

—Anytime.

*   *   *

Chapter 33

In the wake of months of campus turmoil, street rioting, and the Kevin Moran tragedy, keeping up with classes had become a low priority. Although I'd missed several installments of my philosophy class, seeing Kyle motivated me to make an effort to check in on Macomber's class and one or two others.

Due to the Moran killing and the chain of disruptive local events, many professors in the humanities had transitioned their classes into what amounted to long discussions on current events. But not Macomber. He still dominated class sessions with free-wheeling monologues. However, on Wednesday's class he yielded to current events to the extent of offering, late in the hour, a digression taken straight from the front page of the day's paper.

He stood before the class in his usual uniform of sport coat with elbow patches, shirt with open collar, and forest green corduroy pants—bearing wrinkles from consecutive days of use. His unkempt hair bore the look of a man who had just gotten out of bed. But, contradicting the otherwise professorial appearance, were the eyes. Belying the absent-minded look, Macomber's alert, eager, eyes probed around the room from face to face as he spoke.

Holding up a copy of the day's *Washington Post*, he informed the class that Vice-President Spiro Agnew had just given a major speech about campus unrest to a gathering of Republican elite at Fort Lauderdale. Macomber couldn't resist comment because Agnew had cited a philosophy professor from New York University. In defense of his complaint about the failure of campus administrations and faculty across the country, Agnew quoted Sidney Hook from a recent *Saturday Review* article where the substance and tone of Hook's remarks echoed sentiments coming from the UCSB campus administration.

> Shortly after the riotous events at the University of California at Berkeley in 1964, I predicted that in consequence of the faculty's refusal to condemn the student seizure of Sproul Hall, the administration building, American higher education would never be the same again, that a turning-point had been reached in the pattern of development. I confess, however, to surprise at the rapidity of

the change, if not its direction, and by the escalation of the violence accompanying it.

Macomber continued, now reading Agnew's comments.

Now the commonplace seizure of campus buildings has been pushed off page one of newspapers by the burning of campus buildings. Civil disobedience has degenerated into criminal violence. From sit-ins, we have moved to clubs, bricks, bottles, and guns—to violent clashes with police—to burning the Bank of America. Campus anarchy that might have been nipped in the bud at Berkeley with a single act of administrative decisiveness and faculty courage—can now be contained only at considerable cost. But the sooner the price of saving the universities is paid, the better.

Macomber then began his own commentary.

—Now I'm willing to concede that Vice-President Agnew maintains a level of discourse far superior to his immediate superior, Richard Nixon. Can you imagine Nixon citing a professional philosopher? At least Agnew reads! His problem, however, lies in not reading broadly enough. Nevertheless, I'm impressed with a metaphor he uses. Later in the speech he names President Robben Fleming of the University of Michigan as among those to be held in contempt for capitulation to campus radicals. These radicals use building seizures and property damage to achieve their ends. Agnew then says, "As for the vigor of my criticism of President Fleming, it was based on an old Cub Scout theory that the best way to put a tough crust on a marshmallow is to roast it."

Macomber put aside the newspaper and sat on a desk at the front of the class.

—Isn't that marvelous? A roasted marshmallow! You can just picture it. But I think the proper word for the heroism Agnew has in mind is *toasted*, not roasted. We can tell a lot about a culture from its heroes. Look at Humphrey Bogart and John Wayne. What do we like about them? They're tough on everyone, especially themselves. But underneath the tough exterior they have a soft spot—a soft spot for the underdog, the guy who isn't getting a fair shake. They don't like it when the little guy gets stiffed. Charlie Chaplin—the gentle tramp. They don't like it when the Charlie Chaplins of the world get stiffed. Hard and crusty on the outside, warm and soft on the inside. But that's a *toasted* marshmallow, not a roasted marshmallow.

He paused and chuckled slightly in a way that sounded like he was clearing his throat.

—Humphrey Bogart and John Wayne are toasted marshmallows. Roasted gets you brittle and charred on the outside, hot and gooey on the inside. Those marshmallows fall off the stick into the fire. Now in the case of Robben Fleming, the notion that he's a marshmallow, for whom Agnew's verbal fire can provide a roasting, is ludicrous at best. No one person can roast another. Only life can do that. Capitulation to protests is not itself a sign of weakness. It could be a sign of yielding to a better sense of fair play and equity. I'm thinking here of the capitulation to union demands in the early years of the industrial revolution. And wouldn't it be exemplary of an institution of higher learning to have the prescience to yield to a reasonable extension of fair play? The fact that in Michigan student strikes turned to property damage is lamentable. But this violence and other regrettable excesses are not themselves a refutation of the particular case for fair play. Protest, by its nature, sets up a double bind for the opposition. If you concede, have you fallen to coercion or risen to the merit of the demands? How to measure that? Perhaps Flemming saw past the excesses to stay focused on the merit of what was proposed by the students—namely, making higher education more accessible for blacks. Seeing past violent behavior and remaining open to doing the right thing—that requires judgment as well as fortitude. He knows he will catch hell from some quarter, so why not do the right thing? Flemming may have had a tougher crust than Agnew gave him credit for.

Macomber paused, collecting his thoughts, and seeing time was running short, moved to the coda.

—I've just provided an example of philosophy in action. Take an image or a metaphor, offered as insight into a situation, and then rotate it—even stand it on its head—and see what truth might emerge. Quite often what emerges seems every bit as true as the original image—sometimes more so. This is the beauty of the aphorism. An aphorism is a commonplace maxim turned on its head. For example, Plato says art imitates life and Oscar Wilde responds, life imitates art. Kudos to Oscar. And for the *toasted* marshmallow metaphor of the hero, we can thank Vice-President Agnew for the assist.

*   *   *

Chapter 34

Relative calm had returned to the square mile at Goleta Point in the waning days of April. As Pinkerton had predicted, the D. A. finally dropped charges against me and the majority of those arrested on the streets during the evenings following the bank burning in February—thereby cancelling my trial date of April 30th. These relatively minor cases were abandoned in order to focus intently on the more serious offenses. On the last day of April, Chancellor Cheadle requested the County Grand Jury begin a full investigation of the riots surrounding the bank burning and the Moran shooting. Reports circulated on campus that the purpose of this investigation would be to produce indictments for the bank burning in February and the attempted bank burnings in April.

The first day of May also brought renewed tensions on the national level. President Nixon disclosed that on April 30th U. S. troops invaded Cambodia. He announced the invasion as a "limited incursion," part of a maneuver to root out North Vietnamese troops using Cambodia as a sanctuary for launching attacks on South Vietnam. The "incursion" included aerial bombing as well as troop deployment. Defending the decision, Nixon asserted, "We are not a weak people. We are a strong people . . . . We will not be humiliated. The world's most powerful nation will not act like a pitiful, helpless giant."

Nixon's announcement served as a mayday call for anti-war protest groups. Students around the country responded vehemently, sometimes violently. By May 5th over 70 campuses had organized student strikes, bringing these universities to a functional standstill. On many campuses protests held at large noon rallies migrated to campus Reserved Officer Training Corps facilities and some of these buildings were damaged or destroyed.

At USCB a ring of police protection around the ROTC building prevented a crowd of protesting students from assaulting it, so the crowd wound its way across campus to confront the Administration Building once again. As on the night of the Moran shooting, student participation divided between groups trying to prevent violence and others trying to shut down buildings through whatever means necessary. Eventually, a group broke past the student defenders and entered the Ad Building, breaking windows and throwing cans of paint around the lobby. Campus police eventually drove them out of the building. In the process, however, the administration called once again for reinforcements from the County Sheriff's Office and the California Highway Patrol. With additional police, relative quiet returned to campus by late afternoon.

However, national headlines for May 5th belonged to Kent State University. Here campus police were not successful in protecting the ROTC building. On the previous day, students gained access to the structure and set fires. As the ruins smoldered, the governor called in the National Guard. For reasons that remained unclear, four Guardsmen, armed with rifles, fired on a gathering of demonstrators and onlookers, killing four unarmed students.

In the wake of these killings, national outrage and anti-war protest exploded across the country. On May 6th student strikes spread across 360 campuses. In California, Governor Reagan ordered all university and state college campuses closed from Wednesday, May 6th through Sunday, May 10th.

In continuing protests, student as well as faculty leaders organized a march of several thousand on Friday into downtown Santa Barbara. Parts of the group paraded through the Post Office and City Hall while another group closed highway 101 at the intersection with State Street. Police re-routed traffic to avoid a confrontation, but tensions were high on both sides.

With the currents of national and local political events daily demanding new attention, I had largely abandoned exploring any new angles in search of my camera and held out little hope of ever seeing it again. But I decided I would at least follow through on the one lead that remained, which was Caldwell. Aside from the film issue, I couldn't afford to replace the camera and I needed it to continue classes in photo journalism. But either Caldwell was never home or never answered his phone.

I still had no idea what happened to Melanie's photos. If, by some bungling on my part they were among what Newberry took with him, he'd have developed the prints by now. Surely some word would have surfaced about pictures of a naked woman. I had Pinkerton harass them to return the photos. But so far his efforts yielded nothing more than assurances that they would be returned as soon as possible—with no date specified.

I was sure members of the Radical Union still counted me as the one who gave photos from the January strategy meeting to police. But indictments from the Allen demonstrations, anti-war protest gatherings, and the end of April campaign for re-election for student offices drew their attention. The Radical Union suffered a severe political blow when the student elections succeeded in ousting their members from all the positions they held on the Student Legislative Council. Moderates also gained control of the *El Gaucho*. As Bill Allen had said during the first day of the January demonstrations, "Hey, you all really voted today," so also it could be said that with the April elections the students also really voted, sending an unambiguous message across campus about how the majority of students felt regarding the Radical Union and its actions.

On Saturday, May 9th, it was Matt's turn to get served with a subpoena. It required he provide testimony at a coroner's inquest for the death of Kevin Moran at the Santa Barbara County Courthouse on Tuesday. What he had to say about the inquest on his return Tuesday afternoon did not so much mend the fences between us as leave us with uncanny new facts to absorb.

Primarily for the purpose of determining the cause of Moran's death and the source of the bullet, the inquest focused on analysis of facts pertaining to the shooting. Matt told me of the testimony of a criminologist from the California Department of Justice by the name of David Burd.

—You can't believe the safety mechanism on that piece of shit rifle. Burd showed that if you dropped the butt by two or three inches or if you slapped it on the left side, the safety would release.

—You're kidding.

—Then he tells us about the results from the bullet and fiber tests. He found a trace of calcite on the slug along with fibers. The fibers matched the clothing worn by Moran and one fiber matched my shirt. But it's the calcite that makes no sense. The embedded calcite could only have come from hitting a limestone rock. Given the downward trajectory of the bullet and its deformation, no one can figure out what the bullet ricocheted off of to do what it did. To ricochet off a rock, it would seem to have hit the ground, but that would then create an upward trajectory.

—What about the roof or a railing or something else between Moran and the line of trajectory?

—That's just it. They couldn't find anything else in the way. No roof, no railing, nothing else was in the line. Besides, if the roof or any railing had been involved, they would have found some trace of the path of the bullet.

—So what are they proposing, some "magic bullet" theory of their own?

—Burd could only come up with one explanation. Someone must have thrown a rock that was in the air at the time the bullet was making its way toward the bank. The bullet ricocheted off of it, changing its upward course downward toward the bank porch and Kevin Moran.

—Get real! That's really grasping at straws.

—So far, it's the only explanation that fits all the facts.

I was speechless as Matt drew his conclusions.

—Imagine the freaky set of circumstances. Guys defending the bank, a cop with a faulty rifle, an accidental discharge, bullet hits a rock in mid-air, splits and ricochets downward, passes through my shirt, and hits Moran in precisely a place that turns out to be deadly.

—How random is that?

—Yeah, but creating the risk wasn't random.

—You take a chance every time you leave the house.

—But a walk in the park isn't like a walk in Perfect Park, late in the night in April. Radicals created an accident going somewhere to happen. Anyway, that's my opinion.

—And the cops were the accident.

—I don't see the blame as equal.

* * *

Chapter 35

With the re-opening of campus on Monday, May 11th, a faculty group proposed that the administration establish a six week intensive National Crisis course to discuss the war and related domestic troubles. Approximately 2500 students enrolled for the course and sessions began on Wednesday. But since the general mood on campus prevented focus on normal academic routines, almost every liberal arts class converted in one degree or another to National Crisis course agendas.

With the growing focus on political issues, campus faculty found themselves increasingly pressed by events and student insistence to take a position on key issues. Among those who made efforts to channel regular courses toward the relevant current events and express views on administration policies, one professor from the Speech Department, John Macksoud, stood out. His current class on what he called the "limits of language" conducted a broad investigation into the difficulties of separating political and strategic rhetoric from everyday instruction and description.

His class included discussion of public statements made by particular administration leaders and the hot button issue of whether politicking, as campaigning and crusading for particular persons and policies, ought to be a part of university life. As more faculty made public their views on administration positions and national war policy, campus divisions grew. Contrary to the situation earlier in the year, the lines of confrontation on campus no longer fell primarily between administration/faculty on the one hand and students on the other; now more faculty criticized the administration while some students who were formerly neutral went from neutrality to siding with the administration. One day in early May in Macksoud's class proved especially noteworthy in serving notice that members of the faculty could offer a deeper challenge to administration views than had been achieved, or even possible, through Bill Allen's guerrilla tactics.

Macksoud stood beside a folding table at the front of the class. Tall and heavy-set with full beard, he bore some resemblance to Orson Welles. Like Welles, he also spoke with ease and entertaining style—although with a higher pitch to his voice. He had a gift for memorable and often amusing presentation. At times I could even see a potential stand-up comedian in him. He held up what looked to be two photocopied pages.

—This is what I wanted to get into today. Now I read this in the Sunday *News Press*—my wife Jackie read it to me actually—and I was just going to pass it over. I figured what the hell, Sunday *News Press*. But I got this in my box today:

> Dear colleague, we are sending you the attached statement by David Gardner which appeared in the *Santa Barbara News Press* on Sunday, which we feel should be brought to the attention of every member of the faculty.

—This comes out over the signature of Harry Girvetz—who is Professor of philosophy and chair of the Academic Senate Committee on Privilege and Tenure, Glenn Mills—who is in our department, Upton Palmer—who is in our department, and Herman Pritchett—who is in the political science department. This is a little bit long, but bear with me.

Macksoud put the cover sheet down and held the newspaper copy in his left hand.

—Listen carefully. Here we go.

> The rising level of political activity on university campuses around the country is being applauded or deplored depending upon one's conception of the role of the university in society. It is obvious that the university in America is sustaining profound changes in its structure and purpose. Not since the American college was transformed into the American university during the last half of the 19th century have such powerful forces impinged upon the nation's primary institutions of higher learning. Whether or not the outcome of the current struggle will prove to have profited the university and the society it serves will essentially be a subjective judgment for persons of differing persuasions to make.

He stopped and glanced up at the class.

—Now this is the good part.

Shifting the paper to his right hand, he continued.

> As for me, the gain or loss will be whether the university scholar is more free or less free intellectually as a teacher and seeker of knowledge than before. My conception of the university's mission is avowedly traditional. I believe that the function of the university is to seek and to transmit knowledge and to train students in the processes whereby truth may be made known.

This last sentence drew some exclamations from around the room. Macksoud paused, smiled, and went on.

—Note that this next sentence is in parentheses.

(I also believe that this function should be carried on in ways more responsive to the diversity of learning *styles* that characterize our student body than is now the case). Those engaged in this task must be as committed to the welfare of their students as they are to the advancement of knowledge. To achieve either goal, the scholar must approach knowledge with an attitude of concerned and impartial detachment, for such "is the only preservation against the fluctuating extremes of fashionable opinion," as Alfred North Whitehead once observed. Such impartiality, of course, is currently fashionable to condemn as though it were a form of moral indifference or apathy. "Where is your commitment?" one is asked for having failed to vote affirmatively on a faculty resolution condemning escalation of the war.

—Notice the word "escalation."

The answer is not to be discovered in discussing the merits and demerits of military action. Rather, it is to be found within the principles of a competing commitment to the idea of the university as a place where ideas are not voted on but shared and exchanged. And that implies a personal commitment to the traditional values of scholarship. Academic man cannot have it both ways. That is, he cannot argue to politicize the university in behalf of his own political commitments, however, virtuous, without simultaneously compromising his basis of appeal against externally imposed political tests, e.g., loyalty oaths and other contrivances designed to blunt inquiry and the free flow of ideas. As a scholar and a member of the faculty, I am committed to seek and transmit knowledge impartially.

Macksoud looked up, raised his eyebrows, and went on.

In return, I expect the university to protect my freedom in the classroom and my freedom to inquire and to publish the results thereof, which is the essence of academic freedom. As a private citizen, I stand in the same relationship to constitutionally protected rights of free expression as does every other citizen. I enjoy no more lawful rights of free speech than anyone else and I am no less bound by the lawful limits of free expression than anyone else. These critical distinctions between civilly secured rights of free expression and professionally protected rights of academic freedom are terribly misunderstood today. Thus, as Professor Richard Schier has noted, there is confusion within the academic profession generally about "both the basis of political action by teachers, which is that of constitutional freedom, and the basis of academic freedom, which is in the pure sense academic rather than constitutional, and certainly not political." Given present trends, the failure to make these distinctions clear will inevitably transform the university from a place of learning into a base for political action. If this were to occur, the university would at once become socially and politically superfluous. It would have abandoned its authority and special claim upon popular attention. It would, as Professor Philip Rhinelander recently suggested . . .

—No.

Macksoud cut himself off and repeated the name, this time rolling the "R" to evoke images of Teutonic order.

> . . . as Professor Philip *Rrrrrrhine*lander recently suggested, have gone down into the arena where as merely one more gladiator it would in the rough and tumble soon fall victim to institutions more versed in the uses of such power. Is the university then to be wholly insulated from knowing and learning about the political process? Of course not! Political inquiry, expression, learning, and teaching are critical parts of the educative process. But distinctions must be made between political inquiry, expression, learning, and teaching and the use of the university to stage and execute political campaigns, and plan and direct social movements. If one cannot make meaningful distinctions here, then one might as well count the university as a third political party, an institution as politicized as it would be anti-intellectual, with an ethos favoring coercion over persuasion, intimidation over reason, threat over thought, and duress over dialogue. The description may already fit to whatever extent confrontation politics currently dictates the resolution of differences within the university. The commitment to impartial scholarship is perhaps one of the more difficult of commitments to make, not only because it is currently unfashionable with some students, and even with some faculty, but also because

it is more intellectually demanding of the individual than are most other endeavors, political ones included. The university will not long remain a center of learning without the dedication of its faculty to what Rhinelander . . .

—No.

. . . *Rrrrrrhine*lander has called the "exacting moral commitment" to impartial scholarship and the cultivation of young minds. The trend in American higher education, I regret, does not currently favor this view. I am hopeful, however, that by the mid-1970s the American university will with a more sensitive and responsive system of governance together with a reordering of its internal priorities reassert the primacy of scholarship and learning in the university and move into the 1980s with renewed confidence and vigor.

—This is signed David P. Gardner, Associate Professor of Higher Education and Vice Chancellor Executive Assistant, University of California, Santa Barbara. Have you ever heard anything sillier in your life?

I was the first to respond.

—It's a persuasive argument.

Macksoud looked surprised.

—What?

—It is. It's a persuasive argument.

—But look what it rests upon. It rests upon a distinction between the impartial pursuit of truth and knowledge over and against all this political strategizing that is going on. Do *you* see that distinction?

—No. But I've been in this class.

—Do you see a way of going about the impartial search for truth—capital "T"—and knowledge—capital . . . ah, "N"?

I smiled at the small joke as he continued.

—The whole notion of traditional values of scholarship being impartial in the pursuit of truth and knowledge is *nonsense*.

—But most people don't have that viewpoint! Most people who read this are going to respond favorably to it because they believe the university should not only uphold these traditional values but be the shining example of them.

—Yes, but this is why I read it to you. Because it seems to me that you ought to have a little different point of view on this—considering our failure in this class to come up with any examples of impartiality.

—Well I'm not saying the argument is persuasive to *me*. I'm just saying there's probably a wide majority who will find Gardner's thinking persuasive. It appeals to values people already have—and that's part of what we've talked about—how arguments are persuasive when they appeal to the values of the audience.

Macksoud went over to the window, lit up a cigarette, and stared out for a few seconds before responding.

—Well, I don't know. This seems to imply that if Professor Gardner, Vice-Chancellor Gardner, had been sitting here for the whole quarter, he, we must presume, would have been able to do all the things that we couldn't do. He would have been able to generate an unslanted sentence. He would have been able to tell us in pure thought what the relevant argument is, that is, to be able to cast it into several forms. He would have been able to tell us a clear objective set of values by which everybody must be governed. Nonsense! One wonders how somebody who is supposed to be intellectually trained and sets himself up in opposition to anti-intellectualism could conceivably think of truth and knowledge in that way. What I am suggesting is that the type of argument he presents in this letter should not appear to be persuasive to *himself*—because he is in a position to know better.

—But if Gardner acknowledges that impartiality is now fashionable to condemn, that suggests he's heard the arguments against it—and remains unpersuaded. That would seem to mean he believes there are forms of impartiality and objective truth.

Before Macksoud could respond, another classmate, Nathan, switched direction.

—Harry Girvetz. Does he represent our faculty? Is it as bad as he is?"

Macksoud grimaced. He was obviously not willing to participate in putting Girvetz down in an off-handed way. He came, however weakly, to his defense.

—Well, Harry Girvetz is in one sense a symbol of the community in that he thinks he is somewhat radical, thinks he is a liberal, but has discovered the limits of his liberalism.

Nathan hung on the word.

—Liberalism? I don't think he's the least bit liberal.

—Well, I think to some he looks the role. He's been politically of some importance to the university. He's been to some extent instrumental in getting as much faculty power as there is—which, as we have seen, is somewhat limited.

—But people like him have been hoarding the power of the faculty rather than trying to expand it.

—Well, that's what happens when you discover the limits of your liberalism. You begin to discover there are steps you are not prepared to take, and then you begin to move backwards, retracing your steps. You begin to see certain connections between things you thought were right and things being proposed now that don't hold. I think that twenty years ago Girvetz might have said junior faculty have no right to a voice in the governance of the university because they're only tentatively positioned in the educational process. But he moved toward a more liberal position on that and helped secure more power for all the faculty. Now when somebody comes along and says, students have a right to participate in this process, Girvetz says no. In other words, he is unwilling to extend the argument to include *all* the people who have some vested interest in the university.

—In other words he's willing to have power extended to his area and no further.

—I'm not sure he sees it that way.

—Yeah, but that seems to be in effect what happens.

—Well that's what happens, that's what happens. I think you should expect it to happen to you sometime.

Nathan looked shocked.

—I sure hope not.

Macksoud eyed him with a wry smile.

—Well, everybody hopes not, but pretty soon you go out and work for someone else, perhaps a large corporation.

Nathan straightened in his chair.

—You become a fat cat. The senior faculty doesn't know how to respond to a Bill Allen situation. They have for so long been exercising habitual power over these kinds of choices that they don't know what to do when those choices are limited. It's as if someone told you when you have been used to getting in your car and starting it every morning that you no longer have the right to start your car unless you get the approval of somebody else. You would not only be frustrated, you would be nonplussed. You have become too embedded in your habitual way of life. You get to feeling comfortable with that power you have in living your life . . .

Macksoud's words trailed off. Another thought had crossed his mind. He paused for a few seconds. Before he could continue, another classmate, Bruce, spoke out.

—I'm curious on two counts: number one, how many people share our rejection of the idea of plain truth that we're criticizing?

Macksoud was silent but Nathan answered.

—Very few

Bruce repeated it.

—Very few, obviously. The second point is, I'm not quite sure if we're really interpreting impartiality correctly. Perhaps impartiality in the sense people like Girvetz may think of it means, for example, impartiality as offering a multitude of sides or explanations or several modes or avenues of approach. That, to me, is what it would mean to be impartial. A teacher would be impartial if he offered several interpretations of something. Apparently not favoring anyone. So, in that sense, it would be possible to be impartial.

Since this argument had been addressed more than once in one form or another in previous classes, a slightly weary expression briefly crossed Macksoud's face as he answered.

—Now wait a minute. You're saying that it would be possible to do that in such a way that you would use equivalent language in each of these explanations? But you can't do that.

—Not totally, no. But you could give that impression.

—Well sure, but that's not impartiality. That's just cleverness. I would imagine that by investigating in a certain way you could give the *illusion* of impartiality. Say that you have investigated in the area you thought to yield all the alternatives there are. But that won't work. Because if you give three explanations of, say, a statute law, you omit four, five, and six. And there are infinite ways of expressing, say, a legal interpretation.

—Yes, but suppose you leave open the opportunity to add alternatives?

—Okay and then what? Fifteen more, so now you're up over twenty.

—And thereby the opportunity to fill out a more complete understanding.

—No, you're leaving open the opportunity to add yet another slanted alternative. You see how far this process goes?

Macksoud picked up the photocopied letter again, searched for a line, and began reading.

> I believe that the function of the university is to teach and to transmit knowledge and to train students in the processes whereby truth may be made known.

—Yes? How? What are these processes? Aren't they just the same processes that we have been bombarded with since the third grade? Ah yes, this is the "right" word, and oh no, this is the "wrong" word?

Bruce labored on.

—But how, then, do you seek knowledge? Without there being particular processes, are we just here to be trained in whatever processes?

—How can we talk about truth that way?

—Well, truth is certainly something that is out there.

—And to transmit knowledge.

—Transmit knowledge, say, in the sense of history, that sort of thing.

—A description of a series of events?

—Yes, that would be the limit of the transmission, that *something* did happen. But the interpretation, again, is quite different. You should be allowed the freedom to speak the interpretation you want about historical events.

—Perhaps, perhaps, but that isn't transmitting knowledge.

—Well, to the extent that you're transmitting knowledge to me—that's the choice of a particular event in history—by exposing me to a situation that I might then be able to interpret *myself*.

—For a purpose. But the purpose preceded the example, didn't it? I wasn't there transmitting knowledge. I had a specific purpose in mind for which I chose strategically a certain kind of example. If anyone has the impression that I've been saying this quarter that I'm here transmitting knowledge—that is a grossly incorrect impression. I don't say that my way of looking at things is less partial than others. What I am saying is: Can you really buy the statement: to transmit knowledge and to train students in the processes whereby truth may be made known?

Nathan broke in.

—As for Girvetz, all this strikes me as absolutely ridiculous because I happened to be in his philosophy class the first quarter and all he did the whole quarter was to refute the possibility of knowing anything and then . . .

—And then he goes out and . . .

—Yeah, lines up behind Gardner.

Macksoud went over to an ashtray on the desk to put out his cigarette. As he paused I re-entered the exchange.

—But in a class like this you are, in fact, teaching us something. And how would you go about characterizing that?

—I'm teaching you the only thing I can—my way of looking at things, which is certainly not *impartial* knowledge.

—So if the University isn't a place for teaching impartial knowledge, then it can't be a politically-free zone?

—Certainly not! And our experience of late would not contradict that. The attempt to draw a line like Gardner advocates between politically loaded and non-politically loaded instruction is something, as we have seen, that can't be done.

—But isn't that very understanding—the understanding that it can't be done—isn't that itself a kind of knowledge—let's say the kind of knowledge you've been teaching in this class?

—Yes, but again it doesn't lay claim to being an *impartial* knowledge—free of particular agendas—including political agendas.

—So what sort of political agenda are you selling us?

—I'm selling you the agenda that says: *Be absolutely and totally persuaded of . . . nothing at all.*

—That would seem to be a liberal position! So am I right to suppose that, unlike Girvetz, you support students having a role in the Academic Senate and in hiring and tenure decisions?

—I look at it this way. Just as the line between the partial and the impartial cannot be adequately drawn—in the same way I believe the line between faculty/administration and students cannot be adequately drawn. And so there ought not to be a sharp line *arbitrarily* drawn between the two. What faculty member has not continued to learn like a student? And what student has not taught a faculty member? But that doesn't argue that there shouldn't be hierarchy—because differences in power are inevitable, and in many ways productive. But it does argue that the hierarchy should be flexible, capable of orderly change, and that the hierarchy should be permeable by every party that has a stake in the institution. Students should be allowed some representation in decision-making. Legitimacy requires participation.

—So you were a supporter of the substance of the Bill Allen demonstrations?

—As student participation in the tenure process, yes.

—If you don't mind my asking, is the Speech Department aware of your views on that?

Macksoud raised his eyebrows and smiled.

—Yes, I'm sure they're aware.

—So do you think that liberal view will work against you?

—Well, I suppose it could. I'd like to think not since I'm currently up for tenure review.

—So you could become the next Bill Allen?

—No. In his position, I would take a different approach.

—What kind of approach?

—That would be telling.

—You can plead the fifth on this one, if you like. What about the bank? Do you think burning it down was the right thing to do?

—What do you think? Extrapolate from what we've argued in the class.

—Well, suppose we substitute "right" or "just" for "impartial." Actions and judgments always favor a particular set of values. As for violence, things like property damage, I don't know that we can rule out violence in principle. If we did, what becomes of the American Revolution? But when is violence justified?

—Perhaps the better question is: for whom is it justified? It gets complicated, doesn't it? But let's push on to the material for this class. The question you've raised is the start for an entirely new class.

*　*　*

Chapter 36

In the latter part of May, whether in class or out of class, the national political climate and reactions to Nixon's escalation of the war increasingly dominated everyone's attention. National outrage in response to the shootings at Kent State had not even begun to subside when on May 14 two student war protesters were killed by police gunfire at Jackson State University in Mississippi. This tragedy fueled another wave of protests on campuses across the country, sufficiently intense in some locations to force the closure of 75 American colleges for the remainder of the academic session. UCSB remained open but accomplished little in the way of normal academic work. The spread of the war into Cambodia redoubled fears among students like me who faced the draft that the war would not be ending anytime soon. On the local scene, Chancellor Cheadle's activation of a Grand Jury investigation of the bank burning meant renewed efforts for investigating the event, digging up evidence, and handing out indictments.

The Grand Jury task and what I knew about Caldwell convinced me to redouble my attempts to contact Caldwell. So one day the last week of May I caught a ride into town to pay him an evening visit.

As I neared his house, the windows showed no lights. Again no one answered. I walked off the porch and surveyed the house. It was an aging single story stucco house on a narrow lot. The left side of the house sat close to a high wooden fence separating it from the house next door. A section of the fence came to the front corner of the house where it met the stucco as a gate. I approached to take a closer look. Through a gap between the gate and the fence I saw two windows. It occurred to me that if one of those windows were open and the gate closed, a person could get into the house without being seen from the street. And the fence was high enough no one next door could see someone going through one of the windows. I imagined opening the gate and walking to the first window to at least have a look inside. But as I stood at the gate, a voice startled me from behind.

—You looking for someone?

I turned as a man in uniform approached the house from the sidewalk.

—Yeah, I'm looking for Officer Caldwell.

—That's me. What do you want?

—I'm checking with police involved in clearing the streets the night after the bank burning. I'm a photo journalist and I lost a camera when I was mistakenly arrested. I wonder if you recovered any cameras or know of anyone who did?

Caldwell stared at me for a few moments, then climbed the porch and unlocked the door as he answered.

—You look more like a student than some fancy journalist. If you were on the streets that night you were in violation of curfew. As for any cameras, if I knew of any I wouldn't be of a mind to say a thing about them. If you lost a camera, it's likely to stay lost. Officers who were there aren't inclined to be very cooperative with anyone they met on the streets that night. And events since then haven't made any of us feel more cooperative.

I now realized I hadn't prepared myself well enough for this encounter. I searched for a good way forward, but took too long finding it. He closed the door in my face. As I walked away, I was more convinced than ever he had taken a camera that night, just as Lampert had suggested. Whether it was mine or not I might never know.

* * *

Chapter 37

As with the first week of May, the first week of June brought a renewal of barely submerged tensions on and off campus. On June 3rd news leaked from the Grand Jury regarding impending indictments for 17 alleged perpetrators of the February 25th bank burning. If convicted, those indicted faced not only jail time but expulsion from the University. Further indictments were rumored to be in the works but a date for a formal announcement by the Grand Jury had not been revealed. According to one report in the *El Gaucho*, only three names among those indicted were leaked. Reward money played a role in testimony leading to the identification of those three, two of whom claimed to have been in the Santa Barbara County Jail the evening of the bank burning. The impending indictments in addition to the role of reward money leading to apparently false accusations stirred suspicion and anger throughout campus and Isla Vista. If someone in jail the evening of the bank burning could be indicted, it seemed no one was safe from police harassment and severe University sanctions.

The following day, Thursday, Canova and I came across each other at the Isla Vista Market. After the Moran shooting, our paths had progressively drifted apart. For me, it fit my current pattern. Melanie and I had drifted apart. And although Matt and I still roomed together, we mostly avoided conversation.

As we talked, I sensed Canova was extremely angry about the forthcoming indictments. He asked if I was still worried about my own fate in that regard. Before I knew it, I found myself relating my conversation with Caldwell—to which he responded hotly.

—That asshole! It's obvious he has someone's camera—and it could be yours. Since he stole it, you should steal it back.

—The thought occurred to me.

—Do it, man. Stake out his place, watch him leave, then find a way into his house. He has it coming. Just do it!

This felt like a dead end I had been down. So I re-directed.

—You're still hot about the cops, aren't you?

—You kidding me? You know what these guys are doing! Now these stinking indictments! The cops are having a field day! Listen, there's a protest at Perfect Park tonight at five o'clock. You're invited but it could get wild.

—What do you mean "wild"?

—You know what I mean.

—One death on the steps of that bank isn't enough for you?

—One Vietnam is still one too many for me. Surprise me and show up. You've got more at risk here than most, number one.

Before I could reply he walked away.

Anticipating more rioting that evening, I stayed in the apartment. With respect to staying out of jail, that turned out to be a good choice. According to the campus radio station, the gathering at Perfect Park served to collect volunteers to circulate a petition against the indictments. Flyers were also circulated announcing a rally protesting the indictments to be held at noon on Friday behind the UCEN.

Anticipating another assault on the bank, a sizeable number of peacekeepers formed near the Park. The defenders now included a mix of faculty, students, and Isla Vista residents who were sick of the street violence. Matt left the apartment but wouldn't say where he was going. When I fell asleep slightly past midnight, he still hadn't returned.

Friday morning I was awakened by an early call from Officer Lampert. He wanted me to meet him at the Campus Police offices at eleven o'clock. He wouldn't tell me what it was about, but he said it was important. When I arrived, Lampert showed me into a private room.

—Sit down, Dan.

—Why'd you want to see me?

—I have something to show you.

Lampert pulled what looked to be five by seven photographs from a manila envelope. My stomach plunged like it had taken a rollercoaster dip. I imagined, laid out on the table in front of us, my photos from inside the bank the night of its burning. As Lampert actually laid the photos one by one on the table, the sinking feeling got worse. But the photos weren't what I imagined.

—Do these look familiar to you?

I hesitated, but the answer was already written on my face.

—When were they taken?

—Back in January

—Why did you do this?

I couldn't think fast enough to invent anything resembling a defense of Melanie's chaste virtue. So I fumbled forward, trying to minimize the details.

—She asked me to. Said she could pay me.

—Pay you?

—Look, I didn't agree to shoot her naked. She sprung that on me while we were shooting.

—And you thought nothing of it?!

I thought of a sarcastic response to that question, but held it back.

—She asked me not to freak out and just keep shooting.

—Did you ask her why she was doing this?

—Yeah, but only after the shoot.

—And what did she say?

—Maybe you'd better ask her about that.

—I'm asking you, now. What did she say?

I didn't answer.

—I'm going to find out, one way or another.

—I don't feel it's right for me to say anything about it. You need to talk to her about it.

—Believe me, I intend to. But I want your report on it now. What did she say?

—It's not my place to talk about it. She asked me to photograph her. I did that, and that's all I have to say about it.

Lampert opened a leather briefcase and took out another manila envelope. After collecting and placing the photos of Melanie in a stack on the corner of the table, he opened the envelope and pulled out another group of photos. One by one, he placed these on the table. Once again I took the rollercoaster dip as a clammy sweat collected under my shirt.

—Recognize these?

There was no question in my mind. The camera angles, the sequence of shots—they were my photos of the bank the night of its burning. I stared at the photos and could say nothing. What seemed at times like overly paranoid fears about my photos landing in the hands of police had materialized. I couldn't believe it, but there they were.

—Seems to me you're a guy who got around a lot with that camera of yours—until you lost it.

—Where did you get these?

—Can't tell you that right now. What I can tell you is that no one but you and me and a fencepost knows that I have them.

He swept the photos into a pile, tapped them into alignment, and placed them back in the manila envelope.

—My daughter is not always honest with me. I need for you to be.

I got the picture. A friendly inducement to rat her out. It didn't seem like a big deal considering what was potentially at stake for me. He'd probably find out the truth anyway. But I couldn't shake the feeling he was going about everything in the wrong way—and in a very ugly way.

—Look, you're making it an interrogation. Can't you just talk to her? She won't lie to you. I don't get the feeling she'll lie to you. And it's best for all this to come from her.

Lampert got up from the table, put the pictures of Melanie in his briefcase, and leveled a stare at me.

—I'd appreciate knowing what you can tell me before I talk to her. I'm not meeting with her until tomorrow. If you change your mind, call me. Here's a number where you can reach me. If I'm not there, leave a message about when to call you back.

He handed me a card and turned for the door. I couldn't let him leave on that note.

—What's your plan for me?

—That depends on you.

*   *   *

Chapter 38

The noon rally behind the UCEN brought to a head, once again, months of animosity toward the bank and the Vietnam War. Several anti-war groups organized the rally. Canova was among the speakers. Their method of protest consisted of getting everyone at the rally to sign a petition and deliver it to the bank. The petition requested the bank rescind all seventeen indictments. Everyone knew the chances of that happening were nonexistent, but the document created the opportunity for a direct confrontation and the potential for escalation. Following the rally, a group of about 150 marched to the bank and entered the lobby to present the petition. I followed along to see what would happen. To no one's surprise, bank officials dismissed the petition and turned its presenters away. To remove them from the lobby, the bank had to close early. But the crowd remained around the bank and increased in size as the afternoon progressed. By early evening, a familiar situation emerged. The crowd clearly divided between the peacekeepers who wanted to prevent rioting and property damage and the radicals who wanted to close the bank by rendering the building unusable.

Once again Matt joined the ranks of the peacekeepers. Canova and several members of his anti-war group had disappeared, perhaps waiting for a better opportunity later in the evening when the bank defenders might tire and give up. It was unbelievable—how similar everything was to the night Kevin Moran was shot. I felt the oppressive madness of it and thought about leaving. Then Melanie came to mind. I calculated she would likely be home by now. I needed to talk to her before her father did, and I was thankful to have an excuse to leave the area of the bank.

When I knocked on her door she opened it only a foot.

—Hi.

—Can I talk to you for a minute?

—Yeah, what's up?

She didn't move the door an inch.

—Can I come in?

—Okay—for a minute. I'm studying for finals.

She opened the door and motioned for me to sit on the bed that served as the couch in her living room. I sat down as she took a cigarette from a pack on the kitchen table and lit it.

—What are you studying?

—*Medea*.

—I see. I was hoping it might be a comedy.

—Yeah, I'm a real comedian these days.

She spoke dryly and took a drag from her cigarette as I futilely tried to change her attitude.

—Good. That could be handy.

—What does that mean?

I couldn't delay any longer.

—Okay, here goes. I found your photos.

A bit of life returned to her eyes.

—Really?! Where the hell are they, Marleau?

—Well . . . you see, it's like . . . somehow . . . your dad has them.

The look of shock and disbelief on her face rivaled Janet Leigh's in *Psycho*.

—Are you shitting me?

With mixed anger and exasperation she groped to make some sense of it.

—How is that even possible, Marleau??

—He wouldn't tell me how or where he got the photos.

—It doesn't make any sense!!

She dropped the forgotten cigarette on the kitchen floor. Gesturing hands flew in the air as she spoke.

—What did you do, just hand them over to him and say, here, check out your daughter's new wardrobe??

My blood pressure and voice rose to meet hers.

—Stop it. I've been screwed on this deal just like you. I don't know what went wrong. But something's crazy, and I'm going to figure it out.

—I'll tell you what's crazy—my having anything to do with you! How could you mess up any more than allowing those photos to get into my dad's hands? For God's sake. It's too damn freaking much, Marleau!

She picked up her cigarette butt and threw it into the sink with disgust. I got up and walked to the door.

—You're right. It is too much. I feel badly about this.

I hesitated at the door and decided to risk a parting question.

—What are you going to tell him?

—Well he's not going to believe anything but the truth, is he? I didn't want him knowing anything before the fact, before a contract. Now that plan is a mess. He'll find a way to ruin it. Then he'll cut off the money for school.

—You really think he'd do that?

—I don't know. Please leave. I just need to get through this quarter and then figure something out.

I felt small and flattened enough to crawl out without bothering to open the door. In my deflated condition I didn't see what I could possibly do at the scene of the bank, other than be a piece of kindling for the fire, so I returned to my apartment.

As it turned out, the defenders prevented break in or serious damage to the bank. But without their presence, it was clear to all observers during the night that the bank would have been attacked and probably destroyed again. Those intent on destruction didn't disperse until after 3:00am, so those defending the bank were up most of the night. Several residents of Isla Vista who were among the defenders contacted the Sheriff's office before daylight to request that police defend the bank the following evening. The prospect of another all night defense had become too much to manage for the community locals.

*   *   *

Chapter 39

Renewed disturbances on the streets of Isla Vista and around the bank produced a sense of foreboding in the minds of law enforcement that only increased with the news that Tom Hayden would return to campus on Saturday. The response to the refusal to allow Jerry Rubin to speak in April apparently convinced administration officials that silencing members of the famous Chicago trial would not accomplish what they desired. But few in the administration were convinced that allowing such visits would go without consequences either. The lesser of two evils strategy prevailed. Police were put on heightened alert for a possible repeat of the bank burning riots of February.

This time Hayden spoke, as Kunstler had, at the Campus Stadium but to a much smaller crowd. Before Hayden appeared, Phyllis Bennis took the podium to speak about the Santa Barbara 17—those who had just been indicted for the bank burning on June 6th. She read a statement on their behalf.

The statement consisted primarily of a polemic against the Grand Jury, including the partisan and conflicted interests of its elite constituency, and the frontier justice, rush to judgment, baseless charges against the defendants. They underscored the seriousness of the charges against them by reporting they faced a combined total of over 600 years in prison, ranging from 43 to 21 years. According to their statement, the Grand Jury consisted entirely of friends and acquaintances of Superior Court justices rather than, as required by law, a cross-section of the community. Regarding conflict of interest, the statement claimed that the foreman of the Jury was a director of the Santa Barbara National Bank. Most other members were involved in real estate, finance, or insurance businesses—occupations that would disqualify them from serving on a trial jury in this particular case. All told, the Jury acted without good reason, according to the defendants, in order to punish a handful of persons associated with the segment of the population deemed sympathetic with the bank burning.

After reading the statement, Phyllis added remarks of her own that, under the circumstances, seemed to play into the hands of the Grand Jury and the District Attorney. She acknowledged that the defendants were only a few among probably a thousand or more, including herself, who were in or around

225

the bank the night it was burned. Speaking of the crowd, she said, "We were all there. Those of us who did not burn the bank have a responsibility to these 17 to help them in any way we can to get justice for their trial. If anybody is here who did burn the bank, they have an even greater responsibility to help these people attain justice."

As I sat listening in the stadium bleachers, her appeal to the crowd triggered the thought that these indictments, flimsy as they appeared to be, were merely a strategy to pressure others to identify the real perpetrators or perhaps finesse them out of hiding. Nevertheless, failing that, the D. A. would doubtless do everything possible to convict the birds in hand because, like Phyllis, they knew those indicted were at the bank the night of the burning and probably knew who was responsible. And, facing convictions, those indicted might be persuaded to point fingers—especially since they might lose student deferments with expulsion from the university for any conviction, even a misdemeanor, relating to the riots.

In contrast to the brief remarks of the Santa Barbara 17, Tom Hayden embarked on a long-winded and rambling homily for well over an hour. He began with words that left no doubt where he stood regarding the tactic of property damage as a means of violent protest.

> When we were briefly in Cook County Jail, we appreciated very much the uprising that occurred here in the burning of the bank. And we're committed to the carrying out of the objectives and the ideals of the 17 and the others who were on the streets in Santa Barbara that night and other times.

He noted that the so-called Chicago "conspiracy" was only part of a larger "conspiracy" across the land for which others had also been indicted and were being tried. Since many of these activists had supported them when they were on trial, the Chicago Eight now supported all those on trial for similar radical forms of protest. In that spirit, he pledged $5000 for the Santa Barbara 17 defense fund.

Hayden then turned to a discussion of, as he put it, "what is going on." The number of "drop-outs" from society had now increased, according to Hayden, to the point where the word "drop-out" failed to convey the breadth of what must now be described as a "new society," a new "youth culture." The police chiefs and legislative officials of the country recognized these enclaves of radical youth culture and saw places like Isla Vista and Berkeley as "swamps infested with the radical disease and in need of being cleaned out." The Pentagon

226

and the Department of Defense operated from "war rooms" that mapped out the locations of these radical enclaves and established plans for quick militant response to repress these centers of activism and put down what they regarded as insurrections.

Hayden then formed an analogy between the actions of the heads of these "war rooms" and the actions taken by Chiang Kai-shek in the domination of Yunnan province. This comment then triggered for Hayden a set of associations regarding international revolutionary movements with which he clearly felt American left activism could and should be aligned—and from which much could be learned. Specifically, he named the regimes of Mao Zedong and Ho Chi Minh. In the case of Vietnam, he continued to elaborate by forming an analogy between the "repression" in the United States and the "repression" of the Vietnamese, stating that Americans could anticipate what will happen here by observing what has happened under U. S. dominance in South Vietnam. Comparing the struggle for liberation in the United States with the long struggle for freedom and enormous loss of life among Vietnamese, Hayden remarked, "If the Vietnamese have not begun to complain about the repression, if the Vietnamese still talk of a victorious struggle for their own national survival and their own liberation, then we have a long way to go and a lot of blood to shed before we have any right to complain about what has happened to ourselves."

The fervent conviction displayed in these remarks, which the crowd matched in its own response, fueled further speculation about the motives of the Nixon administration. Hayden launched into a history of the Cold War and the pivotal role of the actions of Richard Nixon in the United States' opposition to communism within the country and around the world. Nixon opposed the spread of communism into Vietnam and advocated U. S. military involvement in Vietnam, in support of the French, as early as 1953. Hayden went on to claim that Nixon's order to send troops into Cambodia initiated a secret plan to place American troops in peril precisely for the purpose of enabling him to instigate a crisis justifying the use of nuclear weapons on North Vietnam. And this was only the beginning of the secret plan. The use of nuclear weapons on North Vietnam was intended to agitate the Chinese and provoke a Sino-American confrontation necessitating the pre-emptive use of nuclear weapons on nuclear weapons facilities deep inside China.

Such an attack on China, according to Hayden, had been the goal of the "China lobby" in government since the beginning of the Cold War. This "China lobby," ensconced in the Watergate complex, allied itself with the government of Chiang Kai-shek in opposition to Red China and looked for ways to reclaim the mainland. According to Hayden, Nixon backed the "China lobby" and acted to help create the right set of provocations through the Vietnam conflict in order to launch a nuclear attack against Red China.

Hayden then turned to the student strikes of the month of May which, in effect, stood against the pressing reality of Nixon's secret plan and caused him to falter. Hayden described student actions across the country during the last month as exemplary of a broad "bombastic and militant" trend among protesters. California campuses such as Santa Barbara and Berkeley stood out in the role they played. Hayden praised Berkeley activists for doing "more material damage to university buildings, to the ROTC, to the radiation laboratory, and the counter-insurgency departments than had ever been done before. And these actions were being led, not even by the relatively conservative students, but by the high school and even junior high school students in Berkeley." Hayden continued, noting that throughout the country during this period there had been a great escalation of violence from the time in February when the Chicago trial ended to the time in May when the Cambodian invasion began. Again, Hayden left no doubt about his approval of these violent tactics in relation to government property and his belief that such tactics remained the only effective way to promote the revolutionary agenda.

> This period saw the greatest damage to university facilities, the greatest number of bombings of military installations, draft boards, and university military centers that has occurred in the ten year history of the student movement. It seems there are still a lot of people who believe that revolution is not necessary, that violence is not necessary, that the system should be given one more serious chance at reform, that the universities should somehow be reconstituted, that a new, broader force should be mobilized so as to bring about a policy change by showing the strength of public opinion to the politicians in Washington. I think that this judgment on the part of millions of people is wrong in a very strange sense. It is wrong because people underestimate their own power. It is wrong because people fail to realize that it is precisely the disruption on the campuses that brought Richard Nixon trembling to the press conferences, that made Nixon announce that he was going to get out of Cambodia as soon as possible, that made Nixon run out and talk about sunshine and surfing with all those people at the Washington Monument. It was exactly the disruptions, it was exactly the madmen, the maniacs, the crazies, the people that everybody wants to stay an arm's length away from, who brought about the crisis, who brought about the strikes, and brought

the conditions under which there could even be consideration of the reconstitution of universities. And it's those crazy people we owe our thanks to. Remember the 1966 and '67 situation where it was considered crazy to burn your draft card? Now it's considered crazy to burn a bank. It was those people who were considered the lunatic fringe. At best they were a kind of far out moral conscience that we could respect, but they were not effective. They didn't know how to use conventional channels of change. This brought the reaction from more conservative people that such actions will only bring on fascism, that instead we've got to work for a more responsible and broad-based movement. Then along came Senator Eugene McCarthy, remember him? He said he would offer a more effective way for people to become involved in the conventional political process so they could have an effect on the Vietnam War. So in the Spring of '68 people decided to be "Clean for Gene."

Hayden then remarked that these hopes were dashed in Chicago by the Democratic Party machine led by Mayor Daley and his Gestapo cops. And, upon losing the nomination for President, candidate McCarthy decided his next step would be to cover the World Series for *Life Magazine*. Hayden continued:

That's what happens. That's what happens. The crisis was only intensified by showing our strength in the conventional arenas and leaving the streets behind. But by leaving the so-called crazy forms of protest behind, we left ourselves in a weak position from which we did not recover for over a year, because by the end of 1968 we no longer had a militant anti-war movement on the campuses or in the streets or anywhere else. We had a lot of confusion. We had a lot of people who didn't know what to do. We had lost our bearings, our organizational strength, and had nowhere to go. All this should point up the tremendous mistake we made. But people now should realize that by using conventional avenues of protest and opposition, such as working to get the Senate to cut off funds for Vietnam, they should realize that by these very conventional activities they are undertaking, that instead of calming the social crisis, instead of ending the war in Southeast Asia, they inflame it further by making the generals, the people in the Pentagon and the Whitehouse veto any Congressional activity and go for broke in Southeast Asia. By using the conventional channels today we may create a deeper Constitutional crisis and in that case, if you consider yourself a surfer, you better look around for the bums Nixon was talking about because the bums are the only people who are going to be able to handle the situation under fascism that the surfers are bringing on.

Speaking of the surfers prompted Hayden to transition into taking a critical look at the current youth protest culture and the parallel development of "alienated white culture." Here Hayden cast a stone at youth slogans, saying that the time to put forward the idea of "dope, rock and roll, and fucking in the streets" was over, was long gone, and might even be considered counter-revolutionary. Hayden called for the next step, which was to figure out what would constitute a revolution *within* the Cultural Revolution. He asked everyone to consider what would enable us all to defeat the fascist plan and survive to develop a new society.

As part of his critical glance at the counterculture, Hayden made reference to the recent Altamont Rolling Stones concert and questioned why it had suddenly appeared to many people to be a good idea for the Hell's Angels to serve as the police and security force for the counterculture. Hayden excoriated a "strident, aggressive, power-tripping, male egoism," adding that the only difference between Mick Jagger and the Hell's Angels was the music. These thoughts coincided with his view of the essentially counter-productive, if not destructive, American inclination toward individualism.

> If males in the culture can understand feminism in no other way, we can certainly understand it as part of the revolution in the culture that is necessary if we are going to put ourselves on new footing. There's also no question that if we are going to survive fascism, individualism is going to have to come to an end. Individual creativity, self-expression, doing your own thing have to be very carefully reexamined and redefined in situations where our communities are crawling with police, where our communities are full of eavesdropping mechanisms, and where the very idea of standing out and the macho man mentality is suicidal—not only to the individual but to the community. If rugged individualism is so strong in our culture that it cannot be overcome, then we cannot have a revolution. We cannot do it. Not only because the revolution has to be about the abolition of individualism but because individualism is inconsistent with the kinds of organizations and institutions that we have to build to survive. Here we can take a tip from what the racists say about the

orientals—that they are "inscrutable." Inscrutable means that the white man can't tell a farmer from a factory worker, can't tell the meaning of facial expressions, can't tell an ally from a Viet Cong. Everybody more or less looks and sounds the same to them. What they call the faceless Viet Cong or the inscrutable oriental is nothing but a culture of people who know that their survival as a collective, their survival as a culture, their survival as a national community is at stake, not their own individual egoism.

Hayden went on to tell the story of a conversation he had with a member of the Vietnamese underground against the French when he visited North Vietnam a couple of years ago. The need for strict security was so extreme that the man and his sister each worked in the underground for five years and did not discover the other's involvement until after the French occupation ended. Hayden warned, "Things are not that heavy here today, but they may be tomorrow. But I think we can learn from this so-called oriental inscrutability just what kind of issue is a stake. And the issue is that of solidarity with each other, not a phony, individualistic, do your own thing."

In conclusion, Hayden returned to praising the local radicals for their action in burning the bank. For such bold initiative Isla Vistans now represented part of the "vanguard" in the current state of the "conspiracy movement." He added that he and other members of the Chicago Eight would not continue to give such talks as he had given today because they were no longer exemplary of the kind of radicality he desired to see in the movement. More revolutionary expressions of power were possible and necessary.

> We can be a resource for you but we are not your leaders because in the burning of the bank, in the hitting of the streets, in the organizing of your collectives, we have seen people younger than us becoming the new vanguards of the revolution. And by that I don't mean vanguards in the sense of people giving orders but vanguards in the sense of people who show their leadership and provide the example and show the way through revolutionary action that others can follow. All power to those kinds of vanguards.

If Hayden had wanted to avoid any possible repetition of the Chicago indictment for inciting a riot, he left nothing in the bag that would preclude the possibility of the District Attorney leveling such charges against him. The local authorities certainly anticipated a riot. Following Hayden's inflammatory afternoon appearance, Sheriff Webster installed a ring of police around the bank and kept them stationed there through the evening hours. Nevertheless, late in the evening, a large crowd gathered across the street from the bank. In response, a sound truck drove through the loop area announcing an 11:00pm curfew followed shortly by several officers in a plywood-sided police dump truck. Although tensions between the police and the crowd were high, the constant police presence succeeded in preventing an attack on the bank.

On Sunday the mood in Isla Vista shifted, oddly enough, from street riots to the distractions of a street fair. Scheduled several weeks earlier and staged at the northern edge of Isla Vista near the intersection of Los Carneros and El Colegio Roads, this event, called the Pleasure Faire, offered booths for arts and crafts vendors, stalls for games, and a noon until dusk series of bands—mostly local musicians.

Based on my recent talk with Lampert, I knew he had planned to speak to Melanie on Saturday. I needed to find out what he had said to her and what was in store for both of us. I hadn't told Melanie about the bank photos because I didn't want anything more getting between her and her father than already filled that space. But I was also more than a little curious to see if Lampert leaked any of that news to her or whether he was keeping it between the two of us. So, although, I knew the welcome mat wouldn't be out, I paid Melanie another visit. This time she wouldn't even open the door when I knocked.

—Go away, Marleau. I've got to study.

—It didn't go well, huh?

—What're you talking about?

—You and your dad. You talked didn't you?

—So what? I'm not talking about it.

—C'mon, Melanie. Let me in for a minute. I want to know what happened.

She flung the door open and walked into the kitchen, heading for her pack of cigarettes. I closed the door behind me and leaned against it. I wasn't going to stay long. After lighting the cigarette, she threw me a crumb.

—He's totally pissed off at me. I told him I wanted to be on my own. He said that's what college is for—that I would have plenty of time on my own after I graduate. Then I broke the news that graduating would take longer because I changed my major to drama. Then he got even hotter.

—What did he say?

She drew a puff from the cigarette and blew out the smoke.

—He said that's not what we agreed on. He only budgeted for two more years and I need to get back into education. I said that's why I need to pay my

232

own way. Then he brought up the pictures again and things blew out from there. We started yelling at each other. Then something came in on his radio. He said he had to go.

—So is he going to cut you off?

—I don't know. He'll probably badger me to death to change my major. That'll drive me insane.

She drew from her cigarette again and changed the subject.

—You know, that radio call he got was scary. Something about a guy who brought dynamite into Isla Vista.

—Dynamite?

—I guess they have a suspect and they're trying to find him. The radicals must be tired of trying to burn the damn bank down so now they're going to blow it up. I guess they haven't learned enough from what matches and guns do. They think they can blow it up and nobody will get hurt?

—Maybe they don't care who gets hurt.

—You're getting cynical, Marleau.

—Cynicism—that's what college is for. Look what it's done for you.

—I'm not cynical. I'm angry.

—I can see that. Why don't you come out for a while? Let's go to the Pleasure Faire. You could use a break.

—I've got too much reading to do. Now that I've told the ol' man about my change of major, I'm not going to flunk out of drama.

I opened the door and started to leave, then stopped and closed the door.

—The film—it's my fault. Somehow it must have gotten mixed in with the stuff the Sheriff's office took a few weeks ago. A detective came by my place with a subpoena. They're collecting photos to help indict people for the Allen demonstrations. I'm really sorry.

—Jesus, I didn't know you were subpoenaed. A lot of shit's been coming down everywhere. I guess we just have to get through it.

I nodded agreement. And with little hint of levity, she added the last word as I opened the door again.

—But don't think I won't be getting even with you.

As soon as I left Melanie's place the news she had provided about Lampert's radio call suddenly struck me. It only took putting the mention of dynamite alongside what I knew about Canova's obsession with the bank. What was he up to? I hurried along the several blocks to his store and found him sitting behind his desk reading from a book of Italian poetry. Since there were two customers in the store, I walked to the back and motioned for him to follow me. He gave me a questioning look but followed. As soon as we were behind the curtain separating the room from the rest of the store, I spoke in a stifled whisper.

—Do you know anything about some dynamite that's made its way into Isla Vista?

I watched his face for the slightest sign of recognition. It didn't present much to read, but the fact that he showed little surprise troubled me. He shook his head to indicate no and asked what I was talking about.

—If that's true, you won't mind my taking a look around.

I scanned the place with my eyes and fastened on a piece of fabric he had tacked across the platform that served as a small bed. Impulsively, I grabbed the fabric and ripped it off, exposing several cardboard boxes underneath. Kneeling down, I pulled one out. Canova then pushed me over with his foot.

—What do you think you're doing? Stay out of there!

I stood up and grabbed the front of his shirt with both hands.

—I'm trying to keep you . . .

Before I could finish, he grabbed my shirt and pushed back. Neither of us let go and we rolled to the floor, jerking each other around by our shirts until mine ripped apart. Losing my temper, I punched him in the stomach as he barely missed kneeing me in the groin. After a few more seconds of flailing and knocking over a small table full of candles and books, a familiar voice suddenly stunned both of us.

—Gawd! What are you two doing?

—Melanie?

Canova and I stopped scuffling. I let go of his shirt, sat up, and mumbled a reply.

—I thought you were studying.

She leaned against the doorway, still showing surprise.

—I thought you were at the Pleasure Faire.

As Canova and I stood up, I noticed my ripped shirt dangling below my waist. Before either of us found anything more to say, Melanie turned to Canova.

—I need a copy of Shaw's *Major Barbara*. Can you help me?

Canova tucked in his shirt and politely indicated for Melanie to follow him. He took her to a shelf near the front of the store and pulled out a volume. As he did so, a guy emerged in a bathrobe from under the fabric skirting a rustic table—more precisely a weathered wooden ship's hatch supported by two pillars cut from a palm tree. He held a toothbrush and walked across the floor past me and into the toilet room. Melanie stared in disbelief and couldn't resist comment.

—I hope he's paying rent!

Canova shrugged.

—I thought he had left a couple of days ago.

Melanie handed him some money, shot a smile toward me as I watched from the back of the store, and walked out. Since the two customers who were in the store when I arrived had left, we were now alone in the room. I walked up to him as he put the money in his lock box.

—I don't know what you're planning, but know this. The cops are onto the dynamite. They know how it got into I.V. and if you're involved and that stuff gets used, they'll find you. You'll go to jail for a long time. It's a stupid play, man. That's all I'm saying about it. You can thank Melanie for the tip. Goodbye.

I left the store. Canova stood at his desk and said nothing.

*　*　*

Chapter 40

Sunday evening brought a turning point in the current wave of assaults on the bank. Police continued guarding it during the day, but as evening approached they withdrew and collected in the area of the crowd at the Pleasure Faire. This action came as a result of the need to enforce the curfew, which the Sheriff had tightened from 11:00pm the previous evening to 7:30pm—apparently in an effort to minimize the need for police around the bank that night. Unfortunately for the police, most people were unaware of this change and when the organizers of the Pleasure Faire were informed of it, they asked for an extension to at least 9:00pm. Musicians had been playing most of the day, but the main band entertainment was scheduled for 8:00pm. As word of the 7:30 curfew spread among the crowd, tensions rose.

Finally, only a few minutes before the deadline, police announced an extension of the curfew to 9:00pm. This decision defused tensions and the Faire continued. The final band played until 9:00pm and then, as agreed, stopped playing and packed their equipment. But as people returned to apartments in Isla Vista, a few discovered the bank unguarded. Word traveled and the crowd grew. Shortly after 10:00pm a faction in the crowd launched a heavy assault on the bank.

The front doors were smashed. One firebomb was tossed inside and another on the roof. Once again police in full riot gear arrived in dump trucks to put out the fires, clear the streets, and make arrests. The severity of the attack caused Sheriff Webster to call on the mutual aid system established in the wake of the previous bank riots. This response team included forces from Ventura County, the California Highway Patrol, the Santa Barbara City Police, and the Los Angeles Tactical Squad. These outside forces included many who had experienced the rock throwing rioting of previous Isla Vista disturbances. Short on patience and long on payback, the actions of these men led to many complaints filed on Monday. Reports of police brutality, misconduct, careless use of teargas, and illegal entry reached epidemic numbers.

The crackdown continued through Monday and Tuesday evenings with the return of the 7:30pm curfew and more street patrols by the combined "mutual aid" forces. Although the bank remained secure, street arrests escalated through strict enforcement of the curfew. The 26 arrests on Sunday evening grew to 86 on Monday evening and 142 on Tuesday. Filed reports of police misconduct, which were already legion, also grew and increased in severity of reported abuses. According to newspaper accounts, these reports most often named members of the L. A. Tactical unit as the prime offenders.

The imposition of the curfew also coincided with the beginning of final exams, a number of which were scheduled at times extending beyond the curfew. Administration officials were forced to arrange for special bus transportation between Isla Vista and campus to accommodate evening exams. Late afternoon on Wednesday, June 10, attempts by administration officials and Isla Vista community leaders to move the curfew to a later time met with stiff resistance from the Sheriff's Office and the county Board of Supervisors. This intransigence on the part of the Sheriff and the Supervisors served to ignite simmering frustrations among a broad spectrum of concerned parties ranging from students, faculty, administration, local clergy, Isla Vista community leaders, and residents. As a result, a small group of angry students organized a sit-in protest to begin at 6:00pm in Perfect Park.

Shortly after six o'clock I received a rare phone call from Canova. He called from the bookstore and asked me to stop by because he had something to show me. I asked what it was, but he just repeated that I should get over to his store. When I arrived, we reversed roles from the previous meeting. He nodded for me to follow him to the back room. I wondered if he wanted to take up fighting where we had left off. Instead he opened a cupboard door, pulled out what looked like a photocopy of an eight by ten photograph, and handed it to me.

—Does this look familiar?

At first glance it did look familiar. I scanned it for a few seconds to take in the details. Then I was sure.

—This is one of the photos I took at the ranch during the Radical Union meeting. I remember when I took it, where I was standing, and how everyone is positioned. It's definitely mine. Where did you get this?

—The same place as this.

He reached into the cupboard again and held up a camera.

—I believe this is yours?

I slowly reached out and took the camera. It was missing the strap and the top of the case, but every detail matched down to the slight dent on the viewfinder. A 500 DTL Mamiya Sekor single lens reflex with mid-range telephoto lens. There it was. My camera.

—Where in the world did you get this?

—Sit down. It's a story I'll love telling for a long time.

Holding the camera in my hands in stunned disbelief, I sat down on the floor since a chair wasn't handy. Canova noticed me checking the camera for film as he sat on his makeshift bed.

—Your film isn't in it, but without the camera they'll have a hard time tying any pictures to you.

I thought of Lampert and the prints. Canova had a point. Cameras left identifying tracks on film negatives just as gun barrels left identifying marks on bullets. But if the camera couldn't be located, then all bets were off. A cautious sense of relief crept over me as Canova began his story.

—Monday afternoon I was sick of the cops and sick of Isla Vista, so I decided later that evening to kill two birds with one stone. I borrowed a car and went into Santa Barbara with Cactus, this street guy who hangs out in front of the store all the time. I figured every cop in Santa Barbara would be busy that night. I knew this cop's address from when you and I stopped there before. So we drove to his house. Cactus watched the perimeter as I cased the place. It looked easy enough to break into through a side window I found partly open. Seeing there was good cover with a fence and no lights on, I took a chance and went for it.

—You broke into his place?

—I busted the screen and was through the window in seconds. After searching around for a few minutes, I found the camera in a closet by the back door sitting on a shelf above some coats. I remembered the name and figured from what we knew about this guy there was a good chance it was yours. On the way out, I noticed this photo pinned to the wall along with some others above a small desk. Something about it registered. I thought it might be one of yours, so I took it. I went out the back door and around through the gate. Got in the car with Cactus and we blew out of there like tomb raiders. Haven't felt that high in months.

I stared at Canova, dumbfounded. Then I eyed the camera again. From a flood of questions, one finally surfaced.

—Why did you do it? That was a big risk to take for the chance of finding my camera.

—Well that's just it. You see, it's not your camera. It's mine.

I looked at him stupidly and he grinned back.

—I figure it this way. Remember we had this bet. We agreed that if you got out from behind the camera and joined the movement, then I'd win the camera. After that you wouldn't need it anyway. You were finally in it, really in it—until

238

the Moran killing broke everything apart. I knew the cops would screw things up. And they did it in a bad way that night. I hoped it wouldn't be that way.

I continued looking at him blankly as he reached over and took the camera out of my hands.

—A deal's a deal, man. I won the camera, but I knew if I wanted it I'd need to find the damn thing. When you're playing poker, you've got to take better care of the pot! Look around. You see I haven't burned down my store!

—You haven't managed to blow it up, either.

—That too, not that it's especially relevant.

He switched from staring at me to staring at the camera. I allowed a few moments of silence to pass, thinking, wrongly, he might volunteer more about the subject of the dynamite.

—Listen, since you've been a friend of the movement, I'll consider a trade. You give me something for the camera. Let's think on what that will be for a couple of days.

I smiled and nodded in agreement as he added a question.

—But I have to ask you something. I believe you when you say you didn't give any Radical Union photos to the cops. But how did a copy of your photo end up above Caldwell's little desk?

—That's a good question.

—You been sharing things with Melanie I don't know about?

—She was alone in my apartment, but that was long after the reports of those RU photos getting into police hands. I don't think she could have been involved. We both know who that leaves.

Some ugly feelings bubbled up inside me and I felt the need to move. I got up to leave, but was curious about whether Canova planned to participate in the Perfect Park sit-in.

—You going over to the park?

—Yeah, but I'm finishing up a couple of things here first. I can't miss out on making a statement to the cops. How about you?

—I don't know. Maybe. I'll see you later.

*   *   *

Chapter 41

As I left the bookstore, I heard a helicopter circling overhead and the voice from a police sound truck sweeping through the loop area blasting orders to disperse before the 7:30pm curfew. I didn't plan on joining the protesters. Instead, I wanted to get back to the apartment. Matt would be back from a final exam. He and I needed to talk. But as I walked past the Magic Lantern Theater, I scanned the crowd in the park. Suddenly I was dumbfounded to see Matt sitting by himself between several groups gathered in the park. Finding him among these protesters made no sense. Some of those he was sitting near might have been among those who attacked the bank the night he stood on the porch with Kevin Moran. I picked my way through the crowd and sat in the dirt next to him.

—Didn't expect you to be here. You thinking this crowd will turn on the bank?

—Not likely.

—So what gives?

—What do you think? I know better than anyone how out of control the cops are. I nearly got killed by one of them. I don't want them around anymore than I want idiot rioters around. I'm a bi-partisan defender.

—Bi-partisan my ass! Why don't you get straight with me about your little meeting with the cops?

—What're you talking about?

—I'm talking about how copies of my photos of RU members ended up with the police. I've seen one of them and I didn't give it to them.

Matt glared at me with little change in expression and kept his voice low.

—All right. I did it, but I'm only sorry about how it affects you, not them. I knew you wouldn't be on board with it, so I didn't ask.

—Shit, Matt, what the hell were you thinking? That's so far out of line!

—Those freaks were making things worse not better. I wanted to do something. I wanted to help identify them and put them out of commission. It worked, too. But as we found out, there were plenty more nut cases around here to take their place.

—That really stinks and you know it. What else did you give them?

—That's all. I swear it.

—You didn't give them a roll of film?

Matt thought for a few seconds before answering.

—I did give them one roll—the rest of the RU photos.

—What do you mean, the rest of the photos?

—You said you had another roll. So I included it in what I gave them.

—Jesus Christ! And then you replaced it?

—I didn't want you to notice it right away so I swapped it with a new roll.

—And when I developed that roll, what then?

—I thought you'd figure you screwed up somewhere and it would blow over.

—Unbelievable!! You're the one who screwed up. Those weren't photos of the RU meeting. They were photos of Melanie!

—Yeah? Well, I'm sorry. But what's the big deal? Can't you just take more?

In stifled anger, I blurted out a reply.

—*They were nude photos, damn it!!*

Matt sat motionless, his face unchanging.

—Yes! *Nude*! Get it? And you know who has them now? Her father, the cop!

He managed a quiet response.

—Oh!

As he attempted to reframe the entire set of circumstances, people in the crowd called out for everyone to sit down. The 7:30pm curfew deadline had arrived. A few had given up and joined the ranks of onlookers beyond where the police were gathering at the top of the loop. They began spreading around the perimeter of the park, suited in riot gear. I noticed they were holding clubs. I remained sitting, now along with everyone else in the park. I wasn't finished with Matt yet.

—I wish you could have been the one to explain it to her.

—Yeah, I get it. So what's happening to her? And why *nude* photos?

—It's a long story. She doesn't want her dad running her life, and now she's like in jail with him thanks to you. Not to mention the fact that I'm on her black book shit list.

We had to talk above the police loudspeaker demanding everyone disperse as cops began working in groups, peeling people out of the crowd near Embarcadero del Norte and escorting them to buses bound for jail. Seeing the arrests beginning, Matt moved from sitting to crouching.

—I'm leaving. I didn't come here to break the law. I just wanted to make a statement. If they have another sit-in tomorrow, I'll be back. Are you staying?

—I'm not done making my statement to the cops.

Matt leaned forward.

—Look, for what it's worth, I'm sorry. I may have screwed you on the photos but you and Canova should remember what I didn't do the night Moran was shot. I didn't say a word and I really felt like saying something—especially with Kevin on his back with a bullet in him.

He stood and walked away. I was too angry to move. For a while I sat and stared at the dirt. When I looked up again I glimpsed a face sitting near the outer edge of the crowd. Melanie! I didn't expect to see her here. I got up, stepped around groups of sitting people, and sat next to her.

—Shouldn't you be reading Bernard Shaw?

—He inspired me to be here.

—Really?

—After reading him, I had to be more anti-gun.

—I see.

—Not really. It's what I saw with my own eyes last night. Some cops ripped off my neighbors. I mean they just broke in and smashed a bunch of their stuff and dragged them out in the street and clubbed them. I don't know what they did, but they didn't have any reason to do that. I wasn't going to sit around and watch the same thing again tonight.

—But your dad, won't he be here?

—He is here. In fact, say hello to him.

I looked up to see Lampert looming over us.

—Goddamnit, 'Lanie!! Do you have to do this?

—I'm not moving, dad. So just let it be.

—Fine. You asked for it.

Lampert grabbed her by the belt buckle of her jeans and slid her quickly across the dirt and into the street where two other cops helped hoist her onto a bus. Watching in amazement, I forgot about myself. Two cops then pulled me up and carried me to another waiting bus. Handcuffed and seated on board with many others, I didn't have to wait long before the bus filled to capacity. Then it began the all too familiar route to the county jail.

*   *   *

Chapter 42

The new county jail now had its electrical locks working, so the processing and booking of prisoners proceeded in a timelier manner than had been the case following the bank burning in February—which is to say it took the cops three hours instead of five to begin moving substantial numbers of people from the holding cells. Twenty minutes after I was placed in the holding cell, Canova arrived. He had left the bookstore not long after me and joined the demonstration in the park. But his evening ended similarly with a forced march to a bus under the persuasion of riot clubs. After the bureaucratic formalities of booking were finally completed, we were marched off to the same cell. About a half an hour later the guards deposited three others to fill the ten man capacity of our cell. I was genuinely surprised to see the last man entering the cell.

—Kyle?

—In the flesh.

—You busted at the park?

—Yeah.

—I didn't think protest was your thing.

—It isn't.

Overhearing Kyle, someone spoke from the corner of the cell.

—Then how'd you end up here?

Kyle talked softly, but loudly enough that everyone in the cell could hear him.

—I was part of a faculty group. We were there as observers to watch the cops and report misconduct. After an hour or more of hauling people out of the park the cops got a little testy. They started wailing on a guy with their clubs. I didn't think that was necessary. Maybe he said something they didn't like. Whatever the case, I thought they were out of line. He wasn't cooperating but he wasn't resisting any more than anyone else. So I got in their face about it some and they didn't like that either. Before I knew it, they were busting me with clubs and grabbing my arms.

Given my experience with the cops, I was curious how Kyle handled it.

—So what did you do?

—I was pissed clean off. I was ready to take one of their clubs and frag them with it. But I kept enough wits about me to see where that would lead. Instead, I went limp. That seemed to calm them down some. They put those cuffs on me and stuck me in a bus and that was that. I sat in the bus for a while with a bunch of others, waiting for the ride out. We had front row seats for viewing the colorful festivities. The cops finally wearied of clubbing and dragging people so they fired up their tear gas contraption. A funky cloud of crud wafted out of that thing in the direction of the couple hundred or so left in the park. Most of them hit the ground and laid low while the gas drifted above them. So the cops got frustrated with that and just lit-in to the remnants of the crowd with clubs and mace and gas masks. People yelled and swore at the cops, but it didn't take much longer before the park was clear—except for the cops and a few observers who managed to avoid arrest.

Canova couldn't hold back any longer.

—They're total pigs. The feds, the campus suits, the banks on down to the pigs—it's all the same rip-off. When you see this shit coming down all the time doesn't it make you want to do something more than *observe* it?

Kyle leaned his head against the cell wall and closed his eyes. Everyone heard Canova's question and waited for Kyle to answer. He opened his eyes and leveled one of his patented stares at Canova.

—Since you brought it up, take the bank. Like the Viet Cong the bank is a many-headed hydra. If you're not Hercules, don't try a direct assault. The nature of the beast makes that a losing proposition. I don't know about you, but I don't like to lose. Vietnam taught me that.

—The bank is like the Viet Cong? You're not making any sense.

—They present deceptive fronts that are everywhere and nowhere. If you're going to oppose them, it takes radical strategy. Tom Hayden and his ilk don't think radically enough. Like a French socialist, he thinks "No enemies on the left." Some revolution. Hayden aligns himself with folks like Chairman Mao and Ho Chi Mihn. Those two have engineered more genocide than Stalin and Hitler combined. Radical thinking isn't radical enough if it can't see the flaw in that approach.

—So what are you saying?

—What the radical left does here won't work any better than what the military does in Nam—they're outside-in strategies. What's needed is just the opposite.

—Very clever, but how do you really do that?

—You work change from the inside and turn the machinery on itself. You make allies on the inside—people who see what you see. Do some listening.

Then let your listening inform your acting. I'm not saying any of that's easy. I'm just saying it's effective. And being effective is more the point, isn't it, than, say, making headlines with rock throwing and arson? That sort of thing rouses the beast from its slumber.

—That misses the point. The Bank is a symbol. Burning it down draws attention to what a lot of people don't know—like the bank's fraternizing with the defense industry. The beast isn't slumbering. The people are.

—The symbol is the *burning bank* not the *bank*—and that's a symbol of war. Don't declare war unless you have a clear advantage. When you don't have that, approach is everything—like landing an aircraft. In making war, you get a lot of people angry who might otherwise come around to your cause. Plus you get your head smashed by cops. Academic types should feel obligated to find more effective ways to use their heads than throwing them into street fights with cops.

Kyle paused as more of those arrested marched past our cell and down the corridor to a vacant cell at the end.

—When the means for change come from inside, the means don't corrupt the ends. When self-correction gains traction, it's hard to stop.

Canova wasn't convinced.

—The anti-war movement *is* the beast turning on itself—Americans opposing their own government. Isn't that inside-out enough for you? You're just talking nonsense.

—It's more like civil war. I'm saying to be effective you have to understand the relevant power circle. Then get inside it, see its logic, and direct its force inward. A racing engine slows better with its own brakes than with bodies thrown in front of it.

—Not if it's fascism you're opposing!

—I'm not so sure. Anyway, would a fascist government have bothered giving Tom Hayden a trial? And then failed to convict him of the primary charge—even with a biased judge? And then allowed him to continue advocating violent protest all over the country? We fought a revolution to create a system that could change without revolution. I haven't given up on that yet.

Now visibly agitated, Canova replied brusquely.

—All right, fine. Say you're right. Where are we now in this country—according to your scheme? Are we at war, are we in some kind of self-correction melt down, or are we just flailing around?

Kyle held Canova with an unblinking gaze as he lobbed the question back to him.

—What do you think?

245

Canova exhaled in loud exasperation and butted his head against the cell wall. He was spared further exchange with Kyle by the approach of the dinner meal brigade of macaroni and cheese and Wonder bread.

* * *

Chapter 43

Most of those arrested Wednesday were charged only with curfew violation. The District Attorney set bail at a draconian $1250 for these violators as an additional form of punishment. But late Thursday afternoon Judge Lodge, whose court handled misdemeanor cases, dismissed the curfew charges for those arrested Wednesday. Infuriated by the Judge's actions, the D. A. disqualified him from presiding over future cases relating to street disturbances in Isla Vista.

The curfew violators were released in groups of ten, cell by cell. The process took several hours and the jailors were in no hurry to free anyone. When our turn finally came, we collected our personal items and exited the building. On leaving I was surprised to see Officer Lampert standing outside the door with a group of other officers. On seeing me, he motioned for me to come over to him. He said he needed to talk in private, so he took me to where his cruiser was parked on the south side of the building. As he entered the driver's side he motioned for me to get in on the passenger side. After stepping in and closing the door, I started to speak but he cut me off.

—I'm here to pick up Melanie. She's getting released in a few minutes. Then I saw you. You've been a fine influence on her. What's this, your second or third trip here?

—Second.

—Well make it your last. You and the rest of those knuckleheads and freaks out in Isla Vista are not accomplishing anything constructive. Can you see that at all?

—With all due respect, sir, the cops haven't accomplished much of anything constructive out there either. They've just made things worse.

—That's typical nonsense. I get that from 'Lanie, too. Let me tell you something. Since you're continuing to see each other maybe you're worth the effort. The newspapers have been full of this crap—about police being out of line. For months now every time three or more punks gather in that park there's an attack on the bank or some kind of property damage. Does anyone out there really think it's possible the Sheriff will suddenly believe there's going to be a quiet sit-in next to that bank that won't result in rock volleys and firebombs? For months now, there's been no alternative but curfews and street patrols to clean up nothing more than damned anarchy that passes for political protest. You should see what I've seen and hear the stories I've heard from those who've worked the streets. Can't tell you how many times we've arrested some damn fool who's made it great sport to go out and throw rocks at cops just to see how much he can provoke them and not get caught.

—There's been some of that . . .

—Nobody out there knows a thing about protest. That bank burning was nothing more than a mob lynching, at best. The bank never got due process and if any of those jerks in the street ever had that happen to them you'd hear about it from here to the east coast. If you've got a beef about some professor who's been fired or about housing or about the war or some other thing, *get a lawyer*. That's why we live in a country like this. If you can't do it with a lawyer, then get a legislator. And if you can't change the law, then maybe it's time to quit and go somewhere else. But don't put it on us. We take an oath to enforce the law and if you want a country worth living in, pray for a country that enforces its laws.

—Yeah, that'd be nice. But who do you get to police the cops?

—Okay, wise ass. Maybe some haven't followed the letter of the law in Isla Vista. But that place hasn't been a community. It's been a damn war zone. We've been ducks in a shooting gallery. You're not just on duty out there. You're a damn target—from rocks and bricks to wires strung across streets that would knock your head off. Over four dozen cops have been treated for serious injuries.

—Any been killed?

Lampert jerked himself toward me as if I'd stuck him with a pin.

—All right! Now you're going to get me angry! That Moran kid—he was an accident, a terrible accident. That didn't need to happen if there weren't a bunch of whining, over-privileged, arrogant, juveniles taking the law into their own sorry-assed hands. Don't put that on a group of guys who were trying their damnedest to do a thankless job. And it's no thanks to any of that crowd out there that someone on law enforcement hasn't been killed. And if one of us were killed, I doubt there'd be an Isla Vista community service for him.

The conversation had turned into a lecture. From his point of view the street fighting in Isla Vista was a kind of madness—in every sense of the word. I'd been in the vortex of it myself, so I had little to offer against its measure of truth. I didn't want to refute him, but I couldn't agree with him either. Suddenly I just wanted out of the car. I didn't want to hear any more.

—I'll admit it's gotten crazy in Isla Vista. It's not a balanced community, in more ways than one. If it's any consolation, I'd don't think you'll be seeing me in jail again.

With that remark Lampert cooled off a bit and stared out the window in front of him.

—Okay if I go now?

—Hold it. There's one more thing.

He leaned forward toward me and pulled a manila envelope from under the passenger seat.

—I'm giving these back to you. Don't thank me. Thank Melanie. She convinced me you were the wrong person in the wrong place at the wrong time.

I took the envelope but didn't open it. I knew what it contained.

—Can I ask you how you got these?

—A couple of weeks after the bank burning, Caldwell and I were talking at his house. He showed me the camera. He said he found it among some stuff collected in the San Rafael parking lot the night after the bank burning. He didn't know who it belonged to and he said he didn't care. Since I was interested in the film, we unloaded it and he gave me the roll to develop. I remembered your phone call, so I gave you his name. That's all the involvement I wanted—until I saw what was on the film. Did you ever get in touch with him?

I wasn't good at lying but if ever there was a time for it, now seemed like the right time. After the favor Canova did for me, I didn't want to blow his cover—and that's what would happen if I let on to Lampert anything about knowing where the camera was.

—Huh, yeah, I talked to him one night at his house. He didn't own up to having a camera. But a few days after that I made a decision not to go forward with it any further. I don't want the camera. I'm swearing off photography. I just don't think it's my thing anymore. He can keep the camera.

—All right, Marleau. Let's let sleeping dogs lie. You keep your photos. I'll keep Melanie's photos. And Caldwell can keep the camera.

—That suits me. Thanks!

I waved the manila envelope as I opened the door and stepped outside the cruiser.

*   *   *

Chapter 44

After returning to the jail landing, I discovered the ASIA office had arranged for bus transportation back to campus for students who had been released. Kyle and Canova had apparently already left on one of the buses. As I was about to get on a bus, I saw Melanie coming out of the doorway onto the landing. She strolled over to me and casually displayed what was left of her sense of humor.

—These buses taking us to another jail?

—Yeah. Isla Vista. C'mon if you want to avoid your dad. I just left him in his cruiser parked over there. He's waiting to pick you up. I think he has some words for you.

—Christ! I don't need that right now.

Melanie and I squeezed onto the bus and out of the lot before Lampert returned to look for her. I was probably a close second to her dad on the list of persons she didn't want to hang out with, but I couldn't let matters rest. Sensing her immunity to good behavior, I decided the best approach would be to annoy her further. I pointed to the "no smoking" sign on the bus.

—You going to light up now?

—Drop dead.

—I love your hair. Is that the jailhouse bob?

—You creep.

—Your face has a nice glow to it. Maybe you should make a habit of this.

—What—like you?

—How were the toiletries?

That produced a slight chuckle.

—Gawd! There was no privacy in that cell! Everyone looking at you on the crapper. I had no idea what jail was like. How do people stand it? It's so humiliating.

—I guess we won't count on you for the revolution.

That remark pushed a button.

—I'm not a marshmallow! I can get tough when I need to. That doesn't mean I have to like it.

Seeing her loosening up so much, I chanced genuine flattery.

—I know that. It's one of your most admirable qualities. You expect it in other people, too. Do you get that from your dad?

She skewered me with her eyes. Then she looked away and broke into a laugh.

—Damn it, Marleau! You're really pissing me off!

She turned toward me again and glanced at the envelope I had in my left hand.

—So what's that?

—My photos from the night of the bank burning. Your dad gave them back to me. He said I could thank you for that—meaning our friendship. You didn't know he had these, did you?

—No, goddamn it. He tells me nothing yet expects me to tell him everything. How did he end up with them?

—His friend Caldwell ended up with my camera and gave the film to him. Said he didn't want it.

—I think the ol' man and I need to talk.

Suddenly the bus slowed and began to pull to the side of the road. Melanie and I looked around to see we were being pulled over by a police cruiser with lights flashing. We looked at each other and nodded.

—Perfect! I can't believe he's being such a butt!

—Hey, if you can manage it, meet me for dinner tonight at the Wooden Horse, seven o'clock. Think of it as a down payment on the mess I made of the photo deal.

—We'll see. I'm not sure I'll be in the mood for anything.

Lampert exited the cruiser and walked toward the bus. Melanie left her seat and met him at the entrance. She said something to him too low for me to hear, but the tone wasn't friendly.

*   *   *

Chapter 45

Located above the Isla Vista Market, the Wooden Horse Cafe was the only place in the business area with enough elevation to offer a small sense of getting "above" it all. When I arrived, most people were gathered in the corner near the row of windows facing the street. Curious about the unusual collection of people, I went over to check out the attraction. Through the wall of onlookers, I glimpsed two guys playing chess. Normally chess games at the Wooden Horse attracted as much attention as a sneeze. By shifting position and craning my neck, I could see the player with his back to the window. It was Andy Street—occasional student, occasional hippie, and occasional roommate of Bill Macomber.

When Andy was in town, he usually crashed at Bill's apartment. I had met him there one afternoon last summer. When Bill told him I played chess, Andy suggested we play a game. I had a 1250 rating at the time and played an aggressive queen's gambit opening with white. I lost in 34 moves. Eventually I learned Andy played tournament chess and made extra cash by hustling suckers to play for money. He used my chess ego to lure me into another game in the fall. Wanting the rematch, I had brushed up on chess openings and now knew enough to be dangerous. I signed on to his ten dollar wager and lost in 42 moves playing black. As I scanned the current game, I wondered who he was stealing money from this time.

Edging around the table, I squeezed into a position where I could see the other player. I was surprised to see Kyle. What was he thinking? He was too smart to allow himself to get conned by Street. It was doubtful he knew how to play chess better than Street. No one I knew had ever seen Street lose a game. But I also knew Kyle to be the kind of guy who seldom lost at any competition—especially anything involving mind games or money. Had Macomber somehow egged him into this? Unlikely—since, if he had, he would surely have been here to watch. Did Kyle need money? If so, it wasn't a good idea to try winning it from Andy.

While sorting out these possibilities and waiting for Melanie to show, I noticed three more enter the crowded room—two guys accompanied by a woman with jet black shoulder length hair held back with a red bandana. When she turned her face, I saw it was Angie—the woman I met at Terry's place in

Avalon. One of the guys she came in with was noticeably tall, well over six feet—quite a contrast with her five foot six frame. Angie noticed I was staring at her from across the room. We exchanged nods and I turned back to watch the board. Kyle made a move with his knight. Angie walked over to me and spoke in my right ear.

—Who's winning?

—Andy's a pawn up, so he has the edge.

Since Avalon I had heard a little more about her through the rumor mill—that she was from the Bay Area and that she and Kyle had had a turbulent on and off relationship over the past couple of years. Like Kyle, she exuded an eccentric charisma. Oil and water soul mates, I thought—made for each other but unable to be with each other. From the stir she generated around her, I imagined Kyle already knew she was in the room, even though he had not looked up from the board.

As at Avalon, Angie hadn't chosen clothes to complement her looks—ill-fitting, faded blue jeans and an ugly flannel long-sleeved shirt. But the clothes did little to obstruct her magnetism. She had a soft face but a hard look to her mouth—an intensity that said "Don't cross me." She leaned over to ask another question.

—What's the wager? Andy never plays for the hell of it.

—I don't know. But you're right. They must be playing for something.

The board had reached mid-game positions and might drag on for some time. The positions on both sides were very contained—the kind of board position that leads to a slow and grinding conclusion, the kind of game I knew Andy liked to play. So I figured things were going his way—especially being a pawn up. He would spin a web of mutual protection between his tightly controlled pieces and, like a spider, wait for his opponent to overextend and stumble into the snare. That's how the last game had gone between us. I couldn't get myself to be patient enough. I had to go on the offensive. And when I did I found I had miscalculated—ever so slightly—but enough to lead to a break in my line of defense. In chess Andy was the equivalent of a Kung Fu master who would turn an opponent's thrust to his own advantage. Now he worked the same strategy again.

Angie and I watched for three more moves. No pieces were exchanged and the positions remained closed and difficult. Then, during Andy's move, several minutes passed. This was odd because he usually didn't require much time. I took a closer look at the board position. Although the position was fairly complex, Andy still had the material advantage of a pawn. Finally he reached out and moved his castled king over one square. This seemed an overly cautious move for him. Then Kyle made the same move with his king. I craned my neck to see the entire board. Then it became clear to me what was happening. It was so amazing I spoke without thinking.

—Zugzwang! I think it's Zugzwang!

The tall guy who had come in with Angie pointed at the board.

—What the hell is Zugzwang?

After Kyle moved his king, Andy placed his king on the square where it had been one move before. He offered Kyle a draw.

—Congratulations. A narrow escape.

Kyle nodded in acceptance of the draw. But Andy was not pleased with himself.

—Let's see if you can do that again.

The tall guy seconded the motion.

—Yeah. Another game. Zugzwang? What a rip-off.

Still Kyle said nothing, continuing to stare at Andy. Kyle was like that. He would continue saying nothing when just about anyone else would have felt obliged to say something. The tall guy was annoyed with his silence and tried to prod him into a response.

—Another game. That didn't prove anything. We came to see a winner, not some Zugzwang standoff.

I knew Kyle didn't need anyone speaking for him, but I spoke anyway.

—Forcing a draw against Andy from that board position is like a win.

Someone from Kyle's side of the table agreed.

—Yeah Andy. The bet was you could beat him and you didn't. So you owe.

The tall guy continued to goad Kyle.

—That's no good. You can't end on a draw. What's the deal, Kyle? You don't think you can beat this guy?

The tall guy's focus on Kyle betrayed a clear interest in seeing him lose to Andy. Kyle stood up from the board to face him.

—I'll play another game—with you. But only if we make the stakes worthwhile.

Several others around the table snickered at the suggestion. Before the tall guy could answer, Kyle held his hand out to Andy who then stood up and shook it.

—Another time, then?

Kyle nodded. He turned and walked out of the room followed by a few who had been watching. Angie didn't follow him and instead sat down in a chair at a table nearby that had just emptied and motioned for me to join her. So I took a seat at the table. The two men she came in with had started a chess game at the table Kyle and Andy had just vacated. Aggressive to a fault, Angie spoke first.

—I remember we didn't get a reading done for you back at Avalon.

—No we didn't. You still doing that hocus pocus?

She pulled a deck of Tarot cards from her pocket and set them on the table.

—I don't have time for a full reading. But we do have time for you to draw a card.

She moved the deck nearer to me and spread the cards in a row across the table. But before I could pick a card, Melanie appeared at the table.

—Sorry I'm late, Marleau. You find yourself a fortuneteller or a new date?

—Things happen when you're not on time.

I introduced the two of them, as Melanie continued.

—You could have used a seer back in February, huh Marleau?

—I don't buy into it much. How about you? Maybe you should pick a card. You could use some good news.

Angie objected.

—Can't guarantee good news.

—What kind of a fortuneteller are you?

—The honest kind. Pick with care.

Melanie leaned forward, drew a card from near the end of the spread, and pulled it toward her, face down. Then she looked at me.

—Your turn.

—What nonsense!

I picked a card from the opposite end of the spread and turned it over for all to see.

—The Five of Wands. What does this mean?

Angie didn't answer and instead asked Melanie to show her card. She turned it over to reveal the Seven of Cups. Angie took the cards from Melanie and I, gathered them together with the rest of her deck, and rose from her chair.

—There. I've done the difficult work. The rest is up to you. I've got to go.

I stood up from my chair.

—You can't just leave. We're not finished here yet.

—I need to catch up with Kyle before someone gets him into another game. You're on your own now.

Angie then walked out of the room. After she disappeared down the stairs, I sat down again and turned to Melanie.

—How do you like that?

—I like her style.

—Figures.

—Do you know anything about Tarot?

—Angie told me some—back when we first met. I only remember the four suits align with the four elements—fire, earth, water, air. I think the wands are fire and the cups are water. Judging from the crossing of the wands on the five card, I'd say it has something to do with tests and trials.

—And the Seven of Cups?

—I don't know. Maybe something about the confusion of multiple choices. It's a water suit and water flows in many directions.

—You implying I shouldn't spread myself thin?

—You do look tired.

—I am. Sorry I was late.

—That's okay. How'd it go with pops?

—He doesn't know when to stop policing my life. I'm really sick of it. But I'm going to finish college despite him and take as little money as possible. That means I need a roommate for the summer and fall. You interested?

—Me? You want me for a roommate?

—You got a problem with it?

—I don't know. I hadn't thought about it.

—So think about it.

—I know a nice one bedroom place.

—I was thinking two bedrooms, two baths—with a lock on my door.

—You're a cold fish, you know it? Was I right about you not trusting men?

Melanie smiled.

—Don't take it personally. I'm just not big on men at the moment.

—So glad I came along at the right time.

—Listen, Marleau. I'm infuriated with him for another reason. He left me alone in his cruiser for a few minutes while he talked to another cop. I noticed this envelope under the seat. Guess what was in it?

—Your pictures?

—No. Your pictures! He had copies made of all your bank photos!

—That double-crossing prick! What's he up to?

—I called him on it when he came back to the car. He told me to keep quiet about it, that he kept them for "professional reasons." Gawd, I blew my top!

—What did he mean by that?

—He wouldn't explain. That's when I told him we were done talking. Of course, he had to get in a few more choice words about wanting me out of drama. But now he understands that isn't happening.

After we ate, I walked Melanie home from the Wooden Horse. On the way back to my place, I pondered her suggestion about us being "roommates." Was she kidding? With her apparent attitude toward the opposite sex, why would I want to subject myself to such company on a daily basis? On the other hand, what roommate situation wasn't a mixed bag? And maybe her invitation was a sign of a warming trend.

*   *   *

Chapter 46

The next morning I visited Canova at the bookstore to conclude our business with the camera. While I waited for him to finish sorting through some used books in a box a customer had brought in, another guy walked through the door and immediately spoke to all of us.

—This town is dry as hell. You know any place where a guy can get a drink?

Without a blink Canova opened a desk drawer and pulled out a shot glass and an already opened bottle of Wild Turkey. He proceeded to fill the glass and, while handing it to the stranger, answered his question.

—Right here.

He then swapped a dictionary of medical terms for four books from the box on the floor. The customer picked up his box and left. Canova turned back to the guy holding the shot glass, which was now empty.

—Can you excuse us. We need to talk.

—Sure thing, friend. How about one for the road?

Canova smiled and poured him another. He downed it, bowed politely, and left the store. Knowing why I was there, Canova spoke first.

—What can you give me for it?

—How about we flip for it? Heads I win, tails you lose.

—That's really lame.

—How about this?

I tossed a dog-eared paperback of *The Magus* on his desk. I'd borrowed it from him several months ago.

—I see you took good care of this.

He picked up the book and examined it as if he had pulled it from a trash can.

—You're not getting this camera for nothing, man. I put myself out for it.

—All right, how about this?

I pulled a file folder from my backpack and opened it on his desk, revealing an eight by ten photograph.

—What's this?

He picked up the photo for a closer look.

—Check out the faces.

The photo, taken the night of the bank burning, showed the bonfire at the front entrance. The flames lit the crowd on the side of the fire opposite where I knelt to take the picture. The photo included several people, but two in particular stood out well enough to recognize. They faced each other in conversation. I didn't know the guy on the left, but the one on the right was clearly Canova.

—That's me!

—Sure enough. When I took it I didn't even notice you standing there. Then some guy came up and complained about me taking pictures of the crowd. So I split and went around to the back of the bank. I didn't think he had anything to worry about. But I was wrong.

—Where did you get this?

—From Melanie's dad.

—How'd he get these?

—Caldwell gave him the film a couple of weeks after he got my camera. He said he wasn't interested in the film. But Lampert was, so he had the prints made.

—So how did you get them?

—He gave them to me yesterday when we got out of jail. He said I could thank Melanie for that. He could have made a lot of trouble—and not only for me as it turns out.

—God bless it!!

Canova unlocked his lower right desk drawer, took out the camera, and put it in my hands.

—It's a jinx. Get out of here and don't let me see you and that thing together around me again. I'll keep this.

He pointed to the photo on his desk. When I got to the door, I turned toward him.

—You should stay with the book peddling.

—What's that supposed to mean?

—It means I still have the negative.

His brow narrowed.

—They're still looking for suspects, and Lampert and I are old pals now. You should stay away from certain places.

He shook his head.

—That's crazy. Whatever they throw at me would stick to you too.

—Then we'll share the same cell. We could work on our chess.

—Bull. I know you too well.

As I opened the door, I removed all jest from my voice.

—Ditto. That's why you should be worried.

The look on Canova's face was worth a picture, but there was no film in the camera.

After leaving the bookstore, I stopped by the Rexall Drug, bought a roll of film, and headed for the beach to test the equipment. I wanted to make sure the light meter, shutter, and other internal components were working properly. For all I knew the cops used it as a football the night of my arrest. Walking down the ramp to the beach, I saw Angie approaching. We talked about the bust at the park for a few minutes, then I remembered something I had wanted to ask her ever since meeting her at Terry's place.

—Do you remember at Avalon, when the four of us guys were in the living room? Kyle was talking and you came in and stood at the French doors. You said something to Kyle about how he was telling lies and was full of it. Do you remember that?

—Kind of . . . what about it?

—What did you mean by that?

Angie smiled and stuck her hands in her jean pockets.

—I meant he's a liar and he's full of it.

—Okay. So . . . how was he lying?

—He's never been to Nam. He was never even in the military. He was IV-F with a back injury he got in high school.

—You sure about that?

—Of course. I knew his brother. He's the one who went to Nam. He didn't make it back. Kyle took it hard. They were very close. It was like a part of him died.

—So sometimes he talks like he's his brother?

—Something like that. He's living for both of them.

—So is he confused about who he is?

—Who isn't? But he's not crazy. He's just working through some things.

—Does it bother you when he does that?

—It used to. Now I just call him on it. It's a thing we've got going between us.

—Okay . . . I guess. Thanks for filling me in.

We started walking in opposite directions. Then she called out to me.

—Hey, *you're* not angry at him are you?

—For lying?

—Yeah.

—How could I be? Maybe he was channeling his brother.

—Nice one. You might be ready for that Tarot reading next.

—I don't think so. What isn't written can't be read.

I thought I'd gotten in the last word.

—No, Marleau, it's what's *written* that can't be read.

Macomber would have been proud of her. Angie gave me the peace sign and walked away. I continued down to the beach. It felt good to have the camera back. I leveled the lens toward the horizon and adjusted the focus. Today the rim between the sea and the sky would not resolve to a line. Perhaps tomorrow I would check again.

Epilogue

Whatever happened to:

Daniel Marleau: to be continued (still looking for an education)

Paul Canova: to be continued (still looking for used books)

Melanie Lampert: to be continued (still looking for drama)

Matt Baxter: to be continued (still looking for an explanation)

Kyle Kincaid: to be continued (last seen at a Grateful Dead concert)

Angie Wagner: to be continued (last seen hitching to Berkeley)

John Macksoud: to be continued (like Bill Allen, he failed to get tenure but adopted a different strategy for fighting the decision). From John I borrowed the notion that you can't take a rabbit out of a hat unless there is already a rabbit in the hat (which, apparently, Macksoud borrowed from the film *The Red Shoes*). For more on the life of John Macksoud see the author's web site page at *http://www.gregorydesilet.com/code/John_Macksoud_Eulogy.html*

Bill Macomber: to be continued (like Macksoud, he also failed to get tenure but didn't fight the decision and charted a new course). For further biographical information on Macomber see the author's web site page at *http://www.gregorydesilet.com/code/W_B_Macomber_Eulogy.html*

Bill Allen: In October of 1970 a jury convicted Allen for crimes of disturbing the peace, inciting to riot, and public obscenities committed during anti-Reagan demonstrations at El Paseo in Santa Barbara on March 6. He was sentenced by Judge James Pattillo to six months in county jail (of which three months was suspended for three years pending no repeated offenses). In June of 1971 he was sentenced by Municipal Court Judge Frank Kearney to 60 days in county jail for violation of probation stemming from a May 18 arrest for shoplifting from a Los Angeles hardware store. After leaving UCSB, Allen never resumed college level teaching. He went to Oregon and learned farming and eventually returned to California to operate, with his wife, a 25 acre organic farm near Modesto. In the late 1980s he and his wife helped run a 52 acre organic farm in the foothills west of Goleta. He also became active in sponsoring organic farming consciousness by helping to write the first handbook for California Certified Organic Farmers, serving on boards promoting organic farming, and attending related conferences. Allen is reportedly now living on the east coast.

Bank of America, Isla Vista Branch: A virtually windowless stone and masonry fortress soon replaced the burned down building. In March of 1970 Chairman of the Bank Louis B. Lundborg declared: "We are but one bank, but we have decided to take our stand in Isla Vista." The Bank's stand came to an end in August of 1982 when the branch closed—noting a lack of business during summer months as a major reason. In May of 1983 a company called Food and Fun leased the building and converted it into a video arcade. After several further unsuccessful transformations, the University finally purchased the building and turned it into a lecture hall.

Vernon I. Cheadle: Appointed as Chancellor in 1962, Cheadle served in that capacity until 1977 when he retired. Upon retirement, he continued botanical research at UCSB (he held a Ph.D. in botany from Harvard) and remained active in campus life as a mentor to future administrators. He died July of 1995 at Cottage Hospital in Santa Barbara following complications from a stroke. Allegations of complicity in the development scandal of Isla Vista dogged Cheadle during his entire career at UCSB. Detractors claimed that he profited as a board member of a local savings and loan that funneled development money to individuals and contractors for mutual benefit in the tightly controlled market of Isla Vista. For this account of Cheadle's involvement, see Carmen Lodise's *Isla Vista: A Citizen's History*. Other accounts question this view of Cheadle's involvement (see, for example, the discussion under "Isla Vista, California" at Wikipedia).

Russell Buchanan: With a Ph.D in history from Stanford University, Buchanan came to Santa Barbara in 1938 teaching at what was then the Santa Barbara College. After serving in several Dean positions, he became Vice Chancellor for Academic Affairs in 1961 and filled that office until 1971. At the time of his retirement in 1973, a lecture hall complex that was part of Ellison Hall was renamed in his honor. In 1977 he published a successful monograph entitled *Black Americans in World War II*, which went through three printings in eighteen months.

Robert N. Evans: Evans graduated from West Point with a degree in military science and engineering. He served in Germany as a border operations officer and in Korea with the 23rd infantry regiment, second division, as battalion communications officer and company commander. He received the French Croix de Guerre, Purple Heart, Bronze Star with "V," Combat Infantry Badge, and Parachute Qualification Badge. In July of 1961 he was appointed Acting Associate Dean of Students and Acting Dean of Men. In October of 1971 Evans authored with Geoffrey Wallace, then UCSB campus ombudsman, a pamphlet titled "From Formal Dresses to Patch Pocket Jeans." It began with the sentence: "Hardly anyone needs to be told that in the past few years there have been vast changes, amounting nearly to a revolution, on the campuses of the nation."

Lyle G. Reynolds: Reynolds taught at Santa Rosa High School from 1935 to 1947 and earned an Ed.D from Stanford University in 1953. He came to UCSB as an assistant professor (tennis coach) in 1947 and was appointed to Dean of Students in 1957. In September of 1967 he authored a pamphlet titled "Dean Cites Differences in Today's Students." It began with the following comment, "Today's students are more isolated, experience a greater identity crisis, are less 'collegiate' and are under more pressure than their post-war predecessors." After 30 years as an administrator at UCSB, Reynolds retired in 1976. Reynolds then won election to the Santa Barbara City Council in 1979 and served on the council for eight years. He also founded the Santa Barbara Scholarship Foundation and built its assets to more than $6 million, with $750,000 awarded in college scholarships each year. In the 1990s Reynolds began serving on the governing board of Peabody Charter School, a school that is among a handful in the state to create its own plan for education. Even though in his 80s Reynolds also served as a volunteer playground monitor and sometimes sat in on classes, offering his views when appropriate. Reynolds died in June of 2006 at the age of 94.

William M. Kunstler: At the time of his February 1970 speech at UCSB Kunstler was the director of the American Civil Liberties Union, a position he held from 1964 to 1972. During the 1960s, he built his reputation as a civil rights leader by providing legal representation for the Congress of Racial Equality, Martin Luther King's Southern Christian Leadership Conference, and the Student Non-Violence Coordinating Committee. In the years after the Chicago trial he continued to advocate radical socialism. He also continued representing many famous and controversial persons, including Italian crime family members and accused terrorists and assassins. In the last year of his life, 1995, he appeared on an episode of the television show *Law and Order*, playing himself in the story of the defense of members of the Weathermen Underground for the 1971 shooting of a policeman in a Brinks truck robbery. At the 2009 Sundance Film Festival, his daughters Emily and Sarah premiered a documentary of his life entitled *William Kunstler: Disturbing the Universe*.

Tom Hayden: At the conclusion of the Chicago trial, Hayden (along with Abbie Hoffman, Jerry Rubin, Dave Dellinger, and Rennie Davis) was acquitted of *conspiracy* charges but convicted of crossing state lines with intent to incite a riot (in accordance with the 1968 anti-riot law). He was sentenced to five years in federal prison and fined $5000. However, after an appeal trial in the U. S. Court of Appeals for the Seventh Circuit, Hayden and the other four defendants succeeded in having their convictions overturned when the court ruled in November of 1972 that Judge Hoffman had shown bias by not allowing the defense lawyers to question potential jurors regarding cultural and racial prejudices. In the same year, after having previously visited North Vietnam, Hayden made another famous visit to the war-torn country with actress Jane Fonda. In 1973 he married Fonda and they continued outspoken protest of the war until its ultimate conclusion in 1975. Drawing on experience in her visit to North Vietnam, Fonda gave a talk at UCSB in June of 1974. Hayden and Fonda had one child together who grew to become the actor Troy Garity. In the late 1970s the couple created an organization called the Campaign for Economic Democracy and worked closely with Governor Jerry Brown in promoting ecologically sound energy and environmental policy. After serving several terms in the California State Assembly and State Senate during the 1980s and 1990s, Hayden's political career faltered with failed bids for Governor of California, Mayor of Los Angeles, and City Councilman for Los Angeles. In recent years he has taught courses on social movements as an adjunct professor at Occidental and Pitzer Colleges.

Jerry Rubin: Rubin and Abbie Hoffman were among the founders of the Youth International Party, whose members were commonly referred to as Yippies. After the end of the Vietnam War, Rubin transitioned from revolutionary to entrepreneur, famously stating that "wealth creation is the real American revolution." He went from wearing hippie street theater clothes to Wall Street business suits. Rubin's about-face with respect to "Establishment" values stunned many, including his friend Hoffman. In the 1980s Rubin engaged in several public encounters with Hoffman billed as Yippie versus Yuppie debates. For Rubin, Hoffman was a "revolutionary careerist" and a "legend in his own mind." For Hoffman, Rubin had a "vision of America about as wide as his tie," and had sold out to the era of "designer brains." Rubin and his wife turned to running a business in Manhattan called "The 500 Club" for the purpose of introducing venture capitalists to idea men. Rubin defended himself against accusations of having "sold out" the "Movement" by asserting that he had retained what was best from the 60s, its social consciousness, with what was best from the 80s, its entrepreneurial drive. Rubin continued advocating various left agendas such as eco-consciousness, civil rights, and vegetarianism, stating, "I still have the same value system. I just want to be more effective. I mean, the issue isn't a suit and a tie, for God's sake. Abbie thinks the issue is a suit and tie. He's rebelling for the sake of rebelling." Rubin died unexpectedly in November of 1994 in a jaywalking accident on Wilshire Boulevard in Los Angeles. He was hit by a car and taken to the UCLA Medical Center where he was treated for 14 days but never recovered.

Earnest E. Pinkerton: According to former law associate Arthur Henzell, Pinkerton left Santa Barbara in the 1980s to practice law in San Francisco and is now deceased.

Greg Knell: Whereabouts and career future unknown.

Made in the USA
Coppell, TX
19 November 2021

66020924R00148